LAST OF THE GLADIATORS

LAST OF THE GLADIATORS

A World War II Bomber Navigator's Story

L. Ray Silver

Airlife
England

First published in the UK in 1995
by Airlife Publishing Ltd

British Library Cataloguing in Publication Data
A catalogue record for this book
is available from the British Library

ISBN 1 85310 464 7

Typeset by Servis Filmsetting Ltd, Manchester
Printed by St Edmundsbury Press, Bury St Edmunds, Suffolk

Airlife Publishing Ltd
101 Longden Road, Shrewsbury SY3 9EB

To Lynne,
who walked the cemetery aisles
and climbed Great Knoutberry Hill
with me

our kin

Chris, Keith & Heather, Steven & Margarita,
Eric & Mary, Jane & David, Debbie & Mark

and grand-kin

Brendan, Christopher, Emily, Rachel,
Rebecca, Ruthie, Ryan, Sarah-Jane,
Steven-Thomas and Wesley

Contents

Acknowledgements

A few days after I got home from the war my uncle, Percy Jacobson took me to lunch in Montreal and urged me to write a book about my experiences. His interest was understandable. He was a writer, himself. One of his plays had won a Governor-General's Award and he had been president of the Canadian Authors' Association pre-war. More pertinent, his son Joe and I had both gone overseas to fly with Bomber Command squadrons in the spring of 1941. A year later we were shot down within weeks of each other. I survived; Joe didn't.

As a survivor and one who wrote for his livelihood I owed it to Joe and the 10,000 other Canadian aircrew who died in action to tell it like it was. By the fall of 1945, however, I was planning to publish a weekly newspaper and it engaged all of my attention. Then for many years raising and supporting a family took priority. While I was in my prime in the writing game I never felt I could afford to take time off to write a book.

In due course two people reminded me of my obligation to write of these air-war experiences – the late Wally Floody and my wife, Lynne. In 1970 Wally put his heavy hand on my shoulder, recruiting me to edit *The Camp*, a semi-annual publication for some 2,000 fellow members of the Canadian Ex-Air Force Prisoner-of-War Association. So twice yearly for the next 20 years I waded through my colleagues' aircrew reminiscences to regale them with their own preposterous recollections.

And for more than fifteen years my wife gently nudged me in her own inscrutable way to write this book. Once I started Lynne didn't let me quit. But by then we were both committed. A decade earlier she had walked the wartime cemetery aisles with me. Then at an age when we should have known better we climbed Great Knoutberry Hill in Cumbria to recover bits of the Whitley wreckage that had weathered there like whitening albatross bones.

After that we had visited An de Werdt at Eindhoven. Here was the woman who had risked her family's lives to hide me up and then send me on my way in civilian clothes. Now she was presenting us with a painting of the wartime house where they had sheltered me. It was, the de Werdt family said, 'in thanks because you did not betray us to the Gestapo.'

There we stood a generation later, Lynne and I, blinded by tears of humility. '*They're* thanking *you!*' my wife kept saying. This book is an attempt to set the record straight.

9

ACKNOWLEDGEMENTS

I am indebted to Colonel Arie deJong of the Royal Netherlands Air Force and to Ruud Groen of the *Eindhoven Dagblatt* for their roles in locating the de Werdt family and arranging our visit. We are among the countless Canadians grateful to Col.deJong for invaluable assistance in retracing wartime memories.

When I finally got down to writing *The Last of the Gladiators*, the two people who exemplified how it should be done were the late Kingsley Brown, that relict of bygone Canadian newspapermen and B.A.(Jimmy) James, a born writer who buried his talents in the British Foreign Office for four decades. Brownie's *Bonds of Wire* (Collins, Toronto 1989) and Jimmy's *Moonless Night* (Random House, New York & Toronto 1983) relate their first-hand stories of POW life with superb insight.

But their influence on *The Last of the Gladiators* was much more than style. For half a century Kingsley Brown was my mentor on the arts of living and writing. Just weeks before he died in 1989 Wally Floody introduced me to Jimmy James. When I consider how much effort Jimmy put into helping me get this book published it seems we have known each other a lifetime and it would take much of it to repay his kindness. Donald McIvor of Montreal, a wartime ferry pilot who has authored nine books based on his half-century flying career, was another who helped me in my search for a publisher.

The Last of the Gladiators is mostly about Bomber Command operations because that is what I personally experienced. But I would have been remiss had I failed to recount the remarkable performance of Canadian fighter-ace Don Morrison. I have tried to write of Don's air battles objectively but the fact is I am indebted to him. As an ex-kreigy I share the appreciation that all members of the Canadian Ex-Air Force POW Association – and their families – felt for his leadership. Apart from that I am grateful for the encouragement he provided when my efforts appeared to be faltering. Morrison was one of those born leaders who knew just when to back-pat and when to push without letting the recipient become aware of it.

Back in the North Compound of Stalag Luft III I was involved in producing a fortnightly poster-paper, *Scangriff*, which kept fellow kriegies in tune with home by recounting uncensorous stuff from their correspondence. In organizing this effort I sought out POWs who had been with the news media pre-war. That is how Kingsley Brown and I first met. Two others were Paul Brickhill, who had been a reporter on the *Sydney Sun* in Australia before he flew into adversity and Conrad Norton, a BBC war correspondent who somehow wound up among the grounded fly-boys.

In the bag, Brickhill and Norton collaborated on *Escape to Danger* which was the forerunner of Paul's memorable post-war book, *The Great Escape*. The first half of *Escape to Danger* dealt with exceptional ways in which some of the kriegies had escaped death as they tumbled into captivity.

I was able to put Paul and Con onto three or four such stories including that of

ACKNOWLEDGEMENTS

Jimmy Abbott, whose ride to earth astride the tail of his Spitfire I have briefly recounted in this book, and my own misadventures which intrigued them because they said I 'happened to be a journalist with an analytical mind; a dark young man from Ontario, Canada with all the racy humour and explosive energy of a Hollywood reporter.'

I have relied on Paul's *The Great Escape* and *Reach for the Sky* to jog my own recollections of Wings Day and Douglas Bader as I remembered them in North Compound at Luft III. For the fabulous background of the inimitable Group Captain Harry Day, I turned to *Wings Day* by another fellow kriegie Sydney Smith.

To sharpen my memory of wartime London and of the stoic Brits I read and re-read passages from Angus Calder's *The People's War*. That is where I caught the soul-shaking cry of a Hull air raid warden quoted on an early page of this book.

In 1950 I did a first-person piece for *Maclean's Magazine* that recounted the derring-do of my wartime efforts. I am indebted to Pierre Berton, who was then managing editor, for putting it into perspective. He headlined the article 'I Am The Luckiest Guy Alive' and he ticked off my encounters in three sentences – 'He was thrown into the next county when his plane hit an English mountain. The Gestapo threatened to shoot him after he jumped from a flaming bomber. He's crashed half-a-dozen times by 'plane, train and car; he's fine thanks,' Pierre noted. Forty years later when I got around to writing *The Last of the Gladiators*, I realised that he had set the tone for it.

I am obliged, as well, to fellow newsmen who published some of the reflections regurgitated in this book. Among them were former *Globe and Mail* managing editor Allan Dawson who used 'The Hand That Reaches Out From the Grave' in March 1961 on the seventh anniversary of the *Lucky Dragon* affair that revealed the H-Bombs lethal clout; to former *Toronto Star* managing editor Ray Timson who ran my fortieth anniversary remembrance, brashly headed 'How I fooled the Gestapo' and to *Canadian Churchman* editor Jerry Haymes who carried my account of how 'Aging fly-boys share survivors' laughter' in November 1987. My account of the VE+1 Night reunion with Doug MacFarlane in Brussels first appeared in the Toronto Press Club *Byliner* in 1990 thanks to Jack Hutton. A brief account of my role in 'The First 1,000 Bomber Raid' appeared in *World War II Investigator* in December 1988.

Latterly, Neil Reynolds *Kingston Whig-Standard* editor and Doug Sweet, Op-Ed editor of the *Montreal Gazette* carried my attack on Canadian Broadcasting Corporation's *Valour and the Horror* series in which I cited the theme and title of this book.

Four other newsmen colleagues gave public and private support in 1992 as I spread myself to finish *The Last of the Gladiators* and participate in the aging fly-boys' reaction to the CBC attack on our credibility. They were editorial-page editor Peter Calamai and Queen's Park columnist Jim Coyle of the *Ottawa Citizen*, the Thomson Papers' columnist Derek Nelson and veteran CFRB commentator Bob Hesketh.

ACKNOWLEDGEMENTS

Windsor Daily Star managing editor Michael Dunnell gave permission for reproduction of the 1940 picture of 18 of us en route from Windsor for Air Force training.

I first returned to Britain's wartime haunts in 1968. With Air Ministry and RAF help I tracked the site of our hillside crash to the Yorkshire Dales. So on a May day 27 years later, accompanied by my host Robert Kirkby, the proprietor of the George and Dragon Hotel at Dent and Ron Laing, a Caterpillar tractor driver working on reconstruction of the Great North Road, I climbed Great Knoutberry Hill to reclaim pieces of our shattered Whitley.

Air Ministry duly confirmed by the serial numbers that the aircraft parts were from our Whitley T-4234. It was in 1987 that Lynne and I returned to recover more of the Whitley wreckage. On both occasions – 19 years apart – Eric Wallace of Border Television came down from Carlisle with a camera crew to chronicle these hillside jaunts of rediscovery. Notably Eric's enthusiasm had not diminished in the interval.

On those nostalgic journeys and on half a dozen other visits to Britain in the intervening years we attended reunions of the Royal Air Forces ex-POW Association .This is an appropriate place to say thanks for the hospitality extended on those occasions by James (Dixie) Deans and Roger Simmons and subsequently by their widows Molly and Iris; to Ivan and the late Sylvia Keyes, to Gwyn Martin (author of *Up and Under*), to Calton Younger (author of *No Flight from the Cage)*, to Maurice Butt, to Vic Gammon, to Air Commodore (retd) Charles Clarke and his wife Eileen, and to the late and inimitable Wings Day, DSO, OBE and Albert Medal, who was always ready to receive us at the Royal Air Force Club in Piccadilly.

In the final analysis it is John Beaton, managing editor at Airlife Publishing Limited, who has made *The Last of the Gladiators* a reality. He read two chapters of the manuscript in February 1993 and decided 'This is something we would like to publish.'

Excepting for 'Cindy' at the Regent Palace bar, all of the people in this book have been identified by their right names. Nothing in these pages was coincidental; everything unfolded in an inevitable way. And I have tried to tell it as it actually happened.

1
Last of the Gladiators

Astride their Pennine peaks as darkness fell, the gods of war peered east across the Yorkshire Dales to watch the lumbering Whitleys heading into North Sea winds. Towards dawn they would catch the aircraft limping back, mauled and harried like dogs that had been driven through privet hedges.

At dusk on an August day in 1941 I flew into war in one of those Whitleys. Six hours later it lay smashed on a hilltop in the Dales. Two pilots stared skywards with sightless eyes. We three survivors tasted the first bite of our mortality. The aircraft was 30 miles off course and I was the navigator. The gods laughed.

On the last night of May 1942 I hung by my parachute straps in a moon-washed sky watching Cologne aflame 60 miles away. A morning later like a grounded hawk I was the prey. Pursued by the imagined tread of jack-boots and bayonet thrusts, I ran the woods and ditches to the edge of a Dutch town. In sodden battledress stripped of identity, I stood at a smallholder's door staring into the fathomless depths of a woman's eyes.

'Flyer, downed flyer,' I told her. But she already knew. I brought the smell of death to her doorstep yet it was as if she had been awaiting my arrival. Mother of three small children, wife and sister-in-law of men who would die with her if I was caught among them, she waved me in. An de Werdt taught me what courage really was that wartime day.

A week later at an Amsterdam police building the Gestapo demanded to know who had supplied my civilian clothes? Who had sewn the escape-kit contents – maps and money – into the seams? Handcuffed and shackled, I shook my chains in fear, fury and desperation.

'No one helped. I stole the clothes, you Nazi bastards,' I screamed driving the de Werdt family so deep into subconsciousness it took a generation to relocate them.

Finally tiring of their captive, merely a downed British *flieger*, the Gestapo returned me to the Luftwaffe's custody. The Gestapo had other business – elderly yellow-starred Jews to be run down by their Mercedes staff-car in Amsterdam streets on sunny mid-war days.

So I joined the 'kriegies' – *kriegsgefengeners*, prisoners-of-war; the 10,500

13

Allied airmen who ultimately filled the five compounds of Luft III, the POW camp that spawned *The Great Escape*.

In the early years of World War II – 'before flying got dangerous,' we used to say – four in five Bomber Command aircrew were killed. Those of us at Luft III represented the one-in-seven who survived downed bombers. Four of our crew lived. I tell the three others – half a century dead beneath the tombstones at Eindhoven – how it was in the dozen minutes after they were gone. A fiery pylon arose five miles above Cologne, scarring the horizon of blacked-out Europe. It was at once a torch of hope for enslaved millions and a preface to Armageddon.

We were the last of the gladiators; the last to light fire-storms by hand. To defend humanity, we morally desensitized the human race. Winston Churchill enobled us. Feldmarshal Goering thought of the Royal Air Force and his Luftwaffe as medieval knights jousting in tournament. But we were all warriors, the airmen above and the civilians in the streets.

Latter-day revisionists have described us as callow kids duped to do the devil's work, innocent of the humanity on target below us. Of course, we knew there were people down there. We did what we had to do and to do it we suppressed the human imagery.

Those of us who recall the inferno stoked in Cologne, Hamburg and Dresden – peaking at Hiroshima – remember, too, how Warsaw and Rotterdam were razed. How they died in London streets and in Coventry and in Hull where an air raid warden found his wife.

'She were burnt right up to 'er waist. 'Er legs were just two cinders. I'd have lost 15 'omes if I could 'ave kept my missus,' he said.

So we were directed to the working-class areas of 58 major German cities. The aim was to make a third of the German work-force homeless. The Air Ministry figured that a four-engine bomber would leave 6,000 Germans without shelter. As it turned out seven major raids achieved 70 per cent of the homeless quota. We left 1,596,000 Germans without shelter and killed 200,000 of them. (This was incomparable with the six million they gassed to death; certainly no less humane.)

Mea culpa. But we did not pick the times in which we lived. To fight our battles we could not retread those two million years between the use of wooden clubs and flint-tipped arrows, the 10,000 years between the stone axe and iron weaponry nor those 2,500 years since armies were first marshalled into infantry, archers and cavalry. We could not refly the biplane duels of our fathers' day. Nor could we leap to video games in this age of second-guessing.

We were the warriors available in those desperate years between Dunkirk and Normandy. While Europe lay captive and the Nazi forces raged across the Eastern frontiers killing Slavs and Jews and other *untermenchen* – soldiers and civilians alike – we were the only striking force on the Western Front. For those four awesome years Allied airmen kept the balance of power from tipping to disaster.

We found no glory and we still taste the ashes. But we were ripe for that last war of the gladiators. It lay in our place and time. We could not avoid it.

2

Wasn't It Romantic

LONDON, Spring 1941

On the June day in 1917 that I was born in Montreal's Royal Victoria Hospital, a staff doctor was practising battlefield medicine and writing poetry in Belgium. Within half a year Colonel John McCrae had dropped his scalpel and pen to become humus in the Flanders Fields he had immortalized. *To you from falling hands we throw the torch* . . .

On a March night a quarter century later, within a couple of blocks of the Royal Vic, two World War I veterans to whom McCrae had thrown the torch tossed it to me. Duke Schiller had come out of that earlier war to barnstorm and bush-fly; to carry machinery, prospectors and sick Indians in the winged wheel-barrows that trundled down our northern skies. Danny Duggan had pioneered airmail service on the American east coast.

I met them at Toronto's Malton Airport in the fall of 1940. As a RCAF navigator trainee I calculated courses that Duke or Danny would ceremoniously accept and studiously ignore as they flew the pattern of lights marking Southwestern Ontario towns.

'You're ignoring my courses,' I yelled at Danny one night after weeks of frustration.

'Not really. I read them,' he replied.

'But you don't fly them. You just aim for the lights of the next town.'

'That's true.'

'But I'm supposed to be learning to navigate.'

'So you learn to navigate and I fly to the next town. What has one frigging thing to do with the other?' Danny asked.

I could no more respond to his Boston-Irish logic than I could explain the frustration we felt with the war more than a year old and still 3,000 miles away. The Battle of Britain had been fought without us. Would there ever be another? The first class of the British Commonwealth Air Training Scheme had just graduated and we were the fourth in the stream. There was the gnawing fear that air warfare would end any day without our help.

In the half-year our aircrew class trained for war, Duke and Danny moved on to join the pool of pilots pioneering trans-Atlantic air service. Just a dozen years since Charles Lindbergh blazed the way, Atlantic Ferry pilots were making routine flights to Britain twice a month to deliver American-made bomber aircraft.

'At 500 bucks a flight,' Danny said.

'In American dough,' Duke added.

Now they were waving me off to war from a Mount Royal Hotel suite with ill-disguised envy. 'The Duke and I wish we were in your flying boots,' said Danny lifting his glass.

'But this war we've got it made,' Duke told me. 'Keep your nose clean, kid.'

Within two years they were both dead. Danny was among a half dozen ferry pilots killed when the Liberator carrying them back to Canada didn't make it. Duke overshot on a night landing in Bermuda. One in five civilian flyers on the Atlantic Ferry Service were killed in those war years. Our Bomber Command losses would be four out of five by mid-war. But that spring night of 1941 no one was calling the odds on catching a sky hook.

Clarence (Duke) Schiller had survived the earlier war to fly the uncharted Arctic on bottled instinct, so to speak, and to make his legendary rescue flights. Now he sat tieless in the same blue denim work-shirt he had worn across the Arctic, the Atlantic and the Mount Royal Hotel lobby with equal panache and indifference.

'But not in London last week,' Duke admitted. 'Headwaiter at the Grosvenor handed me a damn tie to wear to dinner.' 'Don't you know there's a bloody war on?' I asked him. 'Yes sir, but it's business as usual here,' he tells me. That's the difference between them and us. They can't get away from it so when the bombs aren't falling they pretend things are normal.' A taciturn man, Duke Schiller fell silent. It had been one of his longer speeches.

Still he didn't feel he had made his point. 'Look at it this way,' he told me. 'This is the second time in our lives Canadians have gone overseas to fight alongside the Brits. When there's a war on we volunteer. But don't ever forget, kiddo, the game is being played on their turf. It's their bystanders that get conked with the foul balls.'

A couple of months earlier Danny had ordered a made-to-measure suit from a London tailor shop. Three or four neighbouring Bond Street stores had been bombed out of existence. 'How soon can you come back for a fitting?' the tailor asked.

'In two or three weeks. Think you'll still be here?' Danny wondered.

'Yes sir. Have been since 1866. Where can we contact you?'

'Well that's a bit of a problem. I'm flying back to Montreal tomorrow.'

'You're what, sir?'

'Flying back to Canada. I deliver bomber aircraft about twice a month,' Danny explained.

'You're flying the bleeding ocean twice a month and you wonder if we'll still be here a fortnight from now. What bloody cheek!' Then they had both doubled with laughter.

Half a century later that exchange between a Boston-Irish pilot and a Bond Street tailor hangs in memory like a rope bridge thrown across a chasm between the Brits and us, between Duke and Danny's generation and mine, between the simplistic society in which I had grown up and the moral minefield into which I was heading. There was a vast ocean to cross.

The day after Duke and Danny waved me off to war I sought out my grandfather, Benjamin Silver, in his walk-up St Marks Street apartment. He was a quixotic man who had fled Fiddler-on-the-Roof country to raise his family in Ottawa Valley towns and Kingston in John A. Macdonald's day. There he would assemble his six children at the Sunday-morning break-fast-table to feed them the atheist dogma of Ralph Ingersoll's *Secular Thought Magazine* before they could touch the food.

Now the *New York Times* lay open on my grand-dad's kitchen table and he pounded it for emphasis as he cited what 'Mr. Churchill' and 'Mr. Roosevelt' had to say. Four of his five grandsons would retrace his odyssey, first to Britain then through Europe. One of them, jogging off McGill playing-field just down the street to join the Air Force, didn't make it back. I was the third of his grandsons to go to war. 'You're going to do a danger-ous job and I hope you rely on your own internal resources to see you through,' he said.

I could sense what was coming next. 'Do you believe in prayer?' my grand-dad asked.

As a child, prayer had meant the now-I-lay-me-down-to-sleep litany that blessed every family member nightly in lieu of seasonal greeting cards. 'No,' I answered after some hesitation.

'Prayer is for fools and cowards,' he told me flatly. 'I am pleased that you will be guided by your own conscience. That you can draw on your own inner strength.'

I sucked in my breath and changed the subject. I was no more up to his expectations than anyone else in the family ever been. Could I person-ally get along without prayer? My grandfather's question would be tested in the sheer terror that stalked a moon-bright sky 60 weeks after he asked it.

Trained aircrew were worth $80,000 apiece that spring so they fed us into the beleaguered North Atlantic convoys a few per ship. Thirty of us sailed to Iceland on the S.S. *Montclair*, a merchant vessel mounting its five-inch guns as cocky as a kid with a sling-shot. The voyage was a week of gun-crew drills and alarms; of smelling the metallic stink of death that tin fish and iron men-of-war spew in their wake.

Iceland was a bleak, windswept pause; Reykjavik gave us a foretaste of war. A merchant ship in the convoy ahead of ours had been blown out of the water. When we tied up they were washing bunker oil from some of her seamen; burying others down a long dirt road.

From Iceland we came over to Britain on the *Royal Ulsterman* without escort; running fast through fog-topped chop, shrugging off the submarine talk but not the foul Atlantic weather. When the babble of voices died that last night at sea the slap of water became apparent. Half a bucket of water sloshed in each of 50 toilet bowls with every roll of the ship.

Morning brought clear sailing and a blue horizon that belied our passage. It's fabric spun by the gods of war, a cultural curtain hung over the North Atlantic. You could sense it when you crossed the meridian 30 degrees west of Greenwich. Time and place changed, daylight and darkness switched, moods and attitudes altered. Europe and North America were twain.

We came through that curtain on a spring morning in 1941. Shrugging off the cloak of night the *Royal Ulsterman* surged into the grey shreds of day. Sniffing the fog-shrouded horizon, her radar caught the scent of the Hebrides. Now she was running fast for the Isles. Underfoot you could feel the ship's roll and yaw lengthen into a purposeful lunge for Britain in a series of long, rolling thrusts.

'Like a gut shaking off colic,' someone said.

As the troopship changed pace so did we. In the early hours of that last morning at sea we shifted sights from our peaceful dominion to an island besieged; from war as a game to the business of war. The curtain closed behind us sweeping the realities of home into nostalgia. At long last we were crossing the horizon. We were moving from the audience to the stage. Drama and dreams were hardening into new reality. Our span of expectation shortened to match that of the war-torn Brits. War had no time for leisurely romance. Come quickly – now! now! – because tomorrow may not come at all.

By mid-morning the sun had burned off the low-lying mist and peeled back layer on layer of stratus cloud. Now the grey sea was flecked with green and the upper cloud leaked sun-lit blue. From the depths of an empty patch of sky, a Sunderland flying boat took shape. It lumbered over our port bow flashing a streak of greeting by Aldis lamp. Gulls came screeching in its wake.

About noon the rocky spine of the Outer Hebrides broke the surface of the sea. Within an hour we were slipping down the passage between the Isles of North Uist and Skye; an hour after that, down past Tiree and the Island of Mull. From these ancestral waters Canada-bound forebears set sail in centuries past. Through these isles Duke and Danny's cohorts had preceded us a generation earlier.

19

With every league of water the sea became a brighter hue, the land more lush, the business of war more evident. Coastal vessels, patrol boats, salt-caked trawlers and barnacled dories hailed us as we came down around the Mull of Oa and the Mull of Kincaid. Suddenly we were in the Clyde flanked by small craft; anointed by a pair of Gloucester Gladiator biplanes out of Stranraer.

The ships of war lay around us in a hundred shapes and sizes from Wemyss Bay to Greenock docks. The flags and pennants were as varied as Britain's allies and dependents that second wartime spring. But it was the ubiquitous barrage balloons, ill-shaped bladders tugging on cable leads from every vessel, that gave them the uniform caps of war. While the ponderous balloons were harmless the steel cables tethering them could slice the wing off a plane. They were not much of a deterrent except at low altitude. I didn't give them another thought until the night we crept back, skimming the North Sea surface in a battered Whitley that Tony doubted would climb across the English coast.

Now the creased faces of the balloons winked at us. Sirens screamed, klaxons sounded, horns tooted. Somewhere below us at dockside a band erupted into *Bless 'Em All*. We came down the gangway to be greeted by firm-fleshed NAAFI girls, their tams saucy on sober hairstyles, ladling out coffee and Eccles cakes. Full-bosomed women embraced us as we had not been held since we were weaned. Younger ones offered full-mouth kisses – warm, wet and not quite wanton. Their Glaswegian accents were unfathomable in the dockside din. But their message was evident.

'Don't mind the clutter, boys,' they said. 'We're an island beseiged but a land alive. Enjoy it while you can.'

The Battle of Britain had been fought by the few and been won. But it had not ended. Blitzed and beset, the beleaguered Brits welcomed us to the family of 50 million crowding their island – Brits themselves, Anzacs, Canadians, Dutch, Free French, Norwegians, Poles – the recruits and refugees from a dozen countries. We really were one family then – intimate, unified, interdependent, mutually respectful.

As Britain's crack train, the *Royal Scotsman*, carried us south we were swallowed up in the blackout, that most pervasive fact of wartime life. Blinds were drawn on the coach windows and we were left in semi-darkness – 'illumined by blue pinpoints of light and the pale ovals of neighbouring faces,' as contemporary writer Vera Brittain put it.

From dusk to dawn for the next four years we shared the blackout with 700 million others across Britain, Europe and the Soviet Union. From the outset the absence of any light that might guide bomber crews – ours or theirs – to a target population created an additional hazard and a pall on wartime life. During the first months of war traffic fatalities in Britain had nearly doubled. Then civilian drivers were allowed to use dimly masked headlights. Yet people still walked into canals, banged into lamp-posts and fell down stair-wells.

While the blackout was particularly hazardous for the elderly it was opportune for the young. Like the war gods' mid-Atlantic curtain it filtered morality and loosed inhibitions. It cloaked clinching couples. The night spoke of adventure, relaxation and sex. The blackout enhanced the wartime night and spread a blanket. War's urgency – do it now – inclined us to lie down.

Back home, a generation before The Pill liberated womanhood and when venereal disease scared everyone, we maintained a two-kinds-of-girls mythology. Nice girls held out for marriage – *de facto*, promised or implied. The exigencies of wartime Britain heightened expectations, blurred moral boundaries and changed viewpoints on relative risks. For the God-fearing believer there was a countervailing factor, of course. Fundamentalists still scrawled their message on the hoardings. 'The wages of sin are death.' Even passing atheists read the graffiti.

We were in the vanguard of the British Commonwealth air training plan – a programme that would put 131,000 pilots, navigators, wireless operators, gunners and bombadiers, more than half of them Canadians – into Royal Air Force operational aircraft. The arrival of our 650 aircrew, yet to be trained for actual warfare in European skies, was less than memorable. Still it was a bright spot of news in a lousy fortnight. British forces had withdrawn from Greece in 'a second Dunkirk' the week before. Londoners were subjected to the worst and last raid of a 34-week blitz the first Saturday night we were there.

A 'bomber's moon' bathed target landmarks and the low-ebb Thames restricted the fire-fighters' water supply. That night 1,436 Londoners died, a quarter-million books burned at the British Museum and $250,000 worth of gin poured from blitzed warehouses into City Road gutters. Westminster Abbey, the Parliament Buildings and the Tower of London were bombed. 2,200 fires raged from Hammersmith to Romford. Still after 587 nights of war we had yet to share their experience. We watched the searchlights and pyrotechnics slash the night six miles away. We had yet to be blooded under Luftwaffe attack.

Londoners remained defiant. When Hitler's deputy Rudolf Hess parachuted into Britain on a crazed one-man peace mission the following week, the Bulmer's cider people ran an opportune newspaper advertisement. *Can you guess / why Rudolf Hess / came by air / from over there ? / The reason's clear / we've Bulmer's here.*

Someone crowned a truncated Bond Street light standard with the head of a display mannequin blown from a shattered shop window. 'I've lost my body, Hitler, not my head,' said the placard beneath it. The hoarding that shielded Eros' statue in Picadilly Circus bore a Cockney oath: 'God damn you frigging Huns.'

As a newspaper reporter pre-war I had chased accidents, covered fires, queried hold-up victims to wring the drama from violent events. Here in London this second year of war violence was to be endured if not ignored. I tried to explain it in a few lines of verse to my folks back home.

That woman in Waterloo, I saw,
standing undismayed with child in hand;
standing amid the shambles of broken brick
– a neighbourhood crushed to fragments,
marking triumph for a Luftwaffe bomber's stick.
Standing not 200 yards from where
a warning spoke familiar words,
'Unexploded bomb. Beware.'
There she joked and laughed amid the mess.
Casually she laughed as well she might have done
had she or child have torn their dress.
And when I asked a naive question her reply
spoke for all England.
'Quit! We'd rather die.'

That Monday we were billeted at an RAF reception centre in Uxbridge, a half-hour subway ride from Oxford Circus, London's hub. Draped with gas masks and forewarned of perils – moral, mortal and militant – we were given a week's free time to adjust our sights to a world at war.

The images of that May week still dance momentous in my mind's eye. It began with Eric and Inez Gibb taking me on tour of London's ancient, war-ravaged core and to dinner among the rich and famous in Soho. The week ended in a Wembley street with a girl named Joan who looked like pre-war film star Hedy Lamarr. She was in my arms.

For Eric and Inez flanking me in long strides, I was news from home even if they over-talked it. Four years earlier I was among the *Windsor Star* news staff at their good-bye, godspeed dinner. Eric was bound for a job with the London tabloid *Sketch*; Inez to mesmerize a BBC audience of kids as she had done on the Mutual Broadcasting System from Detroit.

Keenly-tuned observers, they marched me through the square-mile, medieval borough of Westminster citing its landmarks from the site of King Canute's palace to the Abbey; expounding on a millenium of history and 20 months of war, on Churchill's leadership and how to smother a firebomb on a steep roof.

Didn't they worry about being bombed to death?

'It's really too late to worry, isn't it!' Inez responded.

'We're too busy living,' Eric told me.

At the Czardas in Soho we capped dinner with peaches in brandy. Beatrice Lillie (Lady Peel), her elegant beauty belying her Cockney-image songs, smiled at us from the next table.

'Another airman from Canada, Lady Peel,' Inez told her.

'Another ex-*Windsor Star* reporter,' Eric insisted.

Eric's talk of life and fatalities in wartime London struck a note of *deja-vu*. I had first sniffed a covey of deaths in his company. On a late winter night in 1937 a coffer-dam collapsed at Port Stanley, Ontario, drowning 14 harbour-construction workers. The *Star* despatched me under Eric's tutelage. With a photographer we had sped 100 miles over ice-coated roads to the site. The scene was floodlit and awesomely silent when we arrived. Divers were probing the wreckage. The water would swallow them, then gurgle sardonically like the burping of well-fed frogs as the divers again broke the surface.

I followed spellbound as Eric pursued eye-witnesses, co-workers, rescue-team members and later next-of-kin. His questions were incisive, his voice muted. He asserted an authority that invited answers and the empathy that assured them. What I would never forget was that he approached these deaths as consequential – the logical outcome of mortal men doing potentially dangerous work. In speaking with their co-workers and family, Eric treated each death as the ultimate event that made those workers' lives significant. Unspoken was the obvious corollary that somewhere, sometime, we all must die.

'There is a time to live and a time to die. We choose it,' a writer named Huchsnegger once said. Eric was second-in-command of Canadian Army public relations in the war years. Post-war he headed *Time* magazine's London bureau. He was in charge of their Middle East bureau in the 1950s when he shot his brains out.

If you were at RAF Uxbridge reception centre, or the Polish fighter squadron at Northolt or the Irish Guards' west London base, or if you lived on Eton Court behind Wembley Stadium in those wartime days, you might remember the Orchard Inn at Ruislip. It had a dwarf drummer, a pianist into his second war, and two brass players beyond conscripting. It was three or four stops away from Uxbridge, Northolt and Wembley on the Underground.

Joan would remember it. I do. I look back across the yesteryears into the cigarette smoke hovering above the checkered tablecloths, around the dancers' heads, beneath the multi-coloured lights. It is early and the music is upbeat – *Wish me luck as you wave me good-bye*. It becomes lively as the couples swing through *Beer Barrel Polka* and *Waltzing Matilda*. Later *There'll Always Be An England* will bond us to the Island. Still later *The White Cliffs of Dover* will give us a foretaste of that coastal view homebound bomber crews scanned the edge of dawn to see.

Straight-backed men in uniform, full-blown girls in their very good dresses, are swaying and swirling. The music becomes wistful – *Wishing, If I Had My Way, Maybe*. Now couples lean into each other gently sharing their sexuality, their body heat, the smell of mouth-wash and carbolic soap.

Who's Taking You Home Tonight, asks the proxy voice of the band. *I Want to Say Thanks for a Lovely Weekend*, they sing, putting the ultimate dream into eager heads.

Walking up Eton Court we pass the low brick structure of an air raid shelter. It would offer little protection if a bomb fell nearby but it might shield you from flying debris. Better than being out in the open. It affords a moment of privacy this moonlit night.

'Can we look inside?' I ask artlessly.

'Not much to see,' she laughs. I hear the carefree words but miss the little tremor of anxiety.

In the shadows just inside the doorless entrance we embrace. Not ardently, we might still be on the dance floor. Her lips are warm, affectionate, neither sexy nor sisterly.

'Closer,' I whisper.

'Let me look at you,' Joan replies. We are in a shaft of moonlight now. Her hands bracket my face holding it in focus as she tilts her head back. Moonlight traces her lips, the classic lines of her face. It reflects from her eyes.

'Closer!'

There is no response. But in the half light of the shelter I see an answer shaping in the depths of her eyes. The message is beamed like an Aldis lamp flashing from the folds of night. 'I won't stop you if you insist,' the look tells me. 'But, please, not now.'

I release my hold, take her hand and lead her back onto Eton Court. 'You talk with your eyes,' I tell her. 'It's . . . it's like you were speaking from the soul.'

She laughs and it eases my embarrassment. It is a mix of amusement, cultural confusion, affection. For a moment our roles are reversed. She is the sophisticate, I a gauche young guy on the make. In fact, I am a month away from my twenty-fourth birthday. I was a seasoned newspaperman walking police-court corridors, hearing the deceptions of the self-conned and the hollow tones of the self-lobotomized, when Joan was still in convent school.

But that was three years before. Now her mind travels a short flight back to the soldier who penned her a verse on Dunkirk beach before he died. She sees a west-end London dance hall the night it was smashed by an errant bomb. There is all that plaster dust and debris and a detached stocking filled with the curve of a school-mate's leg.

We kiss goodnight on her doorstep. There is no good-bye but I have a war to get into. I am at the sidewalk when she calls after me.

'Will you write?' she asks.

'Yes I will.'

'But you don't have my address?'

'Oh yes. It's 25 Eton Court.' I am looking at the house number.

'You'll forget,' Joan says and her laughter trails me down the street.

'Oh no I won't.'

Nor did I. Half a century later I can still see the white-on-black house number – 25 – shining in moonlight to the left of the door.

3

Did You Know Him?

ABINGDON, Summer 1941

A death impacts to the degree of its proximity. We attend a neighbour's funeral but blink at genocide half a world away.

That first week in Britain we caught up with fellow-members of the fourth course in the British Commonwealth Air Training Plan. A year earlier 498 of us had been despatched from RCAF Manning Depot to airfields across the country. In another year less than 60 fourth-course alumni would be left and most of us would be kicking sand in German POW camps. Of the dead we recall only those who flashed to oblivion in the nearby night.

A middle-aged flight-lieutenant flying a small desk at Uxbridge handed me a travel chit to Operational Training Unit at Abingdon. 'It's near Oxford and you're going to be on Whitleys,' he said encapsulating the next quarter year of my life in a sentence. Beneath the brush of a handlebar moustache profuse as a peacock's ass I detected a muttered comment. It was either 'You lucky fellow' or 'You hapless bastard.' I couldn't tell which.

Abingdon was a ten-minute ride from Oxford, or a 90-minute walk if you missed the last bus Sunday night. The university town was 50 minutes by Great Western Railway from London's Paddington station. Those distances were relevant that summer.

One of the RAF's oldest and largest airfields, RAF Abingdon sits at the end of the Vale of the White Horse. It is flanked by the chalky Chiltern Hills, dairy and pig farms, and by the ancient market town at its back. The take-off and landing circuit took us over a seventh century abbey, a fifteenth century stone bridge, an ancient school and ageless town hall. We flew that circuit at least half a hundred times – ignorant of the heritage beneath our wingtips but sworn to defend it.

My first glimpse of a Whitley was at 14:20 hours on 3 June 1941. Half a century later I recall my initial impression. It is still vivid as the after-taste of the lunch I lost at the sight of this aircraft that would carry me into battle. At rest it sat wide-winged and close to the ground like a disheartened grasshopper with broken legs. Airborne, it flew tail-high and nose down like a hound dog sniffing spoor. It reminded me of the first model plane I sawed from a piece of two-by-four wood and crossed with a wide board for wings. Painted black with shoe polish it had resembled a flying coffin, which was what RAF airmen dubbed the Whitley.

'Geezus, we're going to do 30 operations in *that*!' I exclaimed.

'Not likely more than five or six,' a war-weary NCO assured me, 'though some lucky bods last eight or nine.'

The Whitley was officially described as 'A mid-wing monoplane designed and equipped for the duties of a heavy bomber. The fuselage is of light-alloy monocoque (one-piece shell) construction, the skin stiffened by continuous fore-and-aft stringers supported by transverse hoops. The three main portions of the fuselage are pin-jointed to the main plane (wing) spar and stern.' So said the manual.

The aircraft was 69 feet long with an 84-foot wingspan. Powered by a pair of Merlin-10 engines, it would – theoretically – haul a 3,500-pound bomb-load nearly a thousand miles across Europe, cruising up to 17,600 feet at 165 miles per hour.

Pieces of Whitley T-for-Tommy-4334 – two substantial fuselage fragments and the manifold intake from an engine – are mounted on an oak plaque hanging now from my office wall. They are mute evidence of the light alloy's durability, and how the monocoque structure would emit survivors like an oyster spitting pearls. Whitley crew and German gunners alike could attest to the uncanny resistance of the pin-joints, light-alloy stringers and transverse hoops that held together under the most concerted flak and fighter assault.

And the aircraft *did* penetrate to Reich targets 800 miles from our Yorkshire base – although none that I knew of ever got above 12,000 feet or 135 mph in level flight. Within those limits it was getting a bit dicey by Christmas 1941 when our squadron converted to four-engined Halifaxes.

But that was in the unfathomable future. On this June day – a year since I signed up and nearly two years since I heard Neville Chamberlain's lugubrious declaration of war and knew I would be in it – a Whitley took me into the hostile skies.

A parody of a wartime song still lingers.

I'd like to fly a Whitley 3
and fly all over Germany
and watch the flak come up at me
It's foolish but its fun.
And if by chance I got shot down
you'd have to wait a while.
So button up your lower lip
and smile my sweetie, smile.

I'd like to fly a Whitley 3
and fly all over Germany
and watch the flak come up at me . . .

The lines keep repeating themselves and I cannot disconnect from them. Half a century later those stupid lines carry me on an endless circuit like a bike on a treadmill. And I don't know how to get off.

At the navigator's table, behind the pilots' backs, I either peered over their shoulders at the instrument panel or through the Perspex windscreen. From this vantage point a Whitley take-off was startling. Its twin Merlin engines bayed in anguish but the nose was reluctant to assume flying position. The sprawling aircraft would shuffle up to speed and lift skittishly at about 90 miles per hour. It always seemed as if the runway had been yanked from under us and that the 'plane was sniffing in search of it.

Pilots, navigators, wireless-operators and gunners, we had been trained separately back in Canada. Abingdon OTU's function was to meld us into bomber crews and cultivate our tribal instinct to collaborate for survival. On a basketball court five players will break into a measured trot; each in his own circuit, all five making a rhythmic advance. As elegantly timed as a minuet, choreographed like ballet, the squad moves harmoniously down the floor. Hockey and water-polo teams advance in the same unified way. That is what we were trained to do in a dozen weeks at Abingdon.

Morning lectures updated us on armaments – theirs and ours; explained the short-wave IFF transmitter beeping Identification Friend or Foe; delineated airfield and beacon locations – ours and theirs; expanded on codes, wireless and RT for Radio-Talk procedures; explained Luftwaffe fighter tactics and how to distinguish their 'planes from ours. We were instructed in first aid; on how to apply a tourniquet and administer morphine.

We were drilled in putting out fires, or if we couldn't, then how to abandon a Whitley by dinghy or parachute. Our survival, personal and collective, hung on an indeterminate balance of all that knowledge, team-work and luck. The gods of war controlled our chances but at Abingdon we learned to lengthen the odds.

We flew the length and breadth of the beleaguered isle familiarizing ourselves with British defence zones, balloon barrages and anti-aircraft sites. Nothing was more instructive than the flash of gunfire and puff of cordite from a British coastal vessel off Skegness or Felixstowe, Dover or the Isle of Wight. Didn't those friggers know a Whitley when they saw one?

'Not frigging likely, mate.'

By day the English countryside was all rolling downs and lush green valleys. Pasturing sheep were unnerved and grazing cattle spooked by the swift passage of the Whitley's pterodactyl shadow. Farmers stopped tractors to watch our progress. Housewives parted the laundry on clothes-lines to wave at us.

By dusk, clouds generally covered the English downs and Midland hills. They mounted the Yorkshire fell-sides and cushioned the Pennine peaks. Night fell on a featureless panorama. Drapes, curtains, shutters, headlight masks and the light-guards atop poles in railway yards painted all Britain black.

Most nights the moonlight seeping through scattered cloud was enough to reflect the distinctive shape of channels, river-mouths, bays and inlets on a coastline never more than a few minutes flying time away. Inland, RAF beacons flashed codes identifiable on our charts. Any other illumination signalled danger. The flick of a searchlight beam slicing the darkness to fix us in a blinding glare told us we had strayed into a forbidden area. The muzzle flash of Bofors or Hispano-Suiza cannon fire announced that a nervous ship's crew didn't give a damn who we were.

Any night there was that random chance that a four or five-second burst of lead, cordite, fire and pyrotechnics from a Luftwaffe intruder would rip the dark with a lethal perforation line, each shell glowing evil like phosphorescent light reflected from shark's teeth in dark depths.

So we gave close attention to morning lectures, pored over the face of Britain in daylight flying. And on long night cross-country flights we practised the evasion and penetration of German defences from the relative shelter of the British sky.

The week we arrived at Abingdon, Hermann Goering switched the weight of his Luftwaffe forces to the East. Reluctantly he accepted defeat in the Battle of Britain. In three weeks the Hun would be at Mother Russia's throat. Within a month Churchill would write to Stalin: 'The longer the war lasts, the more help we can give. We are making very heavy attacks both by day and night with our air force upon all German-occupied territory and all Germany within our reach. About 400 daylight sorties were made (by fighters) yesterday. On Saturday night over 200 bombers attacked German towns and last night nearly 250 heavy bombers were operating. This will go on.'

At this switch-point in the air war the pressure was not on RAF training command. No.10 OTU was programmed to a five-day week and Abingdon's commandant looked perceptively on restive young men who would be a long time dead. So late Friday afternoon or Saturday morning a 48-hour pass was usually there for the asking. London was just over an hour away. And the most beautiful girl in the world lived at 25 Eton Court.

Looking across Abingdon's smoky sergeant's mess one night the first week we were there I saw a familiar face from high-school days. Coulson Adams was a year ahead of me at Kennedy Collegiate and he had left an impressive reputation for athletic, scholastic and sexual achievement behind him.

Recognition was mutual because the *Windsor Star* had already run my picture three times since I enlisted. Because I was the first of its news staff to pursue a fighting role they were determined to fly – patriotically and vicariously – into battle with me.

'Back home you're famous, Silver, and you haven't as much as pooped on the Germans yet. Better send them a new picture for your obituary,' Collie insisted.

A constant smile creased his broad-Scot face like a Hallowe'en cartoon. A second pair of crescents creased the corners of his eyes. His smile disarmed men and charmed women. The eye creases were misleading. They gave a sleepy-eyed, laid-back look. In fact, they were the eyes of a star athlete conserving energy, relaxing in the self-confidence that he can spring like a tiger when action is warranted. In my lifetime I knew two others who wore that deceptive sleepy-smiling eye mask. One was Ontario attorney-general Roy McMurtry who quarter-backed the evacuation of a quarter-million Mississauga residents threatened by chlorine from rail-wrecked tank cars one post-war day. The other was my father. Collie, McMurtry and my dad were all star football back-fielders in their time.

Collie, the eldest of Windsor medical health officer Dr Fred Adam's three sons to become Air Force pilots (one survived the war), approached every challenge with wit and ingenuity. Just two days after our arrival at Abingdon he was inexplicably sharing a room with a fellow trainee pilot a mile down the road from the base entrance. It was in quarters normally occupied by married members of the station permanent staff.

'The off-base digs do have advantages,' he admitted.

'I can imagine,' I said. But my imagination couldn't bridge his. Already he had an arrangement with an older woman near the station. In return for Collie's sexual favours she did his and his room-mate's laundry without charge. Twice a week he dropped off the dirty clothes in a kit-bag and fulfilled his commitment. Twice weekly the woman's daughter delivered the clean laundry to the brave airman her mother had befriended.

Pragmatic, and more aware than I that our dozen weeks at Abingdon were a survival course, Collie tried to keep me on track. Frustrated by the protracted waiting from one stage of our training to the next, I was bored by the morning lecture sessions.

'Pay attention. They're telling us how to stay alive,' he advised.

When I continued to rev-up and take-off in romantic flight after Joan he tried chocking my undercarriage wheels. 'You're aiming to be a widow-maker, Silver,' he warned me.

I was undeterred. On a dozen weekends I would bound down

Paddington station stairs to Joan's embrace. A dozen Saturday nights we danced at the Orchard Inn or crowded a London pub or affected indifference when they posted the red 'Alert' placard in the Criterion off Piccadilly.

The weekend Germany attacked Russia I celebrated my twenty-fourth birthday. Joan cooked Sunday dinner, her mother baked a cake and her sister Eve produced a bottle of wine. I returned to Abingdon starry-eyed and told Collie about it. Soon the mess was in an uproar of celebration. I was stripped stark naked and pursued over an improvised steeplechase route to be squirted with fire-extinguishers from floor level as I jumped the over-turned furniture. 'Happy twenty-fourth birthday,' they kept screaming. 'We hope you live to be 25.'

'How about Joan's sister,' Collie asked me later that week.

'Eve is 30, has a big war job. Not your type,' I told him.

'Does she do laundry?' he wondered.

'Why not come to London with me this week-end and see for yourself,' I suggested. That Friday night both Collie's crew and mine were posted for cross-country flights. It was agreed that I would come by his billet at 9:00 the next morning to pick him up.

There were just two training flights scheduled that night and we took off within minutes of each other. Our crew flew a three-hour cross-country trip that tested my navigation over blacked-out Britain. Within sight of the ground I would pencil in landmarks and the location of flashing beacons on a mercator chart. Above the overcast I would ask for a radio-bearing or, if need be, take a sextant reading and plot a position line based on the angle of light from some distant star. The mathematical logic of astro-navigation had been poured into us at great expense. But it left me skeptical. It was like depending on Peter Pan astride a moonbeam with a flashlight to guide us home.

We were within about three minutes of Abingdon on our last leg when a burst of tracer scarred the blackness with a line of luminous dashes. It was at about the one o'clock position from our Whitley's nose, perhaps a mile away. Three of us called it out at the same time.

'Geezus!'

'That's frigging tracer.'

'Holy god!'

As we spoke the fiery flak line ended in a violent flash that left a momentary yellow blob on the retina of our eyes. Then as suddenly as it had been sighted it was gone.

'Come in L for Lanky. Land now,' the tower directed us. When we checked in with the operations officer he was studiously tight-lipped. We assumed there had been a Luftwaffe intruder in the area but information was dispensed on a need-to-know basis. We didn't ask questions.

About 9:15 Saturday morning I was at Collie's door. While I waited I wondered if his crew had sighted the shoot-up as well. But there was no answer. 'Damn it. Impatient bugger couldn't wait 15 minutes,' I muttered and went on into London alone.

'Coulson Adams, a pal from high-school, was going to come with me. He wanted to meet Eve but we missed connections,' I told Joan.

There was a short, sharp air raid that Saturday night. Anti-aircraft fire, ambulance hooters, the whistle of falling bombs and the rumble of exploding ones merged in an infernal din. Joan shrugged it off with the indifference of a Londoner who had survived 30 months of war. It was my first real awareness of the enemy's lethal intent.

Suddenly we were trapped by a curtain of deafening cacophony and stupefying pyrotechnics. Sound and light of increasing intensity hemmed us in. There was no place to run; no defensive action to take. I would learn that was the difference between bombing a target and being one. No matter how relentless the searchlights might grip you or the flak tear at your innards there was always the perception that you could take evasive action.

To blitz or be blitzed may have been equally lethal. Yet the former had the illusion of gamesmanship. The bomber crew might do something to influence the outcome. The target population was in the indifferent lap of the gods.

Joan and I ducked into an Underground entrance and down the stairs to the subway level. In the blue half-light we stepped carefully over, around and between people bedded down for the night. They covered the subway platform from the tiled wall to within about three feet of the tracks.

'Some of these people have been sheltering here since the blitz began,' Joan said. We sat close as the Bakerloo train rattled through the dimly lit tunnel to North Wembley. Her hand lay on mine stroking it absently.

'The first time the sirens went was the day Chamberlain declared war,' she said. 'Eve and I were caught in the open and thought we would be killed straight off. When it didn't happen in the next few minutes we went on about our business feeling rather foolish.'

The subway car windows were criss-crossed with a plastic film so they wouldn't shatter. 'Billy Brown of London Town,' a cartoon character of insufferable English superiority, leered at us from an Underground system advertisement. 'If you'll pardon my correction that stuff is there for your protection,' he said lecturing us not to peel away the shatter-proofing.

'Pompous little bugger. He infuriates me,' Joan said.

Sunday night I stepped into the blackness from Oxford railway station and found an Air Force jeep idling at the curb. The driver had just delivered an officer from Abingdon and was waiting to take any arrivals back with him.

'We lost another aircraft Friday night,' he told us enroute.

'I saw it from the air. Was that one of ours?' I asked.

'Yes, crew had two Canadians in it. One was a pilot named Adams. Did you know him?' the driver wondered.

Coulson Adams and his crew-mates were buried on a July day that second summer of war. As their caskets were lowered to the grave's oblivion I tossed in my misplaced metaphors. Aircrew were not like a team to perform on a basketball court. We were soft-shelled creatures being trained to evade phosphorescent shark's teeth in the inky black of night.

The day Churchill and Roosevelt drafted the Atlantic Charter Joan and I climbed a Surrey hill, sat close and felt the warm turf beneath us. The wind sang through a power pylon at our backs. Sheep grazed on the Downs below, on pasture a thousand years in the making. We looked into a wide blue sky, saw scudding clouds, the flight of occasional birds and, higher, the condensation trails of aircraft.

'Ours or theirs?' Joan asked.

I didn't know. But it was enough to bring us back to a world at war. And Collie's death had ringed our young lives with a new sense of mortality, an awareness we had never before considered.

We looked again at the Downs and the bird play, letting the quiet of the day check the stir in our blood. We were close and aware in the spring of our lives. We knew that the touch of finger-tips was enough to send hormones coursing through our orbiting systems like neutron bullets triggering the fusion of twin stars. And my genitals ached to do just that.

'Don't be a widow-maker,' Collie called from his fresh-dug grave. 'Be guided by your own conscience,' my atheist grand-dad reminded me. Two millenium of Catholicism gave Joan direction.

'Should we be serious,' I wondered aloud.

'I imagine we are but I wonder if we should,' Joan replied.

'Collie said I was 'aiming to be a widow-maker. That I should cool off.'

'Eve said much the same.'

'What do you say?'

'I don't think either of us can just snap our fingers and check our feelings,' she said.

'No but in another fortnight I'll be on a squadron.'

'Will that cool it?'

'No but it will cut our chances of doing anything about it.'

'Postpone them,' Joan corrected. 'Are you prepared to wait?'

I told her how I had picked up a sense of wartime urgency as we approached the British Isles. How easy it was to accept the do-it-now philosophy when tomorrow we might be dead. 'But if we do it now it's because we lack faith that I'll be here in another month or another year,' I blurted out.

'That is how I feel,' she said solemnly. 'I'm surprised you would think that way.'

'Frankly, I would be too scared to go on ops without some sense of the future – some conviction I'm going to get through okay.'

That was when she produced the talisman of the traveller's faith, the St Christopher medal. Her arms were around me, our cheeks pressed hot and wet with tears, as she fastened the silver chain with the little silver disc around my neck.

'I'm not even a Catholic,' I told her.

'St Christopher carried Christ on his back. I'm sure he can manage a Canadian atheist,' Joan said.

The following week I bought her an engagement ring at Bravingtons, the jewellers in Trafalgar Square. Servicemen queued up on Saturday afternoons to make such purchases. Some became engaged because they and their girls had to have faith in the future. And some did because they couldn't wait.

4

First Operation

LEEMING. August 1941

I flew into war from historic haunts, with a famous squadron, in high hopes.

Leeming, in the Vale of York, sits at the junction of two old Roman roads on Celtic battlements that held off Emperor Vespasian's Ninth Legion in the first century A.D. Since before Christendom this 10-mile-wide valley has been a cockpit of Britain's troubles.

Trenched in antiquity by the River Swale, the Vale of York is the only passageway through Britain's narrow waist. It is flanked by untamed highlands – the Cleveland Hills, wild Moors and Wolds on the North Sea side; the Yorkshire Dales rising to Pennine peaks in the Lake Country that overlooks the Irish Sea.

Even when the Emperor Hadrian built his wall across the Cheviot Hills some 60 miles further north, the Vale of York remained a battleground. Here in 1069 William the Conqueror unleashed his fury. Driving the Brits from six miles of ramparts and ditches surrounding the Leeming encampment, Norman troops struck west through the Dales to raze every farm, burn every crop and slaughter every animal. 'More than 100,000 Christian folk, young and old alike, perished of hunger,' wrote the medieval historian Oderic Vitalis.

No wonder Yorkshiremen still brood. Nine centuries after William's conquest, 20 centuries since Vespasian's, they would watch our Whitleys scurrying out over Whitby, Scarborough and Flamborough Head, carrying the war back to the continent that summer of 1941.

I was posted to RAF 10 Squadron at Leeming in mid-August. War-weary, the *Royal Scotsman* carried me north that second summer of war. Britain's prize train, once all spit-and-polish, chugged out of the grime, the shattered skylights and scarred platforms of King's Cross station. Like a centipede wearing scuffed and dirty shoes it humped and shuffled out on the maze of track that leaves London.

For 13 weekends another train had carried me into Paddington station, into Joan's embrace. Canadian shoulder-flashes and my observer brevet declaring the Commonwealth's response to Britain's need, I had celebrated war – drunk to it, sung to it, romanticized and saluted it without ever firing a shot. Now the *Scotsman* was carrying me north to do battle. Ironically, every milestone marked my passage from the milling mix of war-bent Londoners to Yorkshire's brooding, bucolic fells and dales.

A generation of wartime literature had prepared me for our dockside welcome by firm-breasted Glaswegian girls offering kisses, coffee and Eccles cakes; for the swirling dancers beneath the Orchard Inn's multi-coloured lights, and for the promised matrimonial voyage with Joan when all was done. But just ahead – only hours away now – a Whitley squadron demanded that I attend reality.

RAF Leeming station promised nothing but flight into battle. Like Ouellette Avenue, my home-town's main street in the elysian years between the wars, the *Scotsman* was taking me minute-by-minute from recently famil-iar grounds into the unknown.

Leeming was at the centre of the Four Group bases. It was one of the new airfields from which Bomber Command had launched its attack on German aircraft factories, oil refineries and military communications a year earlier. No.10 Squadron Whitleys led that first assault just as 'Shiny Ten' Squadron Farman and Blériot biplanes had opened the air war against the Hun a quarter century before.

Now a group captain and Leeming station commander, Bill Staton had taken the squadron into World War II. 'The only pilot in 10 Squadron with any notion of the reality of war, Staton had flown Bristol Fighters with the Royal Flying Corps in World War I, become an ace, won the Miltary Cross and still bore the great scar across his head where a chair had been broken over it at a mess party in 1917,' British writer Max Hastings said.

Staton led 10 Squadron on its first night raid – a low-level assault on the German seaplane base at Sylt off the Danish coast – in March 1940. It was dramatic and news-making, but to Staton's despair and Bomber Command's dismay it demonstrated the inability of night-time bomber crews to find and hit their objectives.

Until mid-war, RAF aircrews lacked the navigational aids to reach and identify blacked-out targets. If they got there they were restrained by an Air Ministry order 'to avoid undue loss of civilian life in the vicinity of the target.' After Coventry, Air Ministry dropped that instruction but the targets still remained obscure.

Staton pioneered target-marking with flares. On a Bremen raid he made six bombing runs over the oil installations from below a thousand feet to define the enemy's fuel storage with photo-flares and Very pistol cartridges. There is no evidence that other crews bombed within the marked area but Staton is said to have brought his Whitley home that night at wave-top height, landing with hundreds of bullet holes in its light-alloy, stiff-skin structure. None of the rest of us ever achieved nearly that degree of ventilation.

Staton epitomized the derring-do and Bomber Command's naive belief in pinpoint night-time bombing before Feldmarshal Goering despatched his Kampfgruppe 100 to raze 20,000 homes in Coventry one November night of 1940. That changed the picture. At the outset some may have shared Goering's fantasy that his Luftwaffe and the RAF were like medieval knights jousting in tournament. But as A.W. Smith had predicted in *Harper's Magazine* a half dozen years earlier, 'the unfortunate citizen offers too good a target to be left alone.'

The radar-guided Coventry raid fired British retaliation. More than that, it reinforced the Air Ministry's growing realization that the navigational aids necessary to take a bomber crew three hours across blacked-out Europe to a discreet target had not yet been developed. In 10 Squadron op's room Bill Staton mounted pictures of bombed out sections of London, Southampton and Coventry. 'Go now and do likewise to the Hun,' he bellowed.

The week that Bill Staton moved 10 Squadron to Leeming, Bomber Command's commander-in-chief Sir Charles Portal noted that of ten German aircraft plants targetted for destruction 'only three can be found with any certainty in moonlight by average crews.' From this he concluded that 'since almost all the primary targets are isolated and in sparsely inhabited districts, the very high percentage of bombers which inevitably miss the target will hit nothing else important and do no damage.'

So Portal argued for setting targets over the widest feasible area of Germany. 'It largely increases the moral effect of our operations by spreading alarm and disturbance over the wider area,' he said. Churchill put it more bluntly. 'We shall bomb Germany by day as well as night in ever-increasing measure, casting upon them month by month a heavier discharge of bombs and making the German people taste and gulp each month a sharper dose of the miseries they have showered upon mankind.'

Staton was determined in his fearless, rudimentary way to search out and identify a precise bombing target. But the essential electronic tools – Gee, H2S and Oboe – were yet to be developed. Two years later the Gee box was installed. It enabled another 10 Squadron C/O, Wing Commander D.C.T. Bennett, to pursue pinpoint navigation and precision bombing. In the process he was shot down by a German pocket battleship in Trondheim harbour. But he got back to found the Pathfinders' Force.

With nice regard for a neutral nation, the RAF flew Bennett back from Sweden in the belly of a Mosquito bomber wearing civilian clothes. The clothes were mine. By the time the C/O got back to Leeming I was in a German POW camp. But I didn't begrudge our squadron commander my Harris tweed jacket and grey flannel trousers. I had had ten momentous months with an illustrious squadron.

I arrived at Leeming on 19 August 1941 one of the first thousand Canadian airmen to reinforce RAF Bomber Command's depleted ranks. The Brits welcomed us as Commonwealth cousins but there was a trans-Atlantic cultural gap to be bridged. The squadron's officers were mostly the erstwhile public-school boys we had read of in *Chums* and *Boy's Own Annual* – erudite, gung-ho and inclined to understatement. As station commander, Bill Staton had briefed crews about to raid the Zeiss plant at Jena. 'This place has not heard the sound of gunfire since the Napoleonic War. Make sure it hears it tonight,' he intoned like an Eton history master.

Later, another 10 Squadron commander would tell Max Hastings: 'One was attuned to getting the chop. Every night you were resigned to dying. You looked around your room before you went out, at the golf clubs in the corner, the books on the shelves, the nice little radio set, the letter to one parent's propped on the table.' As a non-commissioned officer I had no golf clubs, shelves of books, nice little radio nor room of my own. But I did spend nearly a year at Leeming, every night of it resigned to dying in the near future.

The Garth, a vine-covered, expansive and battle-worn home of the Lascelles family (royalty once removed), accommodated NCO aircrew. I was directed to a room atop the wide staircase. Here I joined three other air-observers: Newt Turner who arrived at Leeming the same day as I did, a short Jamaican named Johnny Johnson who did not last long enough to be memorable, and a tall, austere Englishman named Robert Alexander Wilson.

Newt was a 30-year-old relic of the Depression-era travelling salesmen circuit and of a peacetime cavalry regiment. He was among those picked to navigate seat-of-the-pants civilian pilots across the Atlantic in American lend-lease bomber aircraft while the rest of us came by ship. Few flyers had spanned the big pond in those days. There was no long-range radar, no computerized air plots for the 10-hour flight. Newt was teamed with Danny Dugan, a veteran of the Boston-New York airmail route. Accustomed to flying a ground-based radio range, Danny eyed the flight-sergeant naviga-tor and was unimpressed. Turner tried to reassure him by demonstrating the Air Force sextant that produced position lines from starlight.

'Geezus, a sextant!,' Dugan swore. 'Christopher Columbus used one of those frigging things.'

Now Turner greeted me with 'Welcome to the flying assholes dormitory.' The term displeased Wilson but it aptly described the O-for-Observer brevet that we wore. The O was attached to half a wing and it might as readily have depicted an observant chap's monocle or a mooning backside. In fact it designated a trade that had become obsolete in the Air Force soon after Billy Bishop quit the second cockpit of an artillery-observing Bristol aircraft in 1916 to take up Hun-killing as a fighter pilot.

FIRST OPERATION

At the outset of World War II, the term 'air observer' was applied to those of us trained in the dual roles of navigator and bombardier. By the end of 1941 the G-set and subsequent radar developments warranted the attention of a full-time navigator as well as a bomb-aimer. These later aircrew wore flying 'Ns' and 'Bs' respectively. At war's end there were perhaps a couple of thousand of us still wearing the flying O that might designate a backside in flight, O for okay or 'up yours!'

Robert Wilson reinforced the prevailing view that observers were the brainy members of bomber crews. He could rattle off statistics like a stock-ticker. And, as Newt Turner added, 'with as much sense of humour.'

I wondered how 10 Squadron's motto – *rem acu tangere* – should be translated. 'It's Latin meaning . . .' Wilson started to explain.

'Italian,' Turner corrected him.

'No. That's the classic Latin they spoke in ancient Rome,' Wilson told us.

'In Rome they speak Italian. I was there once,' Turner insisted. 'In any case I'll tell you what that motto means.'

'If you don't know Latin you can't translate it,' said Wilson.

'Silver, pay attention,' Turner demanded. '*Rem acu tangere*. That means in the air we only eat spaghetti.'

Turner had been by-passed for pilot training because of his age. In a business where everyone wanted to be at the controls I flunked out as a pilot when I put a Link Trainer into a spin at Initial Training School. The son of a player-piano manufacturer, Edwin Link had invented the little flying cockpit. Like a player piano or church organ it was activated by vacuum pumps, valves and motors to simulate flight in a rough sort of way.

Encased by a hooded roof, the joy-stick between my knees and a movie-made sky unfolding before me, I climbed to adversity and tipped to disaster. Link had invented the little flyer in 1929 and it was said that no one had ever before flown it clean off its base. A selection officer considered my potential.

'You were a reporter in civilian life.'

'Yes sir.'

'Well that must take some powers of observation.'

'I suppose so.'

'Good, Silver. You'll be an observer.'

Within 24 hours of our arrival at Leeming, Turner and I were in a pair of hound-nosed Whitleys air-testing for battle. On the 717th night of the war we would see our first action – a 'nursery trip' to bomb the docks at Le Havre. A year since Hermann Goering had failed to clear the skies over the Channel as prelude to invasion, we were making a routine sortie to disrupt any build-up of assault craft in the Channel port.

Most operations took Four Group aircraft quickly out on North Sea routes to Germany. But beginner crews were weaned on coastal targets. Le Havre was a three-hour flight from Leeming, two-thirds of it safely down the length of Britain. 'Mother England keeps nursery crews close to her breast for as long as possible,' someone suggested.

Dick Speer in the tail turret was doing his first operation as well. Earlier in the day we had been crewed up with wireless operator Murray McLaughlin, a veteran of 20 operations, and with our captain Kenneth Liebeck, a 22-year-old from Steinbach, Manitoba. Liebeck was immaculately turned out with new-blue pilot officer stripes on his battledress epaulettes. His dress cap was as yet unmarked by an intercom headset or from use as a beer pitcher.

He shook hands politely and took stock of each of us as he ran through the Whitley crew drill. With his experience as second pilot on six operations, he was prepared to explain any detail, answer any concern. It was evident, however, that idle banter was not in his repertoire. Chit-chat disturbed him.

We were all four of us Canadians on a RAF squadron, all about the same age. But Liebeck's P/O stripe marked a subtle barrier. Dick, Murray and I were flight-sergeants. About to captain his own crew on their first op, Liebeck would temper authority with concern. The easy rapport that encouraged informal exchange, however, was not his style.

A Manitoba farm-boy from a Mennonite community, he could no more adjust to our crew camaraderie than feel at ease in the ribald, irreverent atmosphere of the officers' mess. While his fellow English officers had moved easily from the cricket-pitch, from atop the class structure to service authority, Kenneth Liebeck matured in the abstemious, non-conformist fellowship of a Mennonite congregation where school-boy fun was tin-can curling in sub-zero weather.

Home, school and church imposed Christian principles, a rigid behavourial code and self-discipline. This God-fearing young officer was conditioned to take direction and give it with literal precision. In the fast-changing conditions of air warfare such a lack of flexibility could be fatal.

For the air test I passed Liebeck course directions for Whitby, 20 minutes flying time to the west. Then in the absence of a second pilot I took the jump seat during take-off to lock the throttles forward and lift the undercarriage on the captain's instructions. In a dozen weeks at Abingdon operational training unit I had performed this second-dickey role three or four times, yet the Whitley take-off still startled me. It was on the tip of my tongue to observe that the aircraft lifted its quivering tail like a hamster in heat. But I doubted that Liebeck would appreciate the analogy.

Brakes on, he brought the twin Merlin engines up to 3,000 revolutions per minute, superchargers boosting pressure in the cylinders to nearly six pounds per square inch. Brakes off, we began to roll down the runway. Weighing less than 13 tons without much fuel or a bomb load, the Whitley lifted easily at 90 miles an hour.

We came down through a patch of low cloud to watch the Yorkshire Moors drop sharply into the sea. 'Right on, navigator,' Liebeck told me. After 20 minutes flying on a clear day it would have been difficult to be much off of it. But the captain was building confidence. 'Don't knock it,' I told myself.

Over the North Sea, Dick Speer tested the tail turret's four Browning machine-guns with short bursts and we came back on a reciprocal course. Liebeck flew dead-centre over the intersection of Leeming runways and continued a dozen miles – about six minutes flying time – to where the fells rise sharply in a matter of seconds.

'Are you watching the altimeter and the ground level?' the captain asked. I was.

'Two minutes from here the Dales rise to 2,200 feet,' he reminded me as we turned again for our base.

When we alighted from the dispersal truck at the flight office a tall, slim, red-headed sergeant-pilot greeted us. 'I'm Fletcher, your second dicky,' he introduced himself. His parents had just delivered him from their north country home two hours drive from Leeming. Now he had barely time to shake hands before Liebeck hustled us along to the briefing room.

The briefing was short and informal. There were just two crews scheduled for Le Havre, those navigated by Newt Turner and myself. Veteran Leeming crews were going to bomb Ruhr targets. 'There is going to be a lot of aircraft converging on Four Group bases about the same time coming home. If the weather is rough or you're in trouble don't hesitate to ask for a QDM – a bearing from base,' the operations officer told us.

'But don't clutter the airwaves if you don't need help. 77 Squadron lost a crew the other night because there was too much chatter and base couldn't relocate them for a QDM.'

The met officer told us to expect unbroken cloud up and down most of Britain's length. He was right. He predicted an average wind of about 30 miles per hour from 010 degrees at our flying altitude. As it turned out he was not far off.

So nearly two years since the Labour Day weekend I determined to go to war, I was about to fly into adversity. The Canadian government had spent $80,000 training me to navigate an aircraft and drop bombs on an enemy target. Their investment was now to be tested. It seemed anti-climactic. We had done much the same thing on night cross-country flights from the operational training unit at Abingdon.

If Kenneth Liebeck had any apprehension it would never leak through his implacable demeanour. His doctrinaire evangelical family had raised him and his brother to go to war as Christian soldiers. They would live and die achieving a degree of perfection that the gods were bound to resent.

Murray McLaughlin balanced confidence built on surviving 20 operational trips against the prospects that any of his four crew-mates might screw-up through inexperience. He hoped we would all benefit from what he had learned on some dicey ops but he was not about to offer any gratuitous advice.

Neither Dick nor I had any specific fears. Nothing in our training flights had conditioned us to anticipate trouble on a nursery trip. Seeing another trainee aircraft blown out of the sky six weeks earlier had confirmed the view that war was hell – but only in an abstract way. Like everyone else, Dick and I were certain it wouldn't happen to us.

I had felt more nervously expectant while poised for a high-school swimming race I told Dick Speer as we rode out to the aircraft. 'But you wouldn't pee yourself right there at the pool edge, would you, Silver?' he asked loudly. So much for comradely confidences.

As it turned out our first operation was almost a text-book trip. Daylight was just fading when we took off at 20:02 hours. Cloud closed in below us as we climbed to an operational 12,000 feet. Twenty-five minutes later there was a break in the overcast and enough visibility to see the Humber estuary on the port side. It was sufficient to check our position, the ground speed and consequently, the wind.

'The wind they gave us is holding,' I told Liebeck.

'Good work,' he replied.

It would be nice to claim that I was showing $80,000 worth of expertise but navigation is really just simple subtraction. In those days before radar and Gee-set fixes we caught what ground sightings and radio-bearings we could. Then we compared airspeed and heading with the miles and track covered. The difference was the wind-speed and its direction at flying altitude.

Air navigators were airborne book-keepers adjusting for wind change like accountants adapting to fluctuating interest rates. The sorcerers were the weathermen. Before an operation the meteorologists would predict windspeed and direction for each segment of our flight. As sorcerer's apprentice – like Mickey Mouse trying valiantly to mop up the deluge in *Fantasia* – we tried to adjust reality to the meteorologist's predictions.

Ninety minutes outbound from Leeming, Murray McLaughlin gave me bearings from radio beacons in the Midlands. I recalculated our position and a new wind vector then passed Liebeck a revised course and estimated time of arrival over the south edge of the Isle of Wight. 'ETA Ventnor 21:10 hours,' I announced.

At 21:06 with seven-tenths cloud cover you could look down and see the Solent strait reflecting a trace of moonlight like white space between Southampton and the Isle of Wight. We were on course, a cautious distance from Portsmouth naval guns. Four minutes later we passed over Ventnor and altered course for Le Havre.

'Dead on ETA, navigator,' Liebeck called out.

'I was working on McLaughlin's radio bearings,' I told him.

'Great work, wireless operator,' he told Murray.

Geezus, we were going to do the entire Dale Carnegie course on *How to Win Friends and Build Confidence* before we crossed the Channel. We were, in fact, moving like clockwork and Liebeck's formality reinforced the illusion that we were performing a classroom exercise. The closer we got to the target the farther we seemed to be from reality.

My chart table was immediately behind Liebeck's back and I sat behind Fletcher's jump seat. For the bomb-run he had to step into the well, collapse the seat and let me pass down to the front turret. I adjusted the bomb-sight for windspeed and direction, for our course, airspeed and altitude. A moment or two before the run-up I flicked on the fusing switches for four 500-pound bombs.

Le Havre, like a Gallic snout topping the mouth of the Seine, was clear enough even with seven-tenths cloud cover. Bursts of light flak arced lazily upward, meaningless as fireworks in a distant park. I put Liebeck on the bomb run, fine-tuned the bomb-sight, and called course corrections.

'Left, left five degrees. Five more and steady. Steady,' I called as I guess-estimated that Le Havre docks were passing between the bomb-sight guide-wires.

'Bombs gone,' I announced and he held course for another 30 seconds till a photo-flare triggered our aerial camera. Then the Whitley banked sharply and we were heading homebound again.

'Piece of cake,' someone said.

'We're not back yet,' Liebeck responded sharply. Overconfidence kills. The comment had irked him.

By the time we recrossed the Channel the cloud cover was seamless. I peered down for a fix on the Isle of Wight or the Solent estuary but saw nothing.

'Take over, second pilot,' Liebeck told Fletcher graciously as we re-crossed the Channel. Few captains making their first flight with a new crew were inclined to relinquish controls to an unknown flyer. If Liebeck had any such qualms they remained hidden.

'You'll need all the experience you can get,' he told the second pilot. An erstwhile Manitoba farm-boy raised on tin-can curling, Liebeck was playing cricket with Fletcher, 'doing the right thing' as all Canadian youth had been taught to do, British public-school style in the pages of *Boy's Own Annual* and *Chums*.

I watched the two pilots in the complex manoeuvre of switching positions. First the automatic pilot had to be secured with the controls locked for level flight. Then both pilots had to disconnect their oxygen bayonets and intercom cords from their dashboard positions. Now they exchanged places cautiously, making sure no switches or levers were inadvertently flipped. That done, we flew homeward over unbroken cloud in virtual silence for an hour and 40 minutes.

Midway back I revised our course and ETA for Leeming on the basis of met wind projections for the later hours. The weather boffins were predicting a slight change in windspeed and a small shift in direction across the Midlands an hour or so before midnight. Liebeck passed my directional chit to Fletcher and watched him adjust course and airspeed. 'Thank you, navigator,' Liebeck acknowledged.

'ETA base 10 minutes,' I announced. As we began to lose height, cloud wrapped us in opacity. At about 4,500 feet Fletcher levelled off. Now he and Liebeck began to switch places again. I watched the instrument panel as they went through the cumbersome manoeuvre, disconnecting and reconnecting oxygen and intercom lines.

When I glanced between them the altimeter was registering 3,400 feet and the airspeed needle was nosing 155 mph. Too fast! Perhaps the controls weren't locked for the switch-over and the nose was down. I was sure Liebeck would put it right in a moment.

The captain settled into his seat and I could see him trimming the controls once more. The airspeed was falling back below 135 mph. But the altimeter needle was continuing to drop. Still we were high enough for the Vale of York and we had reason to assume we were on track. There was every reason for a green crew to suck confidence from limited experience.

In fact, we had been flying blind on my navigational theory for more than 100 minutes and that left two imponderables. A six-degree shift in our course from the Isle of Wight could put us 30 miles east or west of our airfield. And the altimeter had been set on take-off more than five hours earlier. The altimeter works on barometric pressure; a barometric change could add or subtract hundreds of feet to its reading. Should the navigator mention this to the captain? Theoretically yes, but I hedged.

Fletcher was still standing in the well putting the jump seat back in position. Liebeck was adjusting the trim tabs to bring the Whitley nose back up. 'I figure we're about four minutes from base and should be on course. But a QDM would confirm it,' I suggested.

'Let's wait on your ETA. They don't want us cluttering the airwaves,' Liebeck told me.

McLaughlin leaned around the bulkhead to talk directly into my ear. 'Mac says it would be no trouble – only moments on air,' I repeated.

'No reason, no need,' Liebeck replied. 'We were dead on track going out and bang on the target. Let's wait on your ETA Leeming before asking for assistance.'

I looked around the bulkhead to watch McLaughlin begin winding in the trailing aerial used for transmission. I glanced again at the instrument panel. Altimeter and airspeed appeared to be holding steady now. I reached for a blue pencil to mark the Mercator chart with the last leg of my air plot. In the dim glow of my chart-table lamp I could see the pencil within inches of my fingertips. I reached again but the pencil remained just beyond my grasp. Some great force was pulling me away from it.

My sense of time, place and gravity was disoriented. Now I was riding the Whitley fuselage as if it was a giant ploughshare cutting ground. Stones and earth seemed to be spraying outward.

Now I was turning in mid-air, flying free, outpacing a horrendous medley of fracturing noises. The grinding, grating, rending, ripping, smashing sounds of disintegration faded into unmeasured moments behind me.

Then I was moving silently, timelessly through space.

'We've blown up,' I concluded. Small blobs of yellow light flicked past like little sky-bursts from fireworks. Was I, too, fragmenting? Was this fleeting sense of identity actually me, my head, or a memory? Was this an early hour of 23 August 1941 or the dawn of eternity?

In the last moment of consciousness I was aware that I had been thrown into the sky with the initial force of an aircraft travelling at more than two miles a minute. Seemingly I was a half mile above the Vale of York. Logic suggested that I would die when I hit ground.

'Eight in ten aircrew die. Now it's happening to you, Silver,' I reasoned. But the primal drive for survival rejects reason. It ignores reality. In absolute astonishment – with the ultimate exercise of ego – I said 'This can't be happening to me.'

When I regained consciousness I was lying face down in cold, damp, gritty dirt. With the instinctive urge of an amoeba seeking light I rolled onto my back. I could feel the night air on my face, the wet turf on my skin. I could see nothing; some weight kept my eyelids shut. My fingers probed and confirmed a scab of mud and blood. Would my eyeballs still be there when I scraped the crud away?

We had been half a mile in the sky and now I lay on the earth. God! my body must have pulped on impact. Gingerly I felt down both arms, across my chest, around my rib cage, down my thighs, my legs. With increasing incredulity I sensed that I was still intact.

I had been lifted free of my flying boots and my fingers closed on a squishy sock where I figured the big toe of my left foot should have been. The conclusion that I had lost a mere toe was somehow satisfying. It seemed earthly evidence that an accident had occurred and, by deduction, that most of me was still intact. Rediscovery of my toe, inches back from the sock-end, was – paradoxically – unsettling.

Certain now that I was going to die of undetermined injuries and blinded by the crusty scab, I waited for oblivion to reclaim me. I waited minutes. When death still stalled I impatiently pulled myself up on shaky legs and shoeless feet. Still sightless I began to shuffle in aimless circles. At least I'd be moving when the sexton waved a spade in my face.

Aftershock is commonplace. When danger has passed we shake our defences back to normality. Everyone reacts a little differently, of course. Invariably trauma triggers my sense of irony; it provokes my melodramatic instincts. And there was something truly absurd about shuffling around unidentifiable ground in stocking feet with unseeing eyes.

I scaled enough crud from my eyelids to reveal the mix of bog, stony ground and wet turf on which I was wandering. With a little more bloody grit removed I squinted into the night to catch a fleeting glimpse of rolling terrain. It terrified me.

'Silver, you've set a world record for a free fall without a parachute – at least 2,500 feet,' I told myself. 'But walk off a cliff in this cruddy dark and you won't live to tell about it.'

The sheer irony that I could be robbed of life and fame by a single misstep was appalling. Flooded with fear I sat in the wet turf. Probing the darkness with stocking-clad toes, I edged forward on my rump like a dog with worms. That reaction was self-limiting. Now I was reduced to a response of comic-strip simplicity. I sat hunched in black solitude on some unknown hilltop and cried 'Help!'

The night swallowed my cries and I felt the utter foolishness of a man shouting at nothing. I was about to quit when a voice came back at me. It seemed to float downward. 'Keep calling and walk towards me,' I demanded.

'Who are you?' asked the voice coming closer.

'What's it matter?' I asked peevishly. 'I've just been thrown from an aircraft.'

'What the hell do you think I've just come out of?' Dick Speer wanted to know.

He still insists he found me a thousand feet from where he had climbed out of the Whitley wreckage. I have been back to that hilltop twice in subsequent years, tramped the boggy ground between the stone wall where most of the wreckage lay and Little Tarn pond beside which Dick found me. I could not have been thrown more than a third of that distance. Tailgunners exaggerate.

I believe that Liebeck saw the 2,200-foot crest of Widdale Fell looming out of the dark and pulled back on the controls. I think we ploughed patches of wet turf and peat bog until we hit the stone wall atop Great Knoutberry Hill. That is when the Whitley came apart, when Liebeck and Fletcher were flung to instant death.

Seated inches behind them I was propelled through the Perspex windscreen – not to drown in the Little Tarn or the Great Tarn on either side of me nor to be dashed on stony outcrop, but to fall on boggy ground.

McLaughlin was thrown through the bulkhead to suffer a torn scalp. Dick Speer found himself hanging in his harness in an overturned turret. Bumps and bruises misshaped his head for days but he suffered no lasting harm. He had helped McLaughlin climb from the shattered fuselage, spotted both pilots' bodies, then answered my cries in the night.

We found a dry patch beside the stone wall and huddled together. As after-shock hit all three of us, our bodies shook spasmodically. My teeth set up an involuntary chatter that threatened to break their enamel till Mclaughlin thrust a glove in my mouth. The risk of walking over a cliff-edge faded as the cloud thinned and our sight lengthened. But in the dead of night there was no evident place to go. And with the pilots dead there was no urgency to move anywhere.

Then I became a little hysterical. 'I navigated us into a mountain. I killed two pilots and wrecked a million-dollar plane!' I told them. Dick and Murray tried not to look embarrassed. They waited in silence for my sanity to return.

'Geezus, what a mess on my first operation,' I muttered. 'If the other 29 trips are like this I'll be a nervous wreck.'

5

Below Ground Zero

DENT, August 1941

Like gods descending, we went down a mountain we had never climbed.

Cloud laundered first light to yellow-grey remnants of dawn. Cloud billowed up the face of Widdale Fell and across its top to wash us in cold steam. We turned our backs on it and started down Great Knoutberry Hill to the southwest, not because we knew where we were going but because this hill had a moderate grade and we had heard trains passing at its base.

'The trains should lead to people,' I reasoned.

'Or to coal and water,' Dick Speer observed.

Despite the awesome evidence of my navigation he and Murray McLaughlin were prepared to follow in my direction. In fact, we had had only one disagreement since daybreak. It concerned my flying boots. I wanted to search through the wreckage for them. Dick was against it. He said there was no way I would find them in the debris and I would wind up cutting my feet on sharp aircraft pieces.

Years later he gave me a better reason. 'Fletcher's body was not intact and I didn't think it would help your mood to discover it,' he explained.

Murray had searched along the stone wall line and come back with a pair of flying boots. 'Do these fit?' he asked.

'Whose are they?'

'Liebeck's.'

'Oh no. I won't wear a dead man's boots.'

'You really are a flying asshole,' Dick told me.

'Are you going to walk down the frigging mountain in your stocking feet?' Murray wanted to know.

When I put the boots on they fitted comfortably but the first step with my left foot brought a pang of pain and my right knee wouldn't bend. Six hours earlier still in evident shock, I had shuffled in aimless circles till Dick Speer found me. Then we had stumbled back to the crash site. Perhaps trauma masks pain. Certainly at the time I was unaware of a foot or leg injury. Now it appeared that I had not escaped unscathed. I staggered a few steps, recovered my balance and cautiously adjusted my stance.

'What's up?' Murray asked.

'Just tripped. The boots are okay,' I assured him.

If I lifted my left foot squarely off the ground the discomfort was bearable but if I let my toes take the weight for another step the pain shot up the nerve chain like an arrow of fire. So lifting my left foot like a draught horse and moving my right leg with a stiff-kneed arcing motion I started down the slope.

Dick and Murray watched silently, muttered with growing distaste and caught up to me. 'Hold it, take my arm,' Dick instructed.

'Bugger off,' I told him. I took a dozen paces before letting out an involuntary yelp. Dick caught me under the armpit. So we proceeded, Dick or Murray moving in to take my weight or guide my stiff-kneed leg around shrubbery and outcrop rock.

We had been descending in wet grass, through hillside brush and on an occasional path for about two hours when we saw a train tracing the west flank of the fell. The locomotive and six cars snaked through the valley at the base of the hill. Like a toy train spied from a child's sick-bed on Christmas morning it made our day.

In another hour we were beside the railway track and within sight of a two-storey stone house alongside it. Time and events telescoped after that. Dent stationmaster's wife met us on the doorstep. She took in the sight of three uniformed figures muddied and bloodied beyond recognition and called out for help.

Seconds later she was joined by her husband and sister. Indifferent to our gore and grime, they thrust us into deep-cushioned upholstery, poured whisky straight from the bottle into our throats and were washing the crud from our faces when others arrived. Within minutes a helmeted member of the Yorkshire constabulary, a Home Guard, a doctor, a nurse and a railwayman were sharing the seldom-used parlour with us. While the doctor and nurse gave first-aid the police constable took notes.

A little scrubbing revealed three faces that might have emerged from anywhere but our Canadian voices fell discordantly on North Country ears. Residents of this remote hill country that summer were mindful of Churchill's repeated warnings. German parachutists might land anywhere, anytime, especially on the desolate Yorkshire fells and moors. So who were we?

'We're from 10 Squadron. Crashed into a hilltop last night. The two pilots are dead,' I explained.

The medical man paused in his bandaging to sit back and study us. 'They're certainly air force,' he told the policeman.

'Aye, they be that. But whose air force?' the constable wondered.

'Where are you from?' the doctor asked.

'Leeming,' I assured him.

'No you don't sound a bit like Yorkshiremen.'

49

'We're not. We're Canadians.'

'Ethel,' said the doctor addressing the nurse beside him, 'you've got a brother-in-law from Canada. Do these men sound like him.'

'Well they don't swear as much but they do sound Canadian,' she advised.

There was a further moment of mutual inspection followed by several minutes of unrestrained laughter as we unbuttoned our strains and stresses all around. More whisky was poured down our upturned throats as medical and laymen forces administered a North Country mix of mountain rescue and hospitality.

We were less than sober when the constable drove us 18 miles west to Kendal Hospital. The road bounds up fells and down dales, dips into steep-sided valleys and mounts the skirt of the Pennines at Kendal. I had a vague feeling that we were not touching bottom in all of the dips.

The Yorkshire policeman was teaching us to sing *Ilkley Moor Bar Tat* and we were retuning his vocal system for *Alouette* when we pulled up at the hospital emergency entrance. When you came to think about it, one song sounded very much like the other.

The doctor on emergency call was a small, feisty lady shaped like a snowman. A good deal of her body weight went to breasts and buttocks but she had the fastest hand with a hypodermic needle I ever encountered. When I recovered consciousness she had closed a gash in my forehead and was bandaging my ankle.

'I removed a piece of windscreen Perspex a couple of inches above your right eye. I've closed the incision with a clamp, not stitches, so it won't scar,' she said cheery as a cricket at an Irish wedding.

I tried to hide my disappointment. Hitting a mountain warranted at least a visible scar. Coincidentally my dad carried the life-long mark of a football boot in almost the identical forehead position. It was a conversation piece that my clamp-closed wound would never be.

'You've got two chip fractures in the left foot. Tiny cracks. Almost hair-line. I've put the pressure bandage on tight enough to hold them in place. No need for a foot cast. Walking will be easier in a day or so,' she told me.

'What's with my knee?' I asked.

'You tell me.'

'I can't bend it.'

'Well that's not surprising. From what I gather you had plenty of opportunity to dislocate it.'

'So can you set it straight?'

'I think it is straight. But the knee is a complex mechanism. It's built to take a lot of weight and to swivel this way and that. Only you can be sure if it's in good working order.'

50

Still, if it seemed to be back in proper position why couldn't I bend my right leg?

It was a bit soon to say. 'You'll have to exercise it. But not for a day or two,' she told me.

The squadron sent a jeep to Kendal Hospital the following morning. Dick and Murray walked briskly out and I vaulted from a wheel-chair to join them. A male nurse with a footballer's forearm thrust me back in the wheel-chair. 'You're travelling by ambulance,' he advised.

Sure enough a two-man ambulance crew arrived from Leeming about an hour later. They seemed to find me incomplete. 'Where's your gas mask?' one asked anxiously. If I had said we didn't carry them on operations they would not have believed me.

'It got lost in the wreckage. Should we go back up there and find it?' I asked. Reluctantly they decided not to but it was an unpromising start for a 55-mile ambulance ride from Kendal back to Leeming.

In fact, the sergeant driver was a North Riding Yorkshireman, as familiar with the oak-beamed pubs that ululate the Sedbergh-Leyburn road through the Dales as he was with King's Rules and Regulations. 'Sorry, flight-sergeant,' he said, 'but we have to strap you on the stretcher while we're in motion.'

'Like hell you do.'

'Give us a few minutes, flight, and it won't be hell, I promise.'

We were on the road before I could muster a reply. Sedbergh was less than 20 minutes drive. We rocked around a couple of corners off the main route and ground to a halt. The rear doors of the ambulance were flung open. The sergeant driver and corporal attendant moved with practiced ease to unstrap me, lift me to the street and stand me gently on my feet.

'Let us take the weight, flight, and let us do the talking,' the sergeant instructed.

You could sense the attention as we came through the swinging doors into the pub lounge. My limp would have been sufficient but there was a small bandage on my forehead to accent my incapacity.

'Another near killed defending Britain,' was all the sergeant said. The foam-topped mugs were on the table in front of us almost before we sat down. The ambulance driver was a temperate man. Two rounds were all he would allow before we moved on.

Garsdale, just a couple of miles north of Dent railway station, was the next stop on the road back. Again the ambulance jolted to an abrupt stop, the service doors were thrown open and I was swung into position between them. The three of us came into the pub in step, albeit a bit hobbled.

'Another near-killed defending Britain,' said the sergeant. There was an appreciative round of cheers and the beer flowed.

As I recall, we repeated the performance at Clough, Hawes, Bainsbridge, Aysgarth, West Witton and Leyburn. In each pub I was introduced as near-killed in Britain's defence and in each we confined ourselves to two rounds of beer and modest acknowledgments. By Bainsbridge or Aysgarth the sergeant was nodding agreeably to the suggestion that we were all equally involved in the air war and implicitly that war was hell. At Leyburn, when the locals were advised that another pigeon had been near-killed in defending the nation, the corporal attendant nodded acknowledgment as well.

When the ambulance run finally ended I was again in a hospital reception area. But this was not Leeming sick quarters. I was in Catterick military hospital half a dozen miles from our squadron site. Built primarily to tend battlefield casualties shipped back from World War I trench warfare, Catterick hospital saw few army patients that summer of 1941. Aircrew from nearby Four Group stations occupied many of its beds.

A nurse wheeled me into a room, tossed me a pair of hospital pyjamas and ordered me into one of the two vacant beds. Then she was gone and for the first time since I joined the Royal Air Force I was utterly alone. An orderly brought lunch and departed before we could exchange a word. A nurse appeared in mid-afternoon stifling conversation with a thermometer. The orderly appeared again with supper and was gone before I could greet him. The three days and four nights that followed were the loneliest I have ever known.

An only child learns to live with solitude but Air Force life had quickly changed that. My first night in the RCAF was at Manning Pool in Toronto's Exhibition Park. More than 3,000 of us bunked in double-deck beds in a vast structure that had been designed to exhibit hogs and sheep. For the first time in my life I shared a bedroom.

'Who's from the west?' someone cried from a dark corner.

'I am' . . . 'I am,' voices answered throughout the arena.

'Screw the west,' they were told.

'Who's from the east?' asked another.

'I am' . . . 'I am,' others responded.

'Screw the east,' they were advised.

I fell asleep my first night in the Service enraptured by a new-found sense of companionship. Not since I quit the womb had I been so enwrapped by humanity. Now a little more than a year later, the sole occupant of a Catterick hospital room, I felt like the last man on earth. Self-pity and hopelessness were my bed-mates. Curled in the foetal position, I sniffed belly-button lint and writhed in a paroxysm of survivor guilt.

'You've really screwed up this time, Silver,' I told myself. 'You've killed two guys and wrecked a million-dollar aircraft. Geezus, that must be a record for one operation.'

'How could you be so gutless not to argue for a QDM when you didn't know where you were?' I asked again and again. 'Why didn't you speak out about losing altitude?' 'How in hell could you miss the Vale of York? It's 10-frigging miles wide.'

By the time I slept I had flailed myself into depression, convinced I would never fly again. Sixteen weeks earlier we had sailed into Gatwick; into the romance and drama of a world at war. Now it was dissipating in a bad dream. In a single season I had lived, loved and flown to war. In a night I had dropped from the game.

The RAF medical service that worked miracles to restore ears and noses burned away by flaming glycol and to rebuild shattered bodies, had not caught up with the behavioural sciences by World War II. Psychology was a dirty word in service hospital corridors. There was only one mental ailment in RAF doctors' lexicon – LMF for lack of moral fibre. Their aim was to make the bed-ridden ambulatory; to put the walking wounded back on the road to their squadrons just as quickly a possible. The wards were swept by eternal vigilance to uproot malingerers.

A doctor briefly examined me my second morning at Catterick. 'What's wrong with your right leg?' he asked.

'The lady doctor at Kendal Hospital thought my knee was dislocated.'

'What do you think?'

'I think it's just a bit stiff.'

'Well let's see how it is now. Try walking to the door and back.'

I did as instructed. My left foot was painful till I got the hang of positioning it again. The right knee seemed stiffer than ever and I had to swing it straight-legged in a wide arc as I moved. The result was not impressive.

'We'll have another look tomorrow or the next day,' he said.

So I remained isolated in a Catterick hospital bed for two more desolate nights, two more empty days. Over and over again I relived the return flight up the spine of England. Again and again I flogged myself like a monk in penance. By the fourth morning I was certain my aircrew days were over; that I would be shipped back to Canada to inglorious ground duties.

For fifteen months I had been primed for air warfare. Then I had screwed up in less than five hours operation. Two years before I had wanted no part of war. Now I would have to fight to stay in it. In the spring of 1939 the *Windsor Star* had transferred me to its London, Ontario bureau where three reporters were expected to compete with the entire *London Free Press* editorial staff. There were days when we did. But we were paced by the *Toronto Star's* one-man news bureau, Art Carty, who raced to assignments in his super-charged Cadillac, and by the *Globe & Mail's* Eric McVeity.

A Royal Canadian Military College graduate and former Mountie, Eric brought self-discipline and a keen intellect to newspaperwork. He was the notably mature and quiet-voiced exception among London's boozy, noisy newspaper crowd. Half a dozen years older than I was, McVeity helped me grow up during our brief acquaintanceship.

We were walking from police headquarters to the court-house one March morning. Hitler was demanding air bases in Iceland and Denmark's premier was warning local Nazis not to press their luck. Lithuania had conceded Memel to the Germans and Hungarian troops were invading Slovakia with Hitler's blessing.

'Looks like we'll soon be marching to war, not the courthouse,' Eric observed.

'Count me out,' I replied.

'The drum beat has already begun,' he said. 'How are you going to avoid it?'

I told him about the three young Communists I had worked with on the editorial desk at Wayne University's *Detroit Collegian*. One year they risked their limbs when mounted police broke up a peace demonstration in Cadillac Square. A year later they had put their lives on the line in Spain.

'They said that was where Hitler and Mussolini had to be stopped and they were probably right. Frankly, I had neither their guts nor their convictions,' I admitted. 'And I still don't.'

'They've been fighting a proxy war in Spain,' McVeity agreed. 'The Reds and the Fascists are testing their weapons far from home. But we'll all be in it before this year ends and it won't have anything to do with political convictions.'

'What then?'

'It's like the Mounties' Musical Ride,' he said. 'When the drum beats and the bugle calls, the men and horses just naturally fall in step. They have been conditioned to do that. You see them forming up and starting to ride off. They're going where the action is and you won't want to be left behind.'

'I'll be glad to report it,' I told him. 'But there's no way I'll fight.'

'You're a born participant, my young friend. There's no way you'll sit on the sidelines and take notes.' Eric knew more about me than I did myself.

On the Labour Day weekend that peace was shattered, my parents travelled from Windsor to Sudbury where I was then *Globe & Mail* correspondent. They wanted to tell me about their decision to take up residence in Detroit. I wanted to articulate my feelings on peace and war. Instead, we listened to the radio commentary and talked over each other's shoulders. Like McVeity, they knew my decision before I did.

When the RCAF established a recruiting depot in Sudbury that September to tap the bush pilot ranks I reported it and – to my own astonishment – sought to enlist. I was not accepted until the following spring. On the June day that France capitulated, 18 of us were despatched from

Windsor to RCAF Manning Pool in Toronto. We were among the two out of every five volunteers accepted. I had won a place and screwed it up on my first op.

Awaking from fitful sleep, I was certain Joan would be at my bedside when I opened my eyes. In old war movies the wounded hero woke to find the girl of his dreams magically beside him, ready it seemed to jump into bed while the hospital staff discreetly waited in the corridor. In fact, three mornings after we failed to return from ops there was not a word from Joan.

Then I realized that the Air Force would advise no one but my mother as next-of-kin. I had been so enwrapped in self-bought misery I had not given a thought to getting in touch with the girl I planned to marry. A nurse brought me a service letter-form and pencil that afternoon but I was too disheartened to use them. A wedding date had been casually discussed but vaguely assigned to that neverland when I finished my 30 ops. Now what could I tell Joan?

Exhausted by self-searching, I was dozing on my fourth day in a hospital bed when the tall shadows of Tiny Clapperton and Angus Buchan, moving on a background of afternoon sunlight, crossed my eyes. Clapperton, a massive man on a six-foot-three-inch frame, was 10 Squadron's ever-cheerful B-Flight commander. Angus Buchan, craggy-featured and almost as tall, was station navigation officer at Leeming. Buchan was an erstwhile mathematics instructor recruited from Edinburgh University at age 28 to help young navigators keep themselves and their crews alive. He was a dour Scot who brooded over his clutch of navigators like a guardian rooster.

'If you're going to get killed let the Jerries do it, don't be done in by bloody bad arithmetic,' Buchan would say.

Tiny Clapperton and Angus Buchan flew the same ops as other aircrew. They understood the Operational Complex – once begun there was an overwhelming compulsion to complete a tour of 30 ops. It was the only route to survival. Clapperton and Buchan saved my sanity that August afternoon.

'Want to talk about it?' they asked.

Self-censure tightened my throat like a noose on each word. But either I shared the reality of the operation with them or I was opting out. Slowly I replayed the trip up and down England, across the Channel and back, recalling courses, airspeeds and ETAs. With Liebeck, there had not been much conversation but I repeated what there was – all except that last brief discussion about a QDM.

'We've talked with Speer and McLaughlin. You've confirmed what they told us,' Clapperton said. 'Incidentally you're ETA was about right because you crashed due west of Leeming when you should have been over base.'

'But you left out something,' Angus Buchan observed, his face impassive.
'What?'

'About asking for a QDM to base and being overruled.'

'The captain was following directions. We were briefed not to clutter the
air-waves if it wasn't necessary.'

'Apparently it was necessary,' Angus said dryly.

'No. No that isn't fair,' I told them, my voice breaking. 'There were
three of us who had some control and two of them are dead. I don't know
what they could have done different. But I know – and you know – I
screwed up.'

'No,' Clapperton contradicted me. 'You were not responsible.'

'But my navigation put us 30 miles off course.'

'Yes you were 30 miles off course after four hours and 37 minutes flying,'
Angus said. 'I've replotted your flight. Your track from Ventnor to Leeming
was six degrees off – six degrees to the west. You know that the compass
and gyro could account for at least a degree or two of that error. You know
that no bloody pilot can hold a course within one or two degrees, it's bloody
impossible. And the wind did shift from the met forecast.'

'No, I can't pass the buck. I screwed up,' I insisted.

'Fortunately that judgment is the flight commander's and mine to make,'
Angus told me, his teeth nearly biting his words apart. 'You're in the clear
and that's for the record.'

'But . . .' I began.

'But, frigging-nothing,' Clapperton interrupted. 'The medicos said
something about a couple of chip fractures and a bad knee. That's no
reason to write you off squadron strength. No reason at all unless you can't
face more ops.'

'Right now you seem to be drowning in self-pity,' Angus told me. 'I hope
you have the guts to come up for air.'

They had both been smiling when they arrived 40 minutes earlier. Their
faces were masked when they left. As their heavy tread echoed down the
corridor I realized Clapperton and Buchan did not share my self-condem-
nation. I had been prepared to write myself off. They weren't. Now I was
clouding the issue with gut-wrenching guilt.

In the 100 hours since we flew into the top of Widdale Fell I had assumed
full responsibility for the crash, written myself off the squadron roster and
virtually disengaged myself from my bride-to-be. While I played these
morbid mind games Catterick medicos decided my knee injury was imag-
inary; that I was malingering. The quicker I recovered flexible knee movement the sooner I got back on ops.

The following morning the same staff doctor examined me again. I
limped as far as the door and back. It was not as difficult as the day before

but my movement did not reassure him. 'Okay, we're sending you to Rauceby Hospital,' he said.

I interpreted this as a positive move and got a long letter off to Joan that afternoon. I had been in a bit of crash and dislocated my knee, I told her. I was being sent to a RAF hospital about 80 miles north of London for treatment. Hopefully I would be out on leave within days.

RAF Rauceby Hospital, about 20 miles east of Nottingham, was a major medical facility. I was bedded down in the orthopaedic ward for NCOs, a narrow room with beds on both sides that seemed to stretch beyond sight. There were possibly 50 or 60 bed-ridden patients. Most, I was told, had sustained broken bones in motorcycle accidents. Among perhaps a dozen aircrew who had been injured on operations I was the only one to come out of a Whitley. The others all seemed to have suffered their injuries in Manchesters, lethal, twin-engined bombers that killed more RAF than the Luftwaffe did in their brief service.

The patient in the next bed to mine had broken his back in a Manchester crash. He was encased in a loose-fitting cast from neck to tailbone. He could roll from one side of the bed to the other and as he did so the cast rubbed layer on layer of rotting skin from his body. At certain times a summer breeze ran down the ward flushing the putrescent smell from my neighbour's cast onto those of us downwind. By the time I left Rauceby I realized such bed placements were not a matter of chance. Everything was contrived to discourage patients from settling in. No one stayed a day longer than they had to.

Rauceby doctors were specialists in putting crash victims back together but knew nothing about what made their heads tick. Where they saw disfigurement they painstakingly repaired it; where bones were broken they helped them mend. The chip fractures in my left foot were mending nicely and x-rays showed no visible damage to my right knee.

Clearly if I didn't need fixing I shouldn't be there. They concluded that I was using my knee as a crutch and they had their own methods of knocking crutches from under ambulatory arm-pits.

I realized that the sooner my knee flexed normally, the sooner I got back on ops. Ironically, the more I tried to flex it the more it seemed to stiffen. Two and three times a day I eased myself off the bed and trudged the length of the ward corridor and back. The more determined I was to stretch the tendons and muscles that restrained my right knee the more I tensed them. The more anxious I was to walk naturally the more aware I was of the pain it was causing.

Medical staff, watching my stiff-gaited efforts and convinced I was faking it, left me alone. A few days of non-treatment were enough. Limping to the nurses' station at the end of the ward, I finally announced 'I want out.'

One of those formidable amazons who rule hospital floors world-wide ordered me back to bed. An hour later a staff doctor examined me again. 'Okay, you can get dressed and exercise in the ambulatory ward,' he said.

While I waited for my clothes I wondered if hospital personnel had cleaned-up my battledress pants and jacket. Beginning to feel the pride of an operational aircrew member once again I couldn't wait to trade the anonymity of hospital pyjamas and bathrobe for my uniform with its observer brevet, rank badges and Canada shoulder flashes.

But my uniform was not returned. What an orderly dumped on my bed was a robin's-egg-blue pair of shapeless trousers, a formless jacket of the same blue colour, a greying white shirt and a narrow tie of reddish-orange hue as if it had been dipped in over-oxygenated blood.

It was a clown's costume; the dress you might see on a self-deprecating, third-rate, stand-up comedian at an English seaside resort. The outfit had been conspicuously crafted to reduce NCOs and other ranks at Rauceby to an untouchable underclass; to make them instantly identifiable as walking wounded of questionable validity.

Horror-stricken, I stared at the loathsome hospital garb. A patient from several beds down the ward hobbled over on crutches. His voice was confidentially pitched, vehement in its intensity. 'Put it on, chum. Wear it in all its hideous absurdity and curse their souls, their kin and their progeny. May their class-warped minds rot in hell,' he said.

Moving closer he dropped his voice to almost a whisper. 'But geezus don't argue. Put it on now, chum. Square your shoulders so that frigging jacket hangs straight. Bend your knees if it kills you so those laundryman-pyjama trousers flap with every frigging step you take. Knot that tie so frigging tight they have to cut it off, chum. Wear it like you'd just been appointed air vice-marshal. If you don't, flight-sergeant, you'll go out of here in a straight-jacket.'

As he talked I could feel anger, dismay and humiliation flood through me. I gagged on them. In minutes a fury of emotion washed away ten days of self-pity and phobic guilt. I wore that lunatic garb in a manner just short of dumb insolence, a court-martial offence. I marched with a stretched knee-bend that mocked them with every tear the pain brought to my eyes.

Descending from Widdale Fell I had levelled out below ground zero. Now there was no way to go but up. Two days later my battledress uniform was returned. It had been cleaned and mended. I was handed a two-week pass, £10 back pay and a transportation chit to London, then back to Leeming.

The man in charge of Rauceby's orthopaedic wing, the group captain who surveyed its serried ranks of convalescing officers and clown-garbed NCO aircrew, looked over my shoulder into the middle distance. He lofted his words above my head and I could pick them off the floor behind me if I wanted the information.

'You're on two weeks sick leave. Then back to 10 Squadron for ground duties. We'll give you another medical examination here on October 10,' he told me.

'Then?'

'Then if your right knee's unkinked so your heel kicks your butt they'll probably let you back on ops.'

6

Not You Again!

WEMBLEY, September 1941

Limping like a puppy that had been stomped underfoot, I hobbled back to 25 Eton Court, Wembley in mid-September. A month earlier Churchill and Roosevelt had set their own agenda with the Atlantic Charter and I had flown bravely off to war. Now the Nazi juggernaut was enroute to Sebastopol; it had captured Kiev and was 20 miles from Leningrad.

'We are making very heavy attacks by day and night with our air force upon all German-occupied territory and all Germany within reach. Thus we hope to force Hitler to bring back some of his air power to the West,' Churchill had told Stalin a few weeks earlier. This was no time for an airman to be limping about London.

The week I was told to kick my own butt back onto operations Churchill was advised to kick backsides in RAF Bomber Command. The advice was based on the report of a British bureaucrat with the improbable name of D. M. Butt. Plotting bomber crew on-target claims against bomb-run photographs for the previous two months, Butt found that only a third of them were actually within five miles of the designated aiming point when they let their bombs go. In the flak-happy Ruhr the figure was one in ten. Moreover, while two crews in five might bomb within five miles of their target under full-moon conditions only one in ten did so on a moonless night.

'This seems to require your most urgent attention,' Churchill told the Chief of Air Staff on 3 September. In his memoirs he would note that 'Several methods had been proposed to guide bombers to their targets by radio aids but until we recognized how inaccurate our bombing was, there seemed to be no reason to embark on such complications.' On the advice of his science guru Lord Cherwell, Churchill ordered the development of the 'Gee' box, a radar set that collected signals from three widely spaced stations in Britain and converted them to little top-hatted, electronic figures that pointed the way on a bile-green cathode-ray screen.

The September week that Churchill approved the Gee box innovation he was advised to let the boffins get on with developing an atomic bomb. Alarmed that German nuclear physicist Otto Hahn now had a substantial stock of uranium oxide on which to base his bomb-making experiments, a

British war-cabinet committee said: 'We are strongly of the opinion that development of the uranium bomb should be regarded as a project of first-class importance and all possible steps should be taken to push on with the work.'

Churchill agreed. 'Although personally I am quite content with the existing explosive I feel we must not stand in the way of improvement,' he told Major-General Sir Hastings Ismay, his Chief of Staff. The heads of the three armed services recommended immediate action to build a pilot plant to make bomb-grade uranium in Britain. This was to be followed by a full-scale plant in Canada.

German scientists were not idle. That same week they tested man-size doses of an insecticide called Zyklon-B on 850 Auschwitz inmates – most of them Russian prisoners-of-war. Death was not instantaneous but it seemed fast enough to make feasible the annihilation of six million Slavs, Jews and gypsies.

The late afternoon train trundling south to London carried its customary wartime overload. I hobbled along a corridor glancing through the glass compartment doors without expecting to find a vacant place. But a middle-aged man in a bowler hat spotted me and leapt from his seat before I could move on.

'Here we are. Here we are, airman,' he insisted. Now two other occupants of the compartment were standing, shuffling about to offer me their seats. Red-faced with embarrassment I paused indecisively. An older couple squeezed out of the compartment as the bowler-hatted man pulled me in. Whether to steady me or to take proprietary possession, his hand grasped my elbow. I shrugged it off, muttering objections.

'Geezus!' I exclaimed. 'I mean thank you very much.' The man in the bowler hat muttered an equally inappropriate response. People resumed their seats and heavy silence cushioned us one from the other till the train puffed into King's Cross station.

Sighing with relief as the train stopped I reached up as inobtrusively as possible to run my index finger around the inside of my collar, then to flick perspiration from my forehead. My fingernail caught momentarily in the small lattice of adhesive-tape above my right eye. It was as if I had pointed a gun at my head. Six pairs of eyes stared transfixed at the small bandage, indisputable evidence that I had been 'near killed' in defence of the realm.

'Geezus!,' I reiterated. Then I closed my eyes and kept them tightly shut until the others had vanished from the compartment. The limp and the forehead bandage made me a marked man.

At the top of the escalator two boy scouts took me in hand and marched me safely out of the station. As the underground train rumbled beneath London streets two elderly ladies seated opposite smiled beatitudes at me.

61

Had they read my reaction I would have been arrested for gross obscenity.

'Well now you do look a bit bunged up,' Joan's mother greeted me. 'Nothing a cup of tea won't mend I hope.'

'Tea would certainly help,' I agreed. 'So would getting that damn bit of adhesive tape off my forehead.'

'Want it off?'

'Definitely.'

Mrs E. removed the bandage with a practiced flick of her wrist. 'Well it's certainly no beauty mark,' she observed. Had things worked out she would have made a wonderful mother-in-law.

That second summer of war Joan was still working in a fashionable west-end beauty salon whose clientele were mostly theatrical people, those British stars of stage and screen dedicated to helping the rest of us carry on. Her sister Eve, a dozen years older, worked closer to home. As secretary of the British Oxygen Company with headquarters in Wembley, Eve author-itatively rationed Britain's limited supply of oxygen to the Air Force, hospi-tals, shipyard welders and other industrial users. Weekdays they were both gone by 7:15am and seldom home before 6:00. But on week night evenings and two weekends that September they helped get me back on the runway.

'When he came here after the crash he looked pale and much thinner but he recovered very quickly. His one aim was to get back into action again,' Joan wrote my mother. 'Since then he has had treatment and six weeks ago he came up to London on his way to have a medical examina-tion and stayed a few days. He looked himself, I have not seen him since but in his letters he says he has done three raids over Germany and seems very pleased about it.'

Joan's comments skipped her family's role in my recovery. I was nursed back to flying fitness on a fortnight's meals that consumed their entire bacon-and-egg ration for more than two months. For two weeks the chesterfield cushions staked out my bed-space on the living room floor. Joan woke me with tea just before she and Eve sped to work in the morning. Their mother fed and clucked after me as she did with her son when he was home on leave. The same age and rank as me, Jack was a maintenance crew chief at a RAF night-fighter station. If he learned that I wore his spare shirts and used his shaving gear during those two weeks, he never mentioned it.

The crash altered the dynamics of my relationship with Joan. Less than a month earlier the operational chapter of our wartime story was about to begin. Until it ran its course the next chapter – vaguely titled 'Love and Marriage' – was not to be written. At the moment my wartime action amounted to one cross-Channel hop; four hours and thirty-seven minutes of operational flying.

Even as we embraced Joan was opening my shirt collar and fingering the

St Christopher medallion. 'It worked,' she said solemnly. I had not thought of it. Now its symbolism was not to be ignored. It bespoke faith; faith in my survival. Conversely, if our faith faltered I wouldn't make it. So we demonstrated our conviction by deferring the mating game.

If we were to remain in a holding pattern like aircraft stacked awaiting landing approval it was not safe to fly too close. I could sense Joan moving almost imperceptibly out of my orbit. The atheist's grandson read the message on the hoardings – 'the wages of sin are death'. With just one in 30 operations completed this was no time to flaunt fate and bed the bride-to-be.

For the next fortnight Joan scrubbed at my pessimism with an upbeat brush. It was irritating but it worked. She found my ailing-ambulatory-airman role ridiculous. Reluctantly I had to agree with her. As I lightened up I unwound. My right knee was still stiff but the leg was no longer flexed like an open jack-knife.

Within a day or two Eve had me on a walking regimen. She was accustomed to issuing orders. I was assigned morning and afternoon walks on Eton Court. Then at 5:30pm, a full hour before she normally arrived home, Eve would return 'to walk me back into flying fitness', as she put it. She would take my arm and move me at a military pace for a mile or more before supper. Enroute, big sister had no hesitation in attending my mind.

'What's this guilt trip all about?' Eve wanted to know.

'Well I do share the blame for flying into a mountain,' I said.

'Rubbish!'

'A plane and two pilots. You call that rubbish!'

'No, but the martyr-boy attitude is.'

'You mean it's a cop out.'

'Of course it is. Your flight commander and navigation officer already told you that.'

'Yeah, they did that.'

'So you better take back more than a mended leg.'

'You mean . . .'

'I mean you're being bloody self-indulgent. It's time you grew up, Ray. You're 24 and there is a war on, you know.'

When I reported back to 10 Squadron a few days later my knee was still not completely unkinked but my head was. Eve had fixed me with candid eyes that seemed to put our minds in frightening closeness. Her words had lashed me like spit in the face.

Leeming's medical officer, a cheery middle-aged squadron leader, greeted me. 'Hi-ho Silver, back for another ride, are you?' he asked.

'I go for a medical at Rauceby in a week and I still can't quite kick my own ass with my right foot.'

'Well now, I've got just the lad to help you do it,' he told me.

The 19-year-old Welshman who took me in charge was an expert masseur. With help of an old brass bed he worked me back into flying shape in the six days available. The bed was, incongruously, part of Leeming's sick-bay furnishings. It had a low cross-bar at its head and I was instructed to grab it behind me with both hands.

'Now bend your knee and kick butt, flight-sergeant,' the Welsh lad commanded politely. I tried but the heel of my shoe still remained a good three inches from my backside. The young Welshman grabbed my leg throwing his weight on it.

'Holy god!' I screamed as tendons and muscles seemed to be tearing apart.

'Not God, just a ten-stone Welsh lad,' he corrected me. Then he threw his weight a little harder. I clutched the bed bar tighter and screamed louder for divine mercy. We didn't seem to be making much progress. But, inch by inch, he stretched whatever had to be stretched. When I reported back to Rauceby on 10 October, two doctors gave me a cursory examination.

'So deep-knee bend,' one commanded.

My back ram-rod straight, toes together, I went into full squat position. 'Again.'

Again and again I went down on my haunches. Ten times my knees bent till the heels of my shoes touched my backside. My eyes were fixed on the opposite wall. I didn't dare shift them until I was certain they were free of tears and fury.

By mid-month I was back on flying duties. I joined a scrub crew to pick up a new Whitley aircraft straight from the Armstrong hangars and deliver it to another Four Group station. Later that week I navigated a Whitley carrying the officer in charge of Humber searchlight command while he tested area defences.

A seasoned pilot jinked the plane port and starboard, up and down, like a hound on a hare's path. The searchlights blinked, lifted, waved and probed the black heights for us. They were never even close. Sensing the commander's embarrassment, the pilot slackened off his evasive action. Still the searchlight beams failed to fix on us. The commander sat in icy silence till we landed.

'Thanks awfully,' he said as he climbed out. An inherent sense of humanity demanded a sympathetic response. But he didn't get it. In our mind's eye we could not divorce his death-dealing shafts of light from German searchlights.

Late that month I was crewed up with sergeant-pilot Ralph Black, a balding Englishman. He was about my own age but his face was care-worn. When not expressing confusion or embarrassment, Black had the harried

look of a loser and it was said he was accident-prone. While welcoming me back, squadron authority was inclined to keep its cracked eggs in one carton.

On the night of 28 October we took off for another trip to the French coast; this time to Cherbourg. The briefing carried one of those injunctions written by RAF groundlings – second-guessers who perceived the air war from desk-top altitude. 'Your bomb-run will take you south-easterly across the harbour area. Just beyond the harbour is a large Red Cross medical complex serving the French civilian population. Be sure you don't over-shoot,' we were told.

How far was 'just beyond'? What about other civilian concentrations? What prompted this particular cautionary instruction? Aircrew who dwelt on such questions missed vital parts of the briefing. It was better to forget what you didn't understand. I wish I had.

Again the route took us down Mother England's cleavage so to speak. There was the short dash across the Channel from just west of the Isle of Wight. Flak ships and coastal batteries stitched the dark depths beneath us with lazy pyrotechnic lines more in greeting than in anger. We seemed to be outrunning the defences as we moved into the bomb run.

'Right 10 degrees . . . and five more . . . steady, steady,' I called as patches of dockside structures seemed to be swept with wispy cloud and flak flashes into the bomb-sight guide wires.

'Steady, steady,' I repeated. Then a swatch of cloud like a wool rug filled my view. 'Wait for it to clear, Silver,' I told myself.

'But there are people down there; you'll overshoot,' a voice from the briefing admonished me.

'Got clouded out. Have to go round again, skipper,' I called.

'Right, we'll make another run,' Black agreed.

'Frigging hell!' said the tail-gunner, a veteran of more than a dozen ops.

'What you guys playing at,' the wireless op muttered.

So we came around again. This time the heavy flak guns were beginning to track us. There were two yellow sky-bursts with the attendant crump-crump sound as we settled onto the bomb run.

'Steady, steady . . .' I instructed. Again there was just too much cloud. 'Geezus, geezus, skipper, I'm going to overshoot again.'

'No dice. Hold-off for another run,' Black instructed.

As we came around for the bomb run a third time, the tail-gunner was flicking his microphone on and off filling the intercom with bursts of screaming invective. Heavy flak was bursting closer and the light flak was streaking up close to our belly.

'You frigging assholes,' the wireless op muttered. The tail-gunner was screaming hysterically now.

'Steady, steady . . .' I called again. Now there were three streams of consciousness. There was the target scene unravelling quickly beneath me. Beyond it thousands of civilian faces were upturned in my mind's eye. And drowning all else was the curdling cry of the hysterical gunner. I shut my eyes and my ears, pressed the bomb-release tit and roared 'Bombs gone.'

As we banked steeply off the target area the gunner was crying, filling our headphones with the hideous noise of human disintegration. The wireless op was condemning Barker and me to eternal damnation, demanding the castration of our heirs and grand-kin.

I swore them a silent oath. If the war was to last a thousand years and I was condemned to bomb targets nightly, never again would I let civilian faces sneak onto the surface of my consciousness in the target area.

In another minute we were headed back to Britain. Again the weather closed in beneath us as it had that fateful night two months earlier. But this time Black kept the Whitley at a safe cruising altitude. We were midway back when the wireless-op picked up a diversion message. A front had wrapped Four Group bases in a thick blanket of cloud. We were to turn south again and land at one of the belt of operational training units that arc Oxford.

The Whitley nosed down through the night till we came out beneath the overcast. Ten minutes north of Oxford we picked up a beacon we identified as being close to a sisterhood of airfields at Bicester, Chipping Warden, North Luffenham and Upper Heyford. Black called down the TR talk channel and Bicester control tower responded.

'Bear 160 from the beacon two minutes flying time till you see the flare path,' he was instructed. We did. The Whitley droned on for nearly four minutes while we scanned the dark countryside to port and starboard. No flare path appeared.

'Back to the beacon P for Peter,' we were told. Back we flew, circling it till they again gave us direction. Again five pair of eyes probed the ground ahead and to both sides of us. But there was no sign of runway lighting.

'Same bearing and distance, P for Peter. This time we're going to give you two minutes of flares,' the controller advised as we circled the beacon a third time. His tone suggested the flares would be at our expense. It was the tailgunner who sighted the flares arcing up in the fading distance behind us. 'Something's popping up off our tail to starboard,' he said.

Again we turned about and overflew the beacon. Two minutes flying in the opposite direction brought us over the flares. As they died the yellow DREM runway markers were obvious.

'P for Peter to Bicester control, thanks for your trouble,' Black told them politely as we waited at the perimeter for a jeep to escort us in. You could hear mumbling and a muted oath behind the control tower microphone.

We waited in silence till the jeep appeared and led us back to a patch of tarmac beside the control tower. We climbed the stairs and trooped into the tower.

'Thanks Bicester,' Black repeated.

'This,' said the controller, his face cold as dead ash, 'is North Luffenham. Don't you friggers read the beacon you're circling.'

We had scarcely landed back at Leeming the following noon when we were called for ops that night. Again it was to be a Channel port, Ostend. This time our route would take us down the east coast from Flamborough Head to the Wash and across Norfolk to Harwich before we nipped across the Channel. It was a route that thrust neither hilltops nor a confusion of beacons at us. It was as trouble-free an operation as benign authority could devise.

Again our take-off was at dusk. The sun was just edging down over the Dales as Whitley Z-9221 trundled around the perimeter like a hound hunting a place to pee. At the edge of the flare-path Black went through the take-off drill, the second pilot double-checking each move.

Behind them I sat idly watching the red-gold strands of dusk laying a carpet for our ascent. The flare-path ended in semi-darkness but the last shreds of sunlight silhouetted a pair of Halifax aircraft parked on a dispersal pad to the right of the runway. These were the first of the four-engine planes which would mark our conversion to big time ops. To the left of the runway just beyond the tarmac perimeter stood a pair of Nissen huts left by the contractor, a reminder that Leeming air field had been built less than two years earlier. Our aging Whitleys were mid-stream in the fast evolving air war.

'Trim tabs?' Black queried.

'Neutral,' the second dickey confirmed.

'Fuel mix?'

'Set rich.'

'Flaps?'

'15 degrees down.'

'Superchargers?'

'Set low.'

'Radiators?'

'Open.'

'Okay. It's brakes on and full power,' Black announced. This always sounded contradictory but I had checked it out to settle an argument with Newt Turner. The Whitley manual said: 'The aeroplane may be prevented from moving until full power is obtained by applying the brakes. This will reduce the chances of a swing developing owing to uneven engine response.'

'Goddamn Whitley doesn't just keep its nose down on take-off. It sniffs the runway from one side to the other,' I muttered to myself as I waited to log the time we were airborne.

Now that I thought about it I could sense the 'plane edging starboard as the tail lifted and we gained speed. Black was a hunched-forward worrier at the best of times. Jockeying 16 tons of aircraft, fuel and bomb-load that was beginning to sway as it approached 90 miles per hour flying speed, he had the look of a man who wished he was elsewhere.

'Needs goosing to port,' the second pilot advised.

'I know,' the skipper agreed.

'You've over-corrected.'

'That's frigging obvious,' Black told him from between clenched teeth.

Twice in our lurching dash down the runway I could feel the 'plane lifting on its undercarriage and my pencil was poised to record the take-off. But as the wheels lifted the swing to starboard was aggravated. Trying to put the Whitley back on track Black swung it to port. For a moment it seemed that we would take-off at an angle of 15 or 20 degrees to the left of the runway. But in the next moment the Whitley was back on its haunches flailing rubber from its tyres.

'Cut power, full flaps,' Black instructed the second pilot.

We were three-quarters of the way down the field, still moving at something like 70 mph, still yawing to right and left. It was obvious we would run out of stopping space.

To our right two brand new Halifax aircraft loomed ever larger. To our left the two Nissen huts took solid shape. The chances were two out of three that we would plough into the four-engine bombers or the corrugated-iron sheds rather than pass between them onto the Great North Road.

At least we weren't going to hit a hillside. We were on the deck and slowing every moment. 'Relax, Silver, 'cause there's nothing else to do,' I told myself, slumping to the floor behind the second pilot's jump-seat.

The gnawing of the propellers on corrugated iron announced our passage through the Nissen huts. The Whitley slewed halfway around and jarred to a stop. The momentary depth of silence that followed was encouraging. It confirmed what the armament blokes had always contended. Not fused, bombs won't go off on impact – unless there is a furious fire, of course.

And unless it splashed onto the red-hot manifolds of the Merlin engines, the 700 gallons of high-test aviation fuel in the Whitley tanks would neither burn nor explode.

Even as we listened for the drip of gasoline from fractured tanks we were moving to put them at a distance. I followed the second pilot out of the escape hatch above us, my head jostling his scrotum in haste.

Jumping from the port wing, the co-pilot and I could see the wireless operator following. The tailgunner had evacuated his turret and hit the ground about the same time we did. You could smell the high-test fuel oxidizing; the scorch of debris on the smoking engines.

I was about 15 feet away from the wing-tip and running fast when the awesome realization hit me. Ralph Black was nowhere in sight. He must still be inside the cockpit. The moment of indecision that followed seemed eternal. To stand in proximity to the smashed and smoking Whitley was to await the impending blast of annihilation. Not to go back was to abandon the pilot, apparently dazed or unconscious.

Perhaps someone else was closer to help? That possibility vanished with the fleeting figures of my crew-mates.

The demons that crawl my torturous head space were still screaming conflict, crying for action, when Black's balding pate emerged from the cockpit hatch. The dying sunlight formed a corona around it, almost a halo to light his habitual look of harassment.

'Get out and run, you stupid bastard,' I screamed. He did.

We were all five running when the crash-wagons roared into view. Firemen were spraying foam as we were ushered into an ambulance. There was just room for all five of us to stand between the stretchers; not enough space to feel for broken bones or blobs of blood.

We could read our unscathed condition on the faces of the medical staff. They were long with disappointment as we filed into sick quarters. I was the last one into the M.O's office.

'Not you again, Silver!' he groaned.

When we first met in the bag, Thomas Breech Miller looked as his 'T.B.' initials suggested. He had a tall man's tendency to stoop and he was a bit hollow-chested. He wasn't tubercular, of course, but his operational experience had left him less than brisk.

Like me, TB was a navigator in a Whitley crew and crashed on returning from a raid early in his tour. He, too, escaped through the top hatch and was running clear of the aircraft when he realized that all of his crew had not escaped. At this point his experience differed from mine. No more heads emerged through the hatch. And now the wrecked plane was afire. TB Miller went back into the flames – twice – to rescue crew-mates.

The Air Force citation accompanying his George Medal tells the story. 'The controls were damaged and the starboard engine was put out of action so the pilot had to make a forced landing. The aircraft landed heavily with undercarriage retracted, came to rest half over a hedge and caught fire.

'The rear gunner and wireless operator were only slightly injured and escaped from the rear of the aircraft. Sgt. Miller was also uninjured and escaped through the top hatch. He then noticed that the pilot and first wire-less operator were still in the aircraft which was now blazing furiously.

'Undeterred, Sgt. Miller re-entered the aircraft through the top hatch and found the captain lying in a dazed condition, wounded about the face and head. Sgt. Miller pulled the captain through the hatch and carried him away from the aircraft. He returned for the first wireless operator who was lying in the rear of the cabin, very badly hurt and his clothing on fire.

'Sgt. Miller succeeded in lifting him through the hatch and carried him to a place safety where he beat out the flames from the injured man's cloth-ing with his hands after attempting to smother them. The flares, oxygen bottles, ammunition and petrol tanks began to explode immediately after Sgt. Miller got clear of the aircraft. He received severe burns to his hands while rescuing his comrades.'

Forty years later TB gave me a first-hand footnote. 'I got the W/Op's clothes extinguished before he was burned very much. I guess my hands were burned more than he was but I couldn't have done his broken legs and arms very much good dragging him out. He was a long time in hospital. I just had burned hands, a broken finger and torn cartilege.'

TB is a former history professor at Lakehead University and his delivery is episodic; he is like a centipede slowly dropping shoes one at a time. Now he continued. 'It was when I had got him extinguished that I had to con-sider our rear gunner who I had not seen. By that time all the adrenalin or whatever it is that makes one a temporary superman had seeped away. I hope I would have gone after him. I'll never know. But I was mightily relieved to find that he was out.'

'I did a few short ops with a bandaged hand,' he relates. 'Strictly speak-ing I hadn't passed the medical board but since they were just Channel ports I suppose the squadron figured it didn't matter or maybe that I didn't.'

In June 1942 their aircraft was brought down by a flak battery off the Dutch coast. The captain attempted the near impossibility of crash-landing a bomber aircraft on a roiling sea. The plane broke in two on impact. TB Miller and the second pilot were thrown clear; they were the only survivors. 'It was just dumb luck that two of us flew through the hole where the air-craft broke in two; dumb luck that we were thrown out the side where the dinghy broke loose; dumb luck that Red Jones, the other survivor, scram-bled into it before it was blown away; dumb luck that he grabbed my harness. I had been braced against the main spar and I thought my back was broken. I got some movement into my arms and legs by the next day which gave me more motive to want us to be picked up.' It did nothing to improve his posture.

We were, all of us, incredibly fortunate survivors. But with those of TB Miller's character you could see God offering a steadying hand in a shaky do.

7

By Starlight

NORTH SEA, November 1941
A week after the Nissen-hut caper I was teamed with Tony Moore.

At first glance Tony was as uninspiring as a Whitley. Five-foot, five-inches tall, with an elfin face and a school-boy grin, he looked like an air cadet which he had been three years before.

But pilots were not selected for their looks. At age 19 Sergeant Anthony Robert Moore was a bomber crew captain. At 20 this 120-pound pilot would be jockeying a 30-ton, two-storey-high, four-engined Halifax – with a wingspan 19 times his own length – off the deck at 100 miles per hour; weaving a course just beyond the Luftwaffe's radar fingertips while holding the aircraft and his crew in check for seven dicey hours. Before his 21st birthday he would be dead.

'God, how young they all were,' my wife Lynne cried on Tony's headstone a generation later.

'No, they lived a great deal,' I told her. And I thought how Tony had spent a lifetime on Icarus' path honing his pilot skills, fine-tuning his response to every yaw and pitch, evolving into a unity of reflex action with the giant aircraft.

He had jumped from a tricycle to a glider in a dozen years; leapt from his bike to an aircraft without time to learn to drive a car. He had extended his tendons, sinews, muscles and nerve-endings till they grasped ailerons, elevators and rudders with the exquisite co-ordination of a bird in flight.

Short men tend to exert authority. Tony exercised it as unselfconciously as the Prince of Wales. In three years he had been plucked from a school desk and thrust skywards to command a million-dollar flying machine. There had been neither time nor inclination to think about it. That was the great difference between Tony and me. I was still an introspective reporter along for the ride. From a precocious childhood I had been demanding of myself and others, 'tell-me-why?'

What we shared was the childhood experience of solitude and self-direction, the parental weight and spoiling privilege of only children in well-off families. As single sons and sole heirs, we had grown up in security and loneliness; rich kids very much on our own. It was a mixed experience but it tended to teach self-confidence. There were no siblings to intimately observe, to ask or give instructions. You picked your own path through the adolescent rubble. And because there was no brother or sister to lead or follow, to compare or confide with, to praise or criticize, you came out on the adult side satisfied that your compass worked; that you could fly damn near anywhere you set your mind on.

From the first day we air-tested together, Tony Moore and I never doubted our own abilities nor each other's. I set a course and he flew it. He would weave – say 50 feet up or down, three degrees to port, five to starboard – constantly varying those logistics of evasion and still average out the course and speed I had given him.

I never felt the need to check the altimeter, airspeed indicator or compass. He never questioned the directional chit I handed up to him. Tony would have flown straight across Europe to Moscow rather than ask me for a turning point. I would have picked myself off another hilltop rather than suggest he nose-up the aircraft. We became a bonded pair that first week, interdependent and mutually respectful.

We did our first op together – Tony's seventh, my third – the night of 8 November. It was yet another nursery trip, another crack at Ostend. There was a half moon and no cloud over the target. The flak spiralled lazily upwards with no sense of menace. Our bomb run was parallel to the coast and I was certain I could actually see the docks thrusting out at right angles to the shoreline. They seemed to float down the bomb-sight guide wires till I pressed the release tit. Then we were homebound.

A week after Ostend we were despatched to another coastal target. But this was different; Emden was a German port. At long last we would bomb the Third Reich. Emden docks are tucked in a corner of the Ems estuary, a little inshore and guarded by the string of Dutch islands that parallel Europe's northwest shoulder from the Hook of Holland to the mouth of the Weser.

Weaned on the Channel ports, novice crews gained confidence or posthumous credit as they penetrated eastwards along the German coast to attack naval targets of increasing formidability at Emden, Wilhelmshaven, Bremerhaven and Cuxhaven. Around the corner from Cuxhaven veteran crews would run the gauntlet of awesome defences for 50 miles down the Elbe estuary to the great port of Hamburg.

As it happened, icing washed out our first attempt on Emden. An hour's flying time from Leeming we were still climbing to operational height in a comparatively clear sky when we caught the edge of a cold front unpredicted for our route. Wads of cloud washed into us thickening to a blanket of endless dimension.

For 20 minutes we continued to climb through a dark broth that obscured the Whitley's wingtips. Still it thickened until the engine nacelles were barely visible. The ice appeared as suddenly as locusts in a summer sky, spreading like bread mould over every surface. 'De-icers on,' Tony instructed Peter Drake, the second pilot.

Even before the pulsating tubing along the leading edge of the Whitley wing could flick gobs of ice into the slipstream to spatter us, rime ice frosted the windscreen, the surface of the astro-dome and the side windows. We were encased like ants in a popsicle thrust through the crystal depths of frigid cloud. Tony and the second-dickey kept their eyes on the blind-flying panel.

'Think you can climb over it?'

'Doubt it,' Tony told me. 'Any other suggestions?'

'No. Let's be British and endure.'

So we continued upwards. There was no sensation of climbing, only the position of the little aircraft silhouette above the artificial horizon and the altimeter needle flicking clockwise like a second hand. If you listened acutely, as Tony was now doing, you could hear the twin Merlin engines starting to rasp. It was the beginning of a mechanical bronchial cough.

Still we edged higher. The air became colder and the ice harder. Watching the windscreen grow more opaque you could visualize the thickening layers of the stuff on the vast Whitley wingspan. You could sense the weight of it. Both engines were coughing more frequently now.

We had levelled out at 11,000 feet altitude when the port engine hacked consumptively and, like a tubercular patient, suddenly died. Tony put his weight on the controls and trimmed the Whitley for one-engine flight. For a few moments the aircraft hung on one engine's power. But the weight of ice was too much. There was a yawing to starboard and you could feel it lengthening into a circular motion. Downwards we began to spiral. The instrument needles whirled madly.

Theoretically a Whitley aircraft would not go into a spin. And if it did, the aeronautics engineers would tell you there was no way to bring it back under control. With a smaller aircraft you thrust the control column full forward to force the downward spiralling motion into a dive, speed and gravity countering the centrifugal force. Bereft of theoretical alternatives our 120-pound skipper applied the conventional response in an unorthodox situation.

The 23-tons of aircraft, fuel and bomb-load did stop spiralling. Now it was dropping at a 60-degree angle and it was 12 seconds from the North Sea surface when Tony began to bring it out of the dive. We levelled off perhaps 250 feet above the water and well below the overcast. Both engines were running again and most of the ice had been blown clear of the Whitley's surfaces.

'How is it?' I asked.

'Like a horse that's dived from a stable roof,' Tony replied.

'What damage?'

'Stretched control cables at least. And a pair of engines vibrating to death.'

'So you want a reciprocal course back to Leeming.'

'You guessed it,' Tony said.

The squadron C/O commended him for bringing us back intact. But we had aborted our flight short of the meridian 4 degrees east of Greenwich – that mid-line on the North Sea crossing that marked an operational flight. Like the Nissen-hut caper this had been an interesting effort but it didn't count towards a tour of ops.

A fortnight later they despatched us to Emden again. Senior crews were assigned to bomb Hamburg that night but we were still to be weaned from a coastal target. The routes were very similar. We would track 095 degrees for 345 miles from Leeming to Borkum, the Dutch island that stands 20 miles off the Ems estuary. Less than a 15-minute flight southeast from Borkum – just half of it across land – would put us on target.

Veteran crews would track a route half a dozen degrees more northerly to the tiny island of Helgoland. From this turning point they would fly 40 miles southeast to Cuxhaven on the bottom lip of the Elbe estuary. Then, for another 50 miles down the Elbe to Hamburg, they would face the most formidable combination of naval and anti-aircraft guns in Germany.

From the dispersal site of Whitley T-for-Tommy we could see the other squadron aircraft taking-off a good half hour before us. We watched them head out for Hamburg with mixed feelings. We would fly much the same North Sea crossing, but from our Dutch island turning point the run-up on Emden would be no more than an extension of our Channel port experience. God, what would it be like making that scary run down the Elbe to blitz a *real* German target?

We took off at 16:40 hrs. The outbound flight was not without incident. An unidentified aircraft appeared to be tailing us for a quarter hour off the British coast. It was undoubtedly another Four Group Whitley but it agitated our tail-gunner and he relayed his uneasiness to the rest of us. Then he reported his oxygen supply was defective. Tony sent Drake back with a portable oxygen bottle.

'Got him settled down?' Tony asked when the second pilot returned.

'Not really. Now he claims his intercom is defective.'

'Tail-gunner, are you going to be okay or do we abort the trip?' Tony asked.

'No. I'll be alright,' he mumbled.

Again we ran into icing at about 10,000 feet altitude. It was not severe but for a few minutes it unsettled the engines. By the time he had them

74

running smoothly again Tony decided against climbing another 2,000 feet to our assigned height. 'If we stay at this altitude we won't need oxygen,' he announced.

As each of us voiced our agreement it was apparent that the intercom was not working properly. George Niness, the unflappable New Zealand wireless operator near the end of his 30-op tour, promised to look into it. A few minutes later he leaned around the bulkhead and passed me a note: 'Short somewhere on my board. Causing big hum on whole system.'

'All of the headsets?' I asked, talking directly into his ear.

'Don't know, but certainly in mine. Which means I can't define radio bearings for you.'

By some fluke the second pilot and I could hear each other quite clearly. But neither Drake nor I could speak through the intercom to Tony or Niness. For the rest of the trip Tony and I communicated by chit or through the second pilot. Drake would lift off his microphone and talk directly into Tony's ear. Tony did the same, raising his voice to bark at Drake or at me.

Based on the weather boffins' prediction of a virtual headwind – from 120 degrees at 35 mph – I calculated the long sea leg would take 198 minutes. 'ETA Borkum 19:58,' I advised Tony by chit.

High cloud allowed only a little moonlight to shine through and about sixth-tenths cloud beneath us gave an intermittent view of the sea two miles below.

Five minutes before ETA Borkum I went forward to the bomb-aimer position where I plugged in my intercom. It worked clearly with Peter Drake but with no one else. 'So you're going to be a relay station,' I told him. 'Who says second pilots are like tits on a bull.'

As we approached the German and Danish coasts the cloud cover virtually disappeared beneath us. In strained moonlight I could see what appeared to be the surface of the sea. But at 19:58 there was no sign of Borkum nor the string of islands to east and west of it. Then, half a minute later, I spotted a tiny island remote from any other land.

'Landfall. But it doesn't look like Borkum,' I announced.

Drake repeated the information to Tony and relayed his response. 'Tony can see it, too. He says it's too small to be Denmark.'

'Set course 120 degrees. 15 minutes to mainland, 20 to target,' I advised, ignoring the sarcasm.

Within minutes, the German coast with its spate of estuaries took shape. Dead ahead was a wide river mouth that could be the Ems, but appeared nearly twice as far away as it should be. Almost joining it on the west was a wider estuary. 'That's wide enough to be the Weser with bloody Wilhemshaven on one side, Bremenhaven on the other and frigging Cuxhaven on the snout,' I muttered.

Lying prone on the Perspex floor in the bomb-aimer position, the turret bathing me in moonlight and with the defective intercom tuning out everyone except Pete Drake, I could consider our position in momentary detachment. Cut off from the intercom, so could Tony.

As we soared towards the German mainland at better than two miles a minute, Tony and I ran through a similar thought process. Much later when we compared notes, it was as if we had tuned in to the same channel of reasoning.

Say the boffins were off on the wind a bit. If it was blowing 25 or 30 degrees more clockwise than they had predicted then we'd be 30 or 40 miles more northerly after the long sea crossing. And both of us realized that with less headwind we would be further east. Tony, like most travelled Brits, had a mental picture of northwest German coastal geography while I had a map at my knee.

Ten minutes flying on the new leg brought us to the same conclusion at virtually the same time. Our first landfall had not been Borkum. It must have been Helgoland, that solitary dot of an island 40 miles off the Elbe and Weser river mouths.

Which meant that on this 818th night of war we were headed for a major target – not in the Ems estuary but down the Elbe. We could forget Emden and test the mighty naval defences of the German Reich. Perhaps penetrate to Hamburg itself.

We could also be court-martialed for making such a decision. That we were not busted to aircraftsmen and left to fill sandbags for the duration of the war, we could thank Angus Buchan, our benign Scottish station navigation officer. Buchan would argue that we had been given a bum wind prediction; that there was sufficient cloud to obscure landmarks; that captain and navigator could not communicate directly with each other on the critical last leg of the operation and that having failed to immediately locate Emden we were entitled to pick a S.E.M.O. – meaning Self-Evident Military Target.

In swathes of moonlight at 10,000 feet the bat-like Whitley floated in to make landfall over the east side of the estuary. I looked down from my Perspex perch dumbfounded. The mud flats were taking shape two miles below and there was not a sign of hostility; no naval guns, no flak, no searchlights seeking us out. The forewarnings of senior squadron crews had obviously been exaggerated

In fact, they sucked us 15 miles downstream to Brunsbuttelkoog, the western terminus of the Kiel Canal. Like an adder's tongue, the garish blue beam of a master searchlight flicked out of the black depths to taste us. Seconds later we were writhing in the cone of a dozen brilliant-white shafts of light. My Perspex cage seemed to dissolve around me. Suddenly it was as if I was hanging stark naked at the end of a fishing line.

Tony twisted the Whitley like a tuna fighting capture. Still the search-lights held us. Anti-aircraft gunfire was almost instantaneous. The lethal perforation lines of light flak climbed the beams of light. Heavy flak burst with a crump-crump so close it drowned the Merlin engine noise. Cordite fumes filled the fuselage.

The cone of lights merged to a single beam. We had been briefed on Luftwaffe fighter tactics. One was apparently coming straight for us, its headlight holding us. 'Silver,' I told myself, 'you're going to be the first one hit. Get the Hun bastard before you go.'

Forcing myself up on one knee, I reached a handle of the two-gun hydraulic controls with my right hand. A four-second squeeze emptied the ammunition pans in eddying streams of yellow fire that swirled ahead of us.

The sound and sight of our own gunfire reoriented me. In the only pos-sible escape manoeuvre, Tony was taking the Whitley down a searchlight beam in close to a 70-degree dive. The bomb-sight altimeter showed we were dropping to earth at six miles per minute from just two miles up. I fused and flicked the bomb-load free with a reflex action.

Balls of fire burst around us. Fabric and equipment were torn free. My navigation stuff along with everything else that was loose in the plane poured into the front turret around me. Then my face hit the bomb-sight as Tony began to pull the aircraft from its dive.

For weeks after Pete Drake would corner others in the mess. 'I couldn't get in position to help him and this little frigger had both feet on the instru-ment panel for leverage,' he would tell them. 'I figured the control column would break and the wings would come off.'

We levelled out literally at roof-top height. The wharf structures and warehousing flipped past half a dozen feet beneath my turret. Geezus, it was like a jet-sped Santa Claus chimney-hopping on Christmas Eve. Now the light flak was bursting above us. Naval guns lashed our Whitley.

'Tell Tony zero on the compass. Straight out to sea,' I roared to Pete Drake.

Tony was already headed out, but getting the Whitley much above wave-top height was not going to be easy. Shells had torn one elevator away and jammed the other. Balloon cables had ripped the rudders beyond control.

Half by skill and half by instinct, Tony wheedled the Whitley up and out the Elbe estuary. Once clear of the headland he jinked and turned on half a dozen headings to evade the radar tracks they were laying to recapture us.

I thrust what nav equipment I could salvage into my pockets and climbed up from the well. Tony winked at me like an elf. 'You know,' he shouted, 'it's highly unlikely we'll get back to England tonight.'

'Just head 270 degrees frigging west,' I told him. 'Britain's a big island, we can't miss it.'

An hour later we had regained 7,000 feet altitude. In our escape from the Elbe the Merlin engines had been run 'through the gate' at super-charged power well past the maker's limits. Yet miraculously they still churned reliably.

'So where are we?' Tony wondered.

The conventional way to answer that question would be to lay down an air-plot – a vector for every leg of the flight, then an accumulative vector for the wind speed and direction. But there had been a dozen minutes of frantic flight over the Elbe, twisting and turning onto several headings. Perhaps they had cancelled each other out; perhaps they had put us 15 or 20 miles in one direction or another from our theoretical position. But theory with a 15 or 20-mile error could take us smack into a British coastal defence.

'I'm working on it,' I said. Then I let him know about the wireless op's troubles. 'Niness says the set has packed up as far as reception is concerned.'

'So now's your chance to practice astro-navigation.'

'Yes,' I agreed. 'But you should know that what I measure with this frigging sextant is the angle of light that left a star before Jesus was born.'

'Sounds ecclesiastic.'

'And what I'm timing is the moment the starlight hits my sextant. If I'm four seconds off we may be sliding our asses down a balloon barrage cable over Teeside or the Humber.'

'That's an incentive for accuracy, Silver,' Tony replied. Then he edged the flak-wracked Whitley another 3,000 feet higher so I could peek at the stars.

The Whitley droned upwards for several minutes until we were above the strata-cumulus overcast. But high cirrus cloud still coated most of the heavens. If I could shoot an astro sight of Polaris, the North Star, I could approximate our latitude; that is, where we would hit the British coast on a north-south line.

But Polaris was lost in the hazy vault of moon-washed cirrus cloud. So were most stars this jinxed night. I *did* fix on an identifiable star which was enough – in theory – to give us a longitudinal position line. That meant a datum point from which I could count off our distance to the English coast-line – providing, of course, that we were aiming for a landfall somewhere between Teeside and the Humber.

I passed the chit to Tony. '*Theoretically* ETA coast is 23:52 hrs. *If we're on track for base,*' it said.

The British coastline leans towards Europe in the south, which meant we would cross it sooner if we were south of track. Conversely, we would have to fly minutes more through the night to a landfall if further north. While my sextant reading gave only an approximate time for the coast, we would likely sight it through broken cloud. In any case, our IFF-set (Identification – Friend or Foe) was equipped with balloon squeakers for just such an emergency. An RAF aircraft blindly approaching British defences was warned off by a high-pitch signal that increased in intensity as you got closer.

'Better turn up the IFF volume,' I told him.

Tony stretched in his seat to reach the IFF control with his right hand. I watched his fingers closing on the brown plastic control knob and felt the aircraft lurching sharply to starboard before Tony regained control. Half a century since that hapless night the image burns bright in my mind's eye. Tony is still holding the control knob. But it has been wrenched free of the set.

'Not much else to go wrong,' he said wryly. As it turned out there was. Virtually all England was cloaked in cloud. We had still to come down through the overcast to get a visual fix of the coast before we ventured inland. And once we lost height there was no way we could quickly regain it.

'If we come in under a low ceiling there's no way I can climb over the coast,' Tony told me.

'So on ETA we break cloud on a reciprocal course,' I said. He agreed.

On the basis of starlight that had travelled the whole of the Christian Era to give us a sextant reading, we were to assume we were at the coast on ETA – somewhere between Teeside and the Humber. Accordingly, at eight minutes to midnight that last night of November 1941, we swung around through 180 degrees and began our descent.

We came down through layer on layer of stratocumulus cloud that filtered the last dregs of moonlight. We came down riding a theoretical beam of starlight. With luck we would see the coast.

The altimeter needle dropped through the 5,000, 4,000, 3,000-feet readings. There was no break in the cloud. Down through the soot-black sky we came.

Tony, Peter Drake and I watched the altimeter needle clicking back like time diminishing. Three pair of eyes watched the needle clicking through the 2,000, 1,500, 1,000-feet marks. Well, at least we had not overshot into the Yorkshire Moors or fells.

But we were still in the bottomless, lightless depths of night. We might yet wipe our backsides on Tyneside, Teeside or Grimsby balloon cables.

At 600 feet, there were ripples of moonlight dancing like wraiths on water below. The altimeter was showing 350 feet when we dropped clear of the overcast. There beneath us the North Sea roiled.

Again we reversed direction and headed towards a shoreline that theoretically was just moments away. Tony kept his eyes on the instruments while Drake and I thrust our heads through side-windows to peer into the slipstream. Two more minutes flight brought the murky outline of the coast into view.

'Land, there's bloody land ahead,' Drake roared.

'It's the coast alright,' I shouted.

'Yes, but whose?' Tony asked dryly, edging the Whitley closer in.

Staying within a mile or two of the coast we flew five minutes north and ten minutes south again. But it was impossible to establish a landmark. It would be suicidal to try flying inland at such a low altitude. And there was no likelihood we could regain a safe height even if fuel reserves permitted.

'So standby to ditch in the sea,' Tony announced with the grin of a school-boy about to take his first summer dive off a seaside dock.

Hopeful that his wireless would still transmit, Niness sent out the traditional SOS call and clamped down the Morse key so RAF Air-Sea Rescue Command could track our continuous signal. Drake remained to help Tony jockey the maimed Whitley nose-up into the sea. Niness and I went back, alerted the tail-gunner and prepared to abandon the aircraft.

With barely suppressed glee I hacked the fuselage door free with a fire-axe while Niness and the gunner readied the dinghy for launching. Then all three of us took up crash positions. We were skimming the sea surface so close we could have dipped our fingers in it.

But now Tony was edging the aircraft closer to shore and we could see, dimly, an unbroken stretch of beach. You could imagine the smooth sandy surface inviting an emergency landing until you remembered the huge concrete erosion-control crosses, the forest of poles to stop enemy gliders and the unseen land-mines.

'Geezus, don't do it, Tony,' I cried out.

A moment later I realized I had misjudged his intention. A searchlight beam moving parallel to the sea surface flicked out from the shore, held our aircraft in its glow and carried us on its northerly arcing path. As the first searchlight's beam returned to shore, a second picked us up. Air-Sea Rescue was answering our SOS and handing us up the coast to an accessible airfield.

Drake summoned Niness and me back to our places. 'It looks like they are going to bring us in somewhere up the coast where the weather is clear. That's what Tony thinks,' he said.

And they did. Successive searchlight arms reached out like those of relay runners to grasp the Whitley and pass it on nearly 60 miles up the coast to Acklington, a night-fighter base just beyond Newcastle-on-Tyne.

At first George Niness and I watched with fascination as Tony fought the half-wrecked controls and nursed the tiring Merlin engines to save our little margin of altitude. But smoke from the wireless panel distracted us. The radio circuitry that had plagued our communications almost from take-off was now burning.

George and I grabbed extinguishers. As the aircraft bucked and shuddered I missed the radio panel and squirted George in the face. The spray from his extinguisher splashed the side of my head. Eventually we doused the flames that were starting to eat through the face of the set.

The pilot side windows were still open to admit the slipstream. A steady blast of air washed down the fuselage to carry the smoke out of the opening where I had jettisoned the door. 'I guess you couldn't smell the wireless panel fire and we didn't want to distract you in the midst of a tricky landing,' I told Tony later.

'That was thoughtful,' he said. 'Anything else I should know about?'

'Well you realized they were trying to bring in two other aircraft beside ours.'

'I only saw one of them.'

'The other hit that dirty great coal pile just off our approach path. It blew up.'

'I thought that was one of the flares they were popping up,' Tony said. He hadn't seen – or anticipated – the 40-foot-high coal pile so close to the landing circuit.

He had brought our Whitley in low and steady on the first try. We bounced a little and were running fast because only half the flap surfaces responded to the controls. But we pulled up well short of the perimeter. As the twin Merlins sputtered and died the five of us sighed in unison.

'Well nothing else can happen tonight. That's for sure,' I said.

I was wrong. By jettisoning the bombs in a 70-degree dive I had left a canister of incendiaries hung-up, still locked on the release hook. The 14-pound phosphorus bombs were shaken loose as we bounced to a landing. Acklington's main runway was aflame for a hundred feet behind us as we climbed from the aircraft.

The following day, Acklington's engineering officer examined the Whitley. He found nearly 50 flak holes of varying sizes. 'Some are in the superstructure, in critical areas. One made a 38-inch long gash beside the flare chute. The de-icing boots on the rudders bear the marks of balloon-barrage cable. The left elevator is partly missing. The right one is jammed. This aircraft is unserviceable and not to be flown,' he reported.

Acklington was the base for radar-equipped Beaufighters. The two-man crews were vectored into the flight path of night-time Luftwaffe intruders, locked onto them electronically and fired aerial cannon into an enemy they rarely saw before their target exploded.

We took the Acklington crews on a tour of our shattered Whitley. 'Christ,' they exclaimed. 'And you guys got to do 30 ops like this?'

'Oh they're all not this rough,' George Niness told them.

8

Dear Fellow Worker

LONDON, Christmas 1941

Our impromptu dive-bomb assault on an Elbe defence point was the last raid by a 10 Squadron Whitley. Five years after it had looked so formidable on the Armstrong-Whitworth drawing board, the aircraft that flew like a hound – and just as doggedly – was obsolete.

As our crew bounced ingloriously back to Leeming in an RAF lorry that 1 December morning, the squadron was ordered to 'stand down.' Over the next few weeks we converted to four-engined Halifaxes aircraft that flew nearly twice as high, 70 per cent faster and carried a 60 per cent bigger bomb-load.

Equally momentous but cloaked in hush-hush security, ours was one of the first two bomber squadrons to be equipped with Gee sets. This innovative black box caught radar signals from three widely-spaced transmitters and projected them as directional bearings on its bile green screen. It was the first really new navigational tool since the 15th-century astrolabe, a prototype sextant, put mariners on course.

Fighter Command had first call on Watson-Watts' Radar (Radio Detection and Ranging). Radar equipped the Spitfire and Hurricane pilots to win the Battle of Britain in 1940. Now it would enable Bomber Command crews to fulfil their purpose.

Throughout 1941, Churchill was reminded that one bomber aircraft was lost for every 10 tons of bombs dropped. And only one bomb in 10 aimed at a Ruhr target on moonless nights fell within five miles of it. We not only missed the target, we screwed-up on the way home. The month I recuperated from hitting Widdale Fell, Bomber Command despatched 2,621 aircraft on operations. 76 were shot down over Europe. Another 62 crashed back in Britain. The following month 68 went missing and 40 crashed returning to base. While I was out of action, 10 Squadron's flying roster was almost completely replaced. Most crews had been wiped out in a dozen ops.

Theoretically, with our Mark IX sextants we could navigate by the stars as mariners had done for centuries. In practice, few identifiable stars were visible on any night. Sighting them from an aircraft that rarely climbed above medium-level cloud was unlikely. Persuading a pilot to fly straight and level over enemy territory for star-shooting was even more improbable.

And converting starlight to a precise position line under operational stress was beyond most of us.

There were exceptions. The star of our air-observer course who had quickly become 10 Squadron navigation officer, Jack Watts could aim his sextant and determine his position as readily as looking up a 'phone number. Later, in a Pathfinder Mosquito hurtling across a flak-starred target-marking path, Jack would operate with ivory-tower detachment. Shot down in the Mediterranean off Tobruk he rolled over and looked at the stars to get his bearings, then swam for shore with a ripped crotch that imperiled his manhood. He subsisted on rainwater for five days till a British desert squad found him in the wake of Rommel's retreating army. Quickly restored to the service of God, king and adoring ladies, he completed 109 Bomber Command operations in four wartime years. Post-war he rose to Brigadier-General.

Air Vice-Marshal Donald C.T. Bennett, who wrote the air navigators' pre-war handbook, organized Atlantic Ferry Command, turned 10 Squadron inside-out as our C/O and subsequently established the Pathfinder Force, was shot down by Tirpitz gunners in a Norwegian fjord. He escaped to Sweden, enroute killing a German border-guard bare-handed. He was another airborne perfectionist who could shoot the stars from first-pilot position while flying the Ruhr's flak-happy gun belt.

A dozen airmen like Watts and Bennett might have won the war years earlier. Forced to use lesser lights, Bomber Command refitted us with higher, faster-flying aircraft and position-fixing Gee sets that season. We were being moved the last mile to total war.

'Analysis of raids on Birmingham, Hull and elsewhere have shown that, on average, one ton of bombs on a built-up area demolishes 20 to 40 dwellings and turns 100 to 200 people out of house and home,' Churchill was told by his science advisor Lord Cherwell. 'We can count on nearly 14 operational sorties per bomber produced; average lift will be about three tons. If these are dropped on built-up areas they will make 4,000 to 8,000 people homeless.'

Accordingly, we would be despatched to 58 German towns where 22 million Germans lived. With the new radar equipment 'these towns should be easy to find and hit,' the Prime Minister was told. We had come a long way since tribal elders defended our hairy ancestors with wooden clubs. Gunpowder had been invented seven centuries past; it took another century to develop a gun to use it. Bronze cannon and rifles appeared in the past 450 years. Nitrocellulose and nitroglycerine were produced in the mid-19th century but were too unstable for military use. Twenty years later Albert Nobel fixed nitroglycerine in a plastic mass to make dynamite. Then he invented the mercury-fulminate detonator to spark it. TNT, picric acid and smokeless powder were developed in the following two decades. Before Queen Victoria died her empire was equipped for war on a grand scale. A dozen years after her death warfare was airborne.

Air warfare began inauspiciously enough. Up to mid-May 1918 when they were subdued, German zeppelins and planes dropped 270 tons of bombs on Britain. They killed about 1,400 people and injured 3,400 others. Eight in 10 British air-raid casualties were civilians. The entrenched British Army had first call on air power till late in the war. Then in the last five months of World War I, the Royal Flying Corps dropped 550 tons of bombs on Germany. *Pro rata* the Germans would have sustained some 2,900 killed and 6,900 injured.

World War II was eight months old before the Luftwaffe was unleashed on the British population. In ten months of 1940–41 the German air force droppped some 50,000 tons of bombs on Britain, killing 43,000 people. Fighter Command was given first call on RAF aircrews and aircraft until the Battle of Britain was won.

Then Bomber Command retaliated. By August 1941 when I joined 10 Squadron, Bomber Command was dropping some 4,200 tons a month on Germany. Still the targets were too scattered, our navigation inadequate and our losses too high to be sustained. By mid-November Air Ministry began to curb our operations. The War Cabinet, it said, wanted aircraft and aircrews built into an effective striking force for the spring of 1942.

The second week of December the Japanese attacked Pearl Harbor, bringing the U.S. into World War II; British battleships *Prince of Wales* and *Repulse* were sunk off the Malay Peninsula while a Soviet army drove the Nazis back 50 miles from Rostov. At Leeming we were preoccupied with the arrival of bigger, faster, better aircraft even while we chafed at the downtime to learn to use them.

Tony and I had no sooner teamed up and gone into action than the whole squadron was idled for training on new equipment. In the previous four months I had survived three Whitleys but completed only four operations. Now there would be a further, indeterminate delay.

It was nearly three months since I had seen Joan, and belatedly I realized how she had slipped from consciousness. Our letters had grown shorter and infrequent. Three weeks before Christmas I was suddenly aware we had not discussed my holiday leave and I 'phoned her. Realizing my own neglect, I was on the defensive and my tone was less than romantic. As we exchanged pleasantries I could sense our mutual withdrawal. The future was so indefinite and our togetherness had been too short.

'What are your plans for Christmas?' she asked.

I had none but was reluctant to say so. Frustrated and restless, unnerved by alternate bouts of high operational activity and enforced idleness, I skirmished. 'Tony has invited me home for Christmas,' I told her. He had mentioned it but there had been no discussion. It was assumed by all concerned that I would spend the holiday with Joan and her family. Now I was injecting uncertainty.

'Oh!' she said and the word sounded hollow. 'Well, let me know what you plan to do.'

So dreams dissolve and romance ends in banality. I 'phoned a few days later to say I would be staying with Tony's family but hoped I would be welcome to come across London to Wembley.

'Of course,' Joan assured.

When I arrived at 25 Eton Court on Christmas Eve only Mrs Eden was home. Joan and her sister returned from Christmas Mass late in the evening. Joan was accompanied by a Canadian army captain; Eve was with a young Air Force officer. Both couples were married within a year.

Tony's home was one of ten vast houses that sprawled on half-acre properties flanking Black Hills Road in Esher, a stylish byway of high-hedged seclusion less than an hour's commuting distance from London's financial centre. As secretary-treasurer of one of England's big three insurance companies, Tony's father Reg Moore was part of the corporate hierarchy keeping Britain afloat in tenuous times.

Tony's mother Dime (for 'Little Diamond,' as Reg had called her) was an update miniature of Mother England. Indomitably cheerful, she considered chirpy optimism a sacred duty that she owed to her husband, son and country. And like Brits of all classes she had met wartime demands with great flexibility. Dime Moore raised egg-laying poultry on the clipped lawns. Hens clucked among the flower-beds.

Dime referred to her son's girl-friend Winnie as his 'fiancee.' It was her pragmatic way of labelling the holiday sleeping arrangements whereby Tony and Winnie occupied adjacent rooms, somewhat distant from four other bedrooms down a serendipitious corridor.

What I remember of Christmas morning breakfast was the naked happiness that lit their faces. Reg and Dime Moore marking their only child's brief homecoming, Tony and Winnie basking in the afterglow of coupling; each of them celebrating the elysian present without regret, apology or anticipation. I fingered the St Christopher medal hanging with my dog-tags. I could not forswear the medallion but I had already given up its donor. That holiday week I went into London, found a girl named Cindy at the Regent Palace bar and got laid.

More consequential was my encounter with Tim Reid that week. He had been city editor of *The Sudbury Star* when I was briefly the *Globe and Mail's* correspondent in his bailiwick. Now Tim was a flight lieutenant doing RCAF public relations work. He was intrigued that I had been the first to report the establishment of a RCAF recruiting office in northern Ontario at war's outbreak and the first to apply for an air-war job.

'Cripes, Silver, here you are actually in the war, not just reporting it,' he observed.

'I figured this would be the biggest story of my life,' I told him, 'and I had to ask myself, "Are you going to get in it or stand around taking notes?"'

We were three deep in a mass of blue uniforms crowding a bar close by Air Ministry offices. My flight-sergeant stripes were lost in the crush and to F/Lt Tim Reid I was just another ex-newsman from Canada. I was aware, however, that I was the sole non-commissioned officer in the place.

Indifferent to military status and hierarchal niceties, Tim looked over my shoulder to introduce another Canadian airman. 'Jim Jeffries shake hands with Ray Silver,' he said. I turned to confront an Air Vice-Marshal across the wide abyss of rank. Under cover of the AV-M's blustering confusion, I reminded Tim we had an engagement elsewhere.

Several drinks later Tim Reid decided how to restore our service careers. 'By all means continue to have fun in the air,' he said graciously. 'But you owe Canada the serious application of your editorial services.'

'Like how?'

'When you get back to the squadron I want you to write a letter to the workers of Canada?'

'Which workers?'

'The men and women who are bent over their lathes and forges to produce the 'planes and armaments that make you an effective warrior,' he said.

'You're drunk, Tim.'

'That's irrelevent.'

It was. Back at Leeming there were further delays in resuming ops and Tim Reid's offbeat assignment filled idle moments. 'Dear Fellow Worker,' I began, 'we are working together on the same job – the business of winning the war. I imagine you're finding, as I am, that it's the biggest job you ever tackled.'

I told them their work was tougher because they couldn't actually see the results of their efforts nor 'the people smashed up by Hun bombs.' Then I described how Canadian-made radio equipment had withstood enemy action, violent aerobatics and terrible weather to 'get us down to earth healthy enough to talk about it.' There was more in this vein. Writing as an anonymous airman I was uninhibited.

Anonymity was the last thing Tim Reid and the government hacks had in mind. What they needed was a live pigeon writing a credible and personable letter. They reproduced 40,000 copies of it, simulated my signature and individually addressed them to war industry workers from one end of

Canada to the other. Replies from some very pretty girls (photographs enclosed), post-war invitations and cigarette packages addressed to their airman pen-pal, were beginning to find me at 10 Squadron when I was shot down.

The old year had ended with such promise; with Halifax heavy bombers and the Gee set to guide us. For Tony and me, however, the new year began ominously. The day we returned to Leeming from leave Tony was advised that his conversion to four-engined aircraft had been deferred.

'Four Group command says no one under five-foot six, can fly a four-engine plane. That's the word from the wingless-wonders,' he told me.

'Is that final?' I asked, dumbfounded.

'No, Squadron Leader Thompson says he'll go to bat for me but I'm not optimistic.'

In the meantime our crew was to remain grounded. Tony was given a range of make-work duties that allowed him to familiarize himself with the Halifax controls and instrumentation. During my previous grounding following the Widdale Fell crash, the station navigation officer Angus Buchan had kept me busy replotting other navigators' operational logs and checking navigational equipment in squadron aircraft.

'Am I jinxed or something?' I asked Buchan. 'The bastards won't let me get my ops in.'

'They're saving you for immortal things,' he told me. 'Now simmer down. I've got a job for you.' I was to take a three-day crash course at Group headquarters on how the Gee set worked and then instruct fellow navigators.

Buchan and Jack Watts, as senior navigators at Leeming, had taken the course and were already testing Gee in the air. One by one the veteran crews completed their conversion while Tony and I were anchored in ground duties. In the first week of January, 10 Squadron bombed the German submarine pens at Brest and St Nazaire, testing new concrete-crushing super-bombs as well as the accurate new means of delivery. By month's end the Squadron was again fully operational though Tony had yet to take a Halifax off the deck.

In mid-February Air Ministry advised Bomber Command that 'It has been decided that the primary objective of your operations should now be focussed on the morale of the enemy civil population and in particular of the industrial workers.' A further note the following day left no doubt of the government's intentions. 'The aiming points are to be the built-up areas, not for instance the dockyards or aircraft factories. This must be made quite clear if it is not already understood.'

A week later Sir Arthur Harris, who had gone from boy bugler to Royal Flying Corp pilot in World War I, was named to the dominant RAF post in World War II. As Bomber Command chief he would implement the government's direction to break the German will for war. In the previous 30 months Bomber Command had lost 7,450 aircrew killed or shot down into captivity. In the next 38 months 72,350 of us would be shot down – one in seven surviving as POWs.

Tony greeted me on my return from guiding a Fleet Air Arm pilot to his Firth of Tay base in a single-engine Skua. I had endured the 90-minute flight in an open-cockpit, kneeling on my map while the wind whistled up my backside at 85 knots. For such aid to the senior service I was awarded a 48-hour pass. On the short train ride inland I met a girl from Broughty Ferry; reward enough for 90 minutes spent in a Skua in the missionary position.

At last, Tony told me, Four Group HQ had waived the height restriction as far as he was concerned. Based on his past performance from gliders to the twin-engined Whitley he would be allowed to fly four-engined aircraft that were 13 times as long as he was and weighed 630 times as much. Squadron Leader Thomson, our flight commander, would be checking him out.

In mid-March, while Tony was still in conversion, I flew with one of the 10 Squadron crews despatched to Lossiemouth, on Scotland's Grampian coast. This was the only airfield big enough to accommodate four-engined bombers within possible reach of Norway's Aaltern Fjord where the German Navy had secured the battleship *Tirpitz*. Naval boffins had developed a special ball-shaped mine and the Halifax were fitted with auxiliary fuel tanks for the nine-hour return flight. At last I was poised for derring-do. For four days we waited for flyable weather. When it didn't materialize, we returned to Leeming.

Air Marshal Harris had glibly told Churchill a month earlier 'I'll sink the *Tirpitz* when I have a spare moment.' As it turned out, the operation tied up some of 10 Squadron's best crews for a month and a half. Half a dozen crews were despatched at the end of March but found the weather impossible. A month later on two successive nights they breached the cloud over Trondheim to make their treacherous runs up the fjord.

Jack Watts was on both raids. 'We began our dive from 4,000 to 150 feet to enter Aaltern Fjord. As we passed its sharp, leading edge, practically brushing it with our wingtip, I punched my stopwatch.' 'At that very moment we flew into a smoke screen that seemed impenetrable. It was like flying in cotton wool. We knew we were thundering alongside a solid wall of rocky cliff and speeding towards an even higher cliff not far ahead. And we were blind. Somewhere, in this ghastly smoke lay the battleship whose masts we might even touch.

'There was no thinning of the smoke and we had reached the end of our timed run. The *Tirpitz* was either dead ahead or beneath us. I pressed the bomb release and we pulled up at full throttle hoping we had not overrun the seconds needed to clear the bloody great wall at the fjord end. I held my breath. It seemed an eternity till we finally broke clear of the smoke screen into the crystalline air of the winter night.'

They were sent back the following night. In place of a smoke screen, the Germans bathed them in searchlight glow and anti-aircraft fire. A Messerschmitt-109 chased them to the lip of the fjord. 'The criss-crossing tracers from ship and shore guns made the air space above the *Tirpitz* a maw of molten metal. Certainly no German night-fighter would fly through that barrage. He broke off but I had not been able to make a satisfactory bomb run. We would have to go round again.'

And they did. Half a century later Watts remembers the Halifax ahead of them. 'It reared up out of the hell-fire of flak to escape the cliff wall but it was engulfed in flames. Flying speed carried it into a high arc and it plummeted in a blazing stall.'

He remembers the canvas camouflage nearly stripped from the *Tirpitz* deck; the way his four mines fell. 'One and two made clean spumes of water, three was dirty and four slightly delayed; it bounced off the cliff wall or rolled off the deck but it was dirty as well.' Dirty meant damaging. Watts won a DFC for his efforts.

In November 1944, RAF and RCAF Lancasters finally capsized the *Tirpitz* in Tromso Fjord. Two and a half years earlier we had counted 10 Squadron losses including those of our C/O's crew who didn't get back. 'Why not just trade a couple of RAF squadrons for the bloody ship,' someone suggested. It would have been cheaper.

I returned from Lossiemouth to rejoin Tony and our new crew-mates. Harry Stacey, an ex-Birmingham postman with a voice like crackling cellophane, succeeded George Niness as our wireless operator. Stacey proved as unflappable as his predecessor. Don Thurlow, a Manchester mechanic with an uncanny eye and ear to diagnose trouble, became flight engineer. Frank Walker was our new tail-gunner.

Thurlow assumed most of the duties previously performed by the second pilot although I sat in the second-dickey seat to assist with throttles and propeller-pitch controls on take-off. My first move on entering the Halifax flight deck was to check the foot-extensions on the rudder bar and make sure they would reach to Tony's feet.

This proved adequate in flight but he couldn't see over the aircraft nose when its tail-wheel was on the ground. So as we taxied I would call out directions, 'Right, Tony,' or 'Left, left, steady', as if we were making a bomb run. Once while we waited on the perimeter for permission to proceed to the runway a NAAFI truck pulled behind our outer starboard engine. The driver opened the service side of the little canteen vehicle exposing its two giant tea urns plus shelves of cakes, snacks and cigarettes.

We had to wait several minutes for clearance. A long line of WAAFs and aircraftsmen had queued up by the time we got a GO signal. 'Hard left, Tony,' I told him, and he gave a burst of the outer starboard engine to turn the Halifax onto the runway. The great Merlin motor roared and the propeller wash caught the NAAFI truck broadside. It teetered on two wheels, the tops were blown from the tea urns and their contents were swept into a giant brown wave. The wave arced over the heads of the scattering ground-crew, carrying cakes and buns in its flow.

Thereafter, Tony sat on a thick cushion to give him a ground view while taxying. A second cushion was thrust between his back and the armoured seat cover to lever him forward till his feet again touched the rudder bar stirrups.

Unlike the Whitley which seemed always to be sniffing the ground, the Halifax sat high on its undercarriage. In the second-pilot's seat I would look in the second-storey window of the control tower as we taxied for take-off and then beside me at the skipper, Tony perched forward in the driver's seat, his feet barely reaching the rudder extensions, his short arms stretched to encompass the controls, his helmet framing a cherubic grin. It was not an imposing sight.

With some 1,800 gallons of fuel in the tanks and a four-ton, barrel-shaped bomb nudging the slightly-opened bay doors, the four Merlin engines would build momentum slowly. 'At 63,000 pounds the Halifax can be pulled off the ground at 100 to 110 miles per hour,' the manual assured us. Tony never doubted it and his confidence was calming.

Where the runways intersected, the undercart wheels would still be gripping the asphalt but the tail-wheel would be up in flight position. I would watch the airfield perimeter approaching and the motor traffic just beyond it on the Great North Road. 'Geezus, did those drivers realize a 110-pound elf was going to pull us over their heads?' I wondered.

At mid-point in the take-off I would hold my breath, then exhale with relief and decry my momentary loss of faith. Once you had been with Tony when he stood the great four-engined bird on a wingtip in a turn or plunged steeply out of a searchlight cone, you knew you were in the hands of a master flyer.

Churchill visited Leeming one April day. Air crews formed up in a hollow square to be inspected. A little man in a siren suit gesticulating with a fat cigar, he peered fiercely at each of us in turn. I watched him staring into Pete Peterson's face, demanding some explanation. Pete was a Canadian sergeant-pilot who had won the Distinguished Flying Medal for his operational performance.

'What was Churchill nattering at you about?' I asked afterwards.

'Oh, he just wanted to know why I got the DFM. But the way he scowled and blew smoke in my face I thought he was either going to take it away or snuff me out,' Pete said.

We had been inspected a dozen times by brass-hats and politicians. It seemed a meaningless ritual yet with Churchill it was different. When he thrust that great beefy kisser of his within an inch or two of you, glowering centuries of British defiance, you knew that there was one guy in charge – one indisputable leader calling the shots.

'I have lived to see four seasons in England,' I wrote my folks that April. 'Last summer, toughened by blitzes and defeats, this island shook its fist in Hitler's teeth and defied him to do more. Autumn brought wishful – perhaps wistful – thinking. There were fleeting dreams of victory soon. Then Hitler went into Russia and we held our breath. Late autumn was shuddering weather. Winter was a grim reality of tanks and aircraft; blood on the frozen ground in front of Moscow and Leningrad; friends being clawed by ice-laden cloud and sweeping fog, taking destruction to the Reich and sometimes being destroyed themselves.'

'Now spring is challenging and offensive,' I wrote. 'Singapore, Java, Rangoon and the seas around them have shorn this island people of any cockiness. Those defeats coaled their fires. Hong Kong taught that we *must* win. Hong Kong, like Coventry, made the Brits fighting mad again.

'So spring has come. More pasture is being broken in Kent and Devon; Britain will do its best to feed the onslaught of Yanks soon to come. You can hear shipwrights' hammers in Scottish firths. In Trafalgar Square they just celebrated something called Warship Festival Week.'

'Grass has begun to sprout in cracks among the rubble piles heaped by demolition workers 18 months ago,' I told them. 'The ceiling above the escalator in King's Cross station, bared in last year's blitz, has been restored. The gaping bomb crater in Temple tube station has been filled in. The other evening I heard a man on the BBC forecasting ever-bigger air raids. A lot of German civilians would die in the destruction of their industry. "But," he said, "we make no excuse for that."'

Then I told my parents about Porritt McGee and Tex Ashe. Porritt was a big, raw-boned 19-year-old, transported in a matter of months from an Alberta farm to the tail-turret of a 10 Squadron plane. He was in Newt Turner's crew and it was Newt who recounted Porritt's operational performance. On the ground we could see McGee's behaviour off ops for ourselves.

Fear chewed at all of us from time to time. With Porritt McGee it was constant. He was certain he was going to be killed. It was just a matter of time and he was filling the interim with music. He played the guitar; played with a sensitivity that belied his big farm boy hands. So far as any of us knew, he had just one piece in his repertoire. It was *Poet and Peasant* and he played it night after night in The Red Lion at Northallerton and a smaller pub we frequented in nearby Bedale.

Stoked on two big mugs of beer, he burned out that classical music like fire from coal. He fed his fear into *Poet and Peasant*, plucking the tenuous, high notes to mask his tears; fingering the guitar struts as if to sharpen his reflexes for the four-gun trigger handle. We watched him pour his innards into that music; heard his fear vibrate and saw it dissipate in smoky pub air that winter.

On a spring night their plane was attacked by a Focke-Wolfe 190 on the approach to a Ruhr target. The Luftwaffe fighter caught them by surprise on his first pass. Porritt McGee heard the gunfire before he saw the 'plane. A bullet went through his right hand, another creased his right cheek. Blood spurted across his face, momentarily blinding him. The big farmboy's left hand swept his eyes clear; the smashed right hand never lost its grip on the turret control.

It was painful but he squeezed the trigger as the FW 190 made its second pass. Now the hand that stroked the guitar, flicked blood from his eyes a second time. He could see the black-crossed plane sweep upwards in flame and shatter to a dozen smoking pieces.

A month later he made his second kill. When we met in Luft III, Newt Turner told me the Albertan farm boy had still been playing *Poet and Peasant* when they shipped out to the Middle East. Newt swears young Porritt was humming it into the intercom the night they were shot down over Crete and only Turner survived.

I wrote home about Leonard Ashe who had come to Canada from Dallas, Texas in the spring of 1940 and was among the 18 of us who signed up in Windsor that June. Tex was a loose-hanging, dryly humorous son of the big state. A Phi Betta Kappa key-holder, he had written a novel, had it published and carried a second manuscript in the battered brief-case he lugged from one flight-training station to the next.

Tex became a Hurricane pilot and I only saw him once after we were all dispersed from Manning Depot. It was in London's Strand. I was with Joan and we both turned to acknowledge his shouted greeting from a cab. He was enroute to a Bach concert and we rode half a dozen blocks with him swapping lies to Joan's amusement.

I wrote my folks: 'Tex Ashe didn't come back from a sweep over France a month ago. One of the guys from his squadron saw him going into a cloud after a Jerry and there was another Jerry on Ashe's tail. Here was a guy who had come 5,000 miles to get into a war and spent his down-time listening to Bach.'

My dad wrote Ashe's family to pass along my comments. A few months later when I met Tex in Luft III he pulled a clipping from a Dallas paper out of his battledress pocket and waved it belligerently under my nose. It seems my folks and his had corresponded during those anxious moments when both of us were still missing.

A Dallas columnist had played up the Canadian-American, fellow-flyers bit. He had quoted my remark about 'this young Texan down from the skies above London where he ploughed the clouds in a six-gun Hurricane, on his way to a Bach concert.'

Ashe wanted to punch me out – as much for my purple prose as for 'peddling bullshit.'

9

A Full Sky!

RUHR TARGETS, Spring 1942

The sea winds, those hand-maidens of the gods, blew hot and cold, capriciously diverting us from paths the weathermen predicted. The Gee set put us back on track. Now we could rip through the cloak of night with Gee's electronic edge. It defined our routes and was indifferent to weather vagaries.

Luftwaffe radar could detect our path as well, of course. When we were eventually sped along the route to Cologne at 11 aircraft a minute on the last night of May it was like shooting fish in a barrel – but just one fish at a time.

The German electronic wizards had produced *Knickebein*, two radar beams they crossed over Coventry to mark it for destruction a year and a half earlier. The Gee system was more flexible. Three British-based Gee transmitters laid radio grid lines across much of Western Europe. When we adjusted our sets we could home on the grid lines. Using special charts – carried in self-destructing canisters to be detonated like the sets, themselves, if we abandoned aircraft – we could ride the radar position lines or apply two of them to fix the target site.

Gee beams would not bend beyond line of sight, which meant that at operational heights we could ride them about 400 miles to the Danish coast or to mid-Ruhr targets. Within that range, the boffins assured us, Gee would give a positional fix with less than six miles error. And they were working on H2S, a second-generation radar navigation set they promised would go further and be finer-tuned if we were still around to use it in the fall.

Air Marshal Harris – 'Butcher' Harris we called him without apology – was named Bomber Command chief in mid-February. When he took stock he had 469 operational aircraft. Except for 33 Halifax and Lancasters, they were all virtually obsolete. But the new four-engined 'planes were beginning to roll off the production lines. As his crews adapted to the new aircraft, and to Gee, Harris fed us cautiously into a new phase of air warfare.

Tentatively he despatched 150 to 250 aircraft per raid; testing Gee to probe the constant haze over Ruhr targets like Essen, Dortmund and Cologne; trying a new mix of armaments – 4,000-pounders to crater roadways and fill them with masonry, new 500 and 1000-lb bombs designed to blow out roofs and windows and 4-lb incendaries to seed fires. Then for most of May he cut back to less than a hundred aircraft per raid as he built his forces for a major operation.

Bomber Command analysts had come to two early conclusions. Moonlight and Gee put significantly more aircraft on target – and more Luftwaffe fighters on our tails. In 60 nights of mostly good weather that spring, Bomber Command lost 298 aircraft, an average 3.7% of the bomber force each night. Flying smaller raids and obscured by winter cloud in the previous quarter, losses had averaged 2.5%. Harris was prepared to lose more crews and aircraft to achieve better bombing on clearer nights.

Still with these relatively small forces the results were not impressive. Eight raids put some 1,550 planes over Essen. Of these, 64 were shot down and just 22 brought back photographs showing bombing results within five miles of the target. A Krupp plant was set ablaze and 63 civilians killed in Essen. Six raids pinpointing war plants in the Paris area did considerably more damage. It was becoming apparent that to strike a punishing blow Harris had to concentrate a critical mass on target. And he had to create the right mix of blast and fire.

That spring 10 Squadron got a new flight commander, a Harwell boffin named Squadron Leader Earl Guthrie. He was a gifted aeronautical engineer who had helped design the Halifax. With great and persistent effort he had won himself an operational posting to see how engineering theory actually worked in practice. Tony was still being checked out for operations the first week of April when I flew with Guthrie one afternoon to test a would-be bomb-aimer on his map-reading ability.

With the advent of the Gee set and bigger aircraft of longer endurance, navigation became a full-time job. Soon a bomb-aimer in each crew would map-read, man the two-gun front turret and drop the bombs. I had been assigned to help train air-gunner volunteers on our squadron for this new role. Guthrie was intrigued with the development of a new aircrew position. How would it work in practice? He had his own navigator but was prepared to take me along on an operation that night in a bomb-aimer capacity.

Anything that would get me operational time was to be jumped at. But I needed Angus Buchan's permission and he refused it. 'No way I'm putting two fully trained navigators into one operational aircraft,' he told me.

'Goddamn it, Angus, I've done only four ops in nearly eight months and I'm still being grounded.'

'No, but you will be if you don't button your lip.'

Tears of frustration stung my eyes and I was shaking with anger as I quit the nav office.

One of 19 recruits departing Windsor, Ontario for RCAF Manning Depot, 24 June 1940. Nine were killed on operations. Texan Bill Ashe, second from left and Silver, far right back row were POWs. *(Windsor Daily Star)*

Fifth air observer (navigation) course at Malton, Ontario, 7 December 1940.

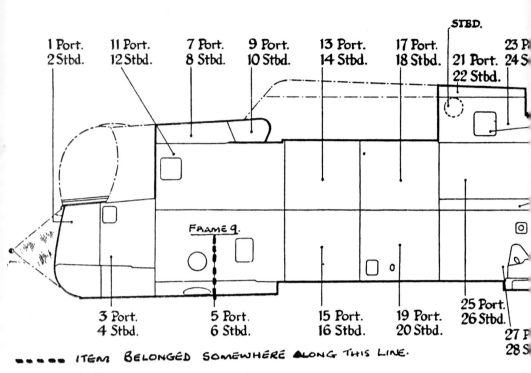

| 1 Port.
2 Stbd. | 11 Port.
12 Stbd. | 7 Port.
8 Stbd. | 9 Port.
10 Stbd. | 13 Port.
14 Stbd. | 17 Port.
18 Stbd. | STBD.
21 Port.
22 Stbd. | 23 P
24 S |

FRAME 9.

| 3 Port.
4 Stbd. | 5 Port.
6 Stbd. | 15 Port.
16 Stbd. | 19 Port.
20 Stbd. | 25 Port.
26 Stbd.
27 P
28 S |

▬ ▬ ▬ ▬ ITEM BELONGED SOMEWHERE ALONG THIS LINE.

Air Ministry identification of piece of wreckage from Whitley smashed on Widdale Fell.

Stationmaster's house at Dent where Silver, Dick Speer and Murray McLaughlin received first-aid and 'whisky straight down the throat' after crash. *(Ray Silver)*

Ray Silver recovers aircraft wreckage from Widdale Fell, now part of Dales National Park, 16 September 1987. *(Lynne Silver)*

Eric Wallace *(centre)* and Border TV crew from Carlisle interview Ray Silver at base of Widdale Fell, 16 September 1987. He had interviewed the author on first search for aircraft wreckage in May 1968.

Left. Pilot and crew captain Tony Moore. Born 28 December 1921, died 31 May 1942, pictured with his mother. He looked like a boy but flew as a man.

Opposite. Author's log entries for May 19

Below. Crew at Lossiemouth, Scotland, three days before they were shot down. *Left to right*: wireless/op Harold Stacey, flight-engineer Donald Thurlow, navigator R Silver, pilot Anthony (Tony) Moore and tail-gunner Frank Walker. Bombardier Jack Ogden and mid-upper gunner Marshall English joined crew two days later. Moore, Walker and English were killed when their Halifax aircraft was shot down on the last night of M 1942.

Date		Aircraft	Pilot	Duty	Remarks	Flying Times	
MAY	1942				(including results of bombing, gunnery, exercises, etc.)	Day	Night
	Hour	Type and No.			Time carried forward:—	199:50	97:45
8	14:1	HALIFAX w 7674	S/Ldr GUTHRIE	navigator	AIR TEST		
9	14:30	HALIFAX w 7611	P/O BAKER	navigator	X-Country (training navigators & bombardiers)	3:00	
15	16:30	HALIFAX w 1056	P/O GOLDSTON	navigator	AIR TEST	:40	
17	10:35	HALIFAX w 1049	P/O GOLDSTON	navigation X	AIR TEST	:40	
17	14:30	HALIFAX w 1099	P/O GOLDSTON	navigator	Air firing Filey Bay	1:00	
18	21:1	HALIFAX w 1090	P/O GOLDSTON	navigator	AIR TEST		
19	22:05	HALIFAX w 1098	P/O GOLDSTON	navigator X	OPS-MANNHEIM		7:05
29	11:30	HALIFAX W —T	SGT MOORE	navigator	returned aircraft from Lossiemouth	2:00	
30	13:00	HALIFAX W —T	SGT MOORE	navigator	AIR TEST	:50	
30	11:30	HALIFAX W —T	SGT MOORE	navigator	OPS-COLOGNE not completed.		
					Total Time....		

No. 10 Squadron,
Royal Air Force,
Leeming,
Northallerton,
Yorkshire.

Reference :-
10S/6/171/Air.

31st May 1942.

Dear Mrs Silver,

It is with the deepest regret that I have to
confirm the sad news already cabled to you by Air Ministry,
that your son Warrant Officer Lionel Raymond Silver failed
to return this morning from an operational flight over
enemy territory.

The aircraft of which he was the Observer left
base at 23.31 hours on 30.5.42 and no messages were
received from it after that time.

I do not wish to raise false hopes, but there is
the possibility that the crew had to abandon their aircraft
and land in enemy territory, and are prisoners. In this
event he will, in due course, be permitted to communicate
with you.

May I offer you my deepest sympathy during this
time of anxious waiting, and express on behalf of all
the members of his squadron the fervent hope that we may
soon have good news of him.

Yours very sincerely,

Wing Commander, Commanding,
No. 10. Squadron. R.A.F.

Mrs. M. Silver,
5, Winchester Avenue,
Westmount,
Quebec,
CANADA.

10 Squadron commanding officer Wing Commander J. B. Tait's letter to Mrs
Silver informing her that her son's crew was missing.

An de Werdt and Ray Silver at Budel. *(Lynne Silver)*

An de Werdt points out the escape route Ray Silver failed to take 45 years earlier. They are flanked by *Eindhoven Dagblad* editor Ruud Groen to left of Silver and de Werdt family members. *(Lynne Silver)*

Senior officer in the North compound when Luft III was evacuated in January 1945, Canadian Group Captain Larry Wray kept us intact and moving as slowly as possible in the hopes that Russians would overtake us. They didn't but Wray badgered our German captors every step of the way. *Below*. Ray and Lynne Silver visit three crew-mates' graves at Eindhoven cemetery. *(Eindhoven Dagblatt)*.

'Station nav officer won't let me do it,' I told the flight commander.

'Well then you don't. Perhaps another time,' Guthrie said pleasantly.

I didn't know the target was to be Wilhelmshaven, nor that Guthrie had planned a diversionary role for himself. He would fly the single Halifax on a low-level, bomb-run to distract the formidable naval defences from the main bomber force which were attacking from 16,000 feet. He did and they destroyed him. None of his crew survived.

I presented myself to the station nav office next morning and awaited Angus' arrival. He greeted me as if we had just met. 'I heard . . . I heard about the flight commander going missing,' I blurted.

'We win some, we lose some,' Buchan told me. It was all he ever said on the subject. He was himself killed on ops a few months after that. Half a century later I wish he was still around, not just because he saved my life on that occasion, but because he had handled me with such bloody graciousness.

A week after the Guthrie encounter, Tony and I did our first Halifax operation. We were among 200 aircraft sent to Dortmund at the centre of the Ruhr's heavy industry belt. Ours was one of eight 10 Squadron Halifax assigned to test the accuracy with which the Gee set could put us on a Ruhr target. The briefing officer was most emphatic.

'Navigators will rely entirely on their Gee sets from take-off to landing no matter what visual identification you get,' we were told. 'For the last leg you will set the target co-ordinates and home on them. Regardless of what you see below you wait on the Gee set to tell you that you're centred over Dortmund. That's what you bomb on.'

We did. I kept Tony on the Gee-set course. It took us about a dozen miles to the north of what I was certain was Dortmund, over what I think was the great rail junction at Hamm. There was certainly plenty of flak from both locations.

As instructed we flew on till the Gee screen told us we were at the intersection of three position lines that should have been the target. It was more than 30 miles northwest of what I was sure was Dortmund. Nonetheless, I dropped our bomb-load where the Gee set told us to.

132 aircraft claimed to have dropped their bombs that night where Gee said Dortmund was. Bomb-run photographs traced a 40-mile stretch of the Ruhr – all of it beyond the target city. Ironically, the way the Gee sets consistently missed Dortmund that night proved that they were at least giving a constant reading. We were at the beginning of a learning curve that would rapidly put the RAF on target that season.

At the end of April we were among more than 500 aircraft sent, over a four-night period, to bomb the Baltic port of Rostock. We were routed north of the deadly defence belt that ran from Kiel to Hamburg. Gee worked well in keeping us on track. Our raid was on the fourth night and the Luftwaffe were more than ready for the predictable bomber stream.

An Me-110 fighter met us as we crossed the North Sea coast of the German-Danish peninsula. Tony saw it coming in on our starboard quarter and reacted instantly. He turned into its path and continued into a steep bank. Suddenly the Halifax was standing on its starboard wing-tip and the German fighter shot past. By the time he got turned around we were out to sea. The Luftwaffe pilot made a second pass. Again Tony spun on a wingtip like a matador turning inside the bull's lethal radius.

Then we were diving into cloud; jinking, twisting, spinning out of radar's reach. For nearly three minutes Tony had the four Merlin engines 'through the gate' at over-power. When he levelled out Thurlow gave him the bad news. 'You've blown the outer port engine. It's going to come apart if you don't turn it off.'

As he feathered the outer port propeller to stationary position you could feel the vibrations coming from the other port engine. 'I don't think that one is going to last too many minutes more,' Thurlow told him.

'You don't think we should push on to Rostock then?' he asked me.

'Target's 160 miles, about 40 minutes, Tony. And home's about 400 miles back the other way,' I advised. 'We're practically over Sylt right now.'

Sylt is the long, thin island that brackets the Danish-German coast. It had a major seaplane base which was a reasonable alternative target. We had an undisturbed run on it but I could see nothing identifiable. My maps showed the seaplane base midway up the island at Westerland where a spur of land thrusts eastwards. I fused the bombs and let them go. In a few moments we could see the debris rising a mile into moonlight. It was the only time on operations I could see the crud flung skywards by our bombs. What I saw were great lengths of trees bowling end over end like cabers.

'Geezus, we came all this way for that?' I muttered but no one heard me.

In mid-May we were sent to Mannheim, a major industrial city on the Rhine. It was a good 125 miles beyond Gee's dependable range but the set took us across the Low Countries and much of the Ruhr with pinpoint accuracy. Nearly 200 aircraft were despatched, including all available Halifaxes and Lancasters. We were briefed to fly at 18,000 feet, a record altitude at that stage of the war. And we were advised to rely on our Gee sets for as long as possible. We were also advised that all the aircraft were scheduled to bomb Mannheim within a 45-minute period.

'You'll be testing Air Marshal Harris' new bombing theories tonight,' we were told. 'The threat of collision over the target might be slightly greater but what we want to determine is the saturation point at which the German defences are swamped.'

There was a fair amount of moonlight but we flew above six-tenths cloud cover. The Gee set kept us readily on track and we crossed the Dutch coast just below Rotterdam. From the coast to the heart of the Ruhr is about 125 miles, roughly a half hour's flight. Mannheim was another half-hour beyond that. Bomber Command strategists were feeding us at about six planes a minute down Happy Valley, that series of radar boxes in which the Luftwaffe ran its fighter patrols.

Homing on Gee was like making a bombing run or flying a compass course. You set the parameters and gave corrections left or right to maintain the setting. Within minutes Tony had the heading to keep us on track. He wove steadily to keep enemy radar off our tail, always averaging the swings to port with slides to starboard; moving as far upwards one minute as he had dipped down a minute or two before. Ten or a dozen miles to port, the Rhine was visible between cloud banks. It was a quiet night.

'Aircraft ahead!' the mid-upper cried. This was Roddy English's first operation.

'Whose?' Tony asked.

'Could be an Me-110 but it's travelling the same way we are.'

'Keep your eye on it,' Tony told him. 'If there's one tailing the guy ahead of us, there may be one on our tail,' he cautioned Frank Walker in the rear turret.

'I'm watching,' Walker assured. His voice had a grim edge to it. The tail-gunner was older, about 30, and his wife was expecting their first child momentarily. He had been 'phoning her every morning for a week and was trying desperately to get a 48-hour pass when the baby was born.

'Oh, Christ!'

'Holy shit!'

The cries hit our intercom at the instant a bomber aircraft exploded ahead of us. There was that same flooding of the eye's retina that I had experienced the night Collie Adams died; like a curtain of light ending an act in a divine comedy. Tony took us a thousand feet down into altocumulus cloud. There we droned on; deathly silent, vitally alert.

Four Group had assigned an 18,000-foot altitude for our bomb run over Mannheim. We regained it in cold, clear air under a half moon. Broken cloud lay a couple of thousand feet below. Group aircraft had maintained our time-on-target schedule. Geezus! As a I went forward to the bomb-aimer's position I could see two other aircraft, a Halifax and what looked like a Lanc, within less than a mile to starboard.

All three of our aircraft were ploughing half a dozen square miles of sky seeking the target city below. My eyes were peeled for a glimpse of moonlight on the Rhine, some suggestion of Mannheim's harbour area or the structures east of it. My five crew-mates' eyes locked on those other two aircraft – and then a third four-engined bomber crossed in front of us.

Now there were four navigators churning the same patch of sky, square-searching for the target three and a half miles below. How could we miss hitting each other? On the third pass I could see the sharp line of Mannheim edging the Rhine. I put Tony on the bomb run, fused our load, and fine-tuned the bomb-sight.

The last leg took 150 seconds. I know because I heard each second ticking in my head. At about 90 seconds into our approach fear emptied my bladder. I could feel the hot urine scalding my thighs. I was aware of piss running into one flying boot as I pressed the bomb-release.

10

This is it!

COLOGNE, 30/31 May 1942

At 16,000 feet the sky was a moon-washed blue and the Maas River a silver wire twisting south through Venlo and Roermond in the depths below. It was a tableau to be painted on cathedral ceilings; a macabre illusion. The cold, clear canopy covering Europe this thousandth night of war carried airborne plague.

In this bit of Holland thrust down the Maas valley between Belgium and Germany, Roermond is a cathedral town built on battlements from seven centuries of war. In the War of the Spanish Succession it was an often changing pawn. Then, free of Spain, it became the capital of Austrian Gelderland. Subsequently it was French for some years. In July 1914 the Hun swept southwest around this political peninsula. But in World War II Roermond was the first Lowlands town to hear jackboots on cobblestones.

Now on this late night of May, 1942 it would hear the drone of a thousand aircraft. We were headed for another cathedral city, aiming to raze Cologne in a 90-minute blitz.

Venlo was a Luftwaffe fighter base guarding the Reich's western frontier. For the fourth time this May, Venlo's Messerschmitt-110s and Junkers-88s were being summoned to intercept an RAF bomber stream enroute to the Ruhr.

Our track from Four Group's Yorkshire airfields crossed the Dutch coast due west of Rotterdam. Hearing the recurrent wasp-like hum of aircraft heading east into the moon-filled night, Rotterdam burghers could only guess our destination. Had they seen the fiery column rising 140 miles to the southeast as the night wore on, it might have evoked mixed emotions.

Two years and two weeks earlier, Rotterdam's 600,000 men, women and children had seen the red flares of surrender lit on the city's perimeter and heard General Winkleman announce capitulation. In bright May sunshine they awaited the invaders' arrival.

Sharp at noon 30 German 'planes rose from Rotterdam airport, circled to 4,500 feet and shuttled systematically back and forth across the city. Never breaking formation, they dropped general-purpose and incendiary bombs on each pass. At 2:30pm they were finished. The 15th-century Groote Kerk cathedral, the 18th-century Exchange and the 19th-century

Stadhuis lay among the rubble of 2,600 other buildings. Under the rubble lay a thousand men, women and children – not all of them dead.

Thus Goering's flyers sought to impress Paris and London of Nazi intent with a noontime raid on a Dutch city in May 1940. Thus RAF crews were despatched to raze the cathedral city of Cologne in a midnight assault two years later.

The raid that fired up Cologne with more than a thousand aircraft on the last night of May was based on the success in setting the Baltic ports of Lübeck and Rostock aflame with much smaller forces earlier that spring. Late in March some 200 aircraft were sent to Lübeck in moonlight. Gee-equipped aircraft led the way, defences were light and many crews bombed from very low levels. Two-thirds of the bombs were incendiary and the attack centred on the *Alstadt*, a district of ancient, timbered houses in narrow streets. More than 60 per cent of Lübeck's buildings were damaged or burned out; more than 300 people were killed. A U-boat outfitter was destroyed. Damage was set at 20-million pounds sterling. The cost was a dozen aircraft.

Air Marshal Harris considered the Lübeck raid to be Bomber Command's first real success. In four nights a month later he set 520 bombers onto Rostock, 60 miles further east along the Baltic coast. It was on one of those nights that a Luftwaffe fighter deterred us and we bombed Sylt. Most of the aircraft penetrated to Rostock's *Alstadt* area of old, wooden houses in narrow streets. Again the incendiaries were strategically employed. Some 2,300 buildings were razed or damaged. More than 200 people were killed.

This, said Dr Goebbels was *Terrorangriff*, a terror raid. 'Community life in Rostock is practically at an end,' he told his diary.

For a month Halifax T-for-Tommy had been parked on a Lossiemouth dispersal site waiting a tyre replacement. Another crew had flown it to the Scottish base for a raid on the *Tirpitz* at the end of April. A burst tyre scrubbed their participation, while back at Leeming we had been assigned another aircraft. Now near the end of May our crew were sent north by rail to fly T-for-Tommy home.

'What's up?' Tony asked.

'Can't say, except every servicable aircraft in Bomber Command is going to be needed,' he was told.

Tony, Stacey, Thurlow, Walker and I had just been joined by Marshall English who was manning the mid-upper turret. Against precedent he took our picture when RAF transport dropped us on Lossiemouth doorstep. Just as it was Navy tradition to ban whistling on board ship, it was a RAF super-stition not to photograph bomber crews in mid-tour. No one told us about that. Walker and I had even piled up a bit of dirt and positioned Tony between us so we all looked a uniform height. How ironic that Tony never saw himself standing tall among us.

We flew back to Leeming the following morning, landing in tension palpable as a headwind. You could hear it in the clipped comment from the control tower: 'Move it, T-for-Tommy, you're not the only scooter in the queue.'

An hour after our return we were airborne again to familiarize our new bomb-aimer with his duties. Jack Ogden had joined us in that capacity. He was among a dozen ex-air-gunners we had been instructing for the past month in map-reading and bomb-sight technique. He was the keenest of the group and I had pressed Tony to recruit him. The son of the police superintendent at Peel, Isle of Man, Ogden was a lean, taciturn youth who spoke only when he had something important to say and he said it in the fewest possible words.

'Think you'll like the front turret better?' I asked.

'Sure beats dragging your ass as fighter bait,' he told me.

Marshall English and Jack Ogden joined readily into the easy relationship the other five of us had developed. But as we moved into the stepped-up activity at Leeming that day Frank Walker's distress added to the tension. When we trooped into the mess Walker was informed that his wife had borne him a daughter. I turned to congratulate him and caught the conflict working his tight facial muscles. It was a mix of paternal pride, a husband's concern and deep-seated fear.

Walker and his wife had been ten years trying for a child. Now when it happened he needed to be with her. The news had sent him sprinting to the orderly room. Half an hour later he was back, frantic and frustrated. 'All leave is cancelled. They won't let me go. Not even a 24-hour pass to Leeds,' he told us from the depth of a Yorkshireman's misery.

'You'll make it by the week-end. 'Phone her meantime,' I said.

'Week-end . . . be . . . too . . . bleeding . . . late,' he replied. There was a terrible note of conviction in the way he spaced out his words.

In fact all leave had been cancelled; not just at Leeming but throughout Bomber Command. Some 80 squadrons were locked onto about 40 airfields waiting for 'something big to happen.'

By tea-time the rumours of an impending invasion were persistent. 'We're going to invade France – army, navy, air-force,' we were told. The invasion appeared to be postponed, called-off, reinstated, stood-down, re-alerted and deferred by the time we went to bed.

'Briefing is at 13:00 hours, in a hangar with a bloody air commodore,' we were advised at breakfast. And so we were briefed. More than 25 crews from 10 and 77 Squadrons trooped into a hangar that had been hastily fitted out with trestle tables, chairs and a podium.

'Tonight, gentlemen, more than a thousand aircraft will bomb Cologne. This is double the largest bomber force previously launched on an enemy target. What is more, you will all be on and off it within 90 minutes. Tonight we are going to swamp the Hun,' the air commodore from Four Group headquarters advised.

He told us that 10 and 77 Squadron Halifaxes would be the last aircraft on the target. 'Defences will be overwhelmed by the time you arrive,' he said with non-participant confidence.

'The aiming point is the *Neumarket*, the market place here on the map,' we were told. 'Or the cathedral if you can see it,' an intelligence officer added facetiously. The 'new' market was actually built at Cologne's core in medieval days, some time after the Normans first burned the town. The cathedral – constructed over seven centuries half a mile from the market-place – was left unscathed by two Royal Flying Corps raids in World War I. It was not targetted this time because there was no pretence at precision.

We were being sent to the centre of Germany's third largest city. There we would first smash masonry to block the streets; blow away roofs, doors and windows to create fire-carrying corridors. Then we would seed a fire-storm with incendiary bombs.

We would do this mindful of Warsaw bombed to submission at war's outset, recalling the destruction of Coventry's cathedral and all else around it a year later, and remembering the corona of fire arcing St Paul's and other Wren churches during raids that killed 30,000 Londoners. In proxy for subdued Czechs, cowed Slavs, sullen French, defiant Norwegians, trapped Jews, we would ride the valkyrie eastwards into this moon-washed night because Churchill could despatch no other warriors to fortress Europe that third year of the war. Enroute to Cologne we returned the salute of human arms poking through Rotterdam rubble.

Thurlow did the take-off drill with Tony, calling out pressures and tem-peratures, boost and fuel gauge readings, magneto drop, supercharger response, the vacuum reading behind each pump. He was a machine doctor who treated each of the Hercules engines as if they were Olympic entrants in the decathlon.

You could picture him in a white coat in the pits at LeMans, manufac-turer's manual in hand. Thurlow went by the book; things were right or wrong. It was not his role to adjust specs, vary King's Rules and Regulations nor take liberties with the script. Under subsequent interrogation Thurlow was a model of reticence. He couldn't remember the names of his crew-mates. That nearly got me shot.

Once again I checked out the fit of Tony's feet in the rudder-bar stirrups; took the jump seat as Thurlow called off the instrument readings and sat poised to lock the throttles and propeller-pitch controls for full-power take-off.

Half an hour past midnight they gave us the green light and you could feel 31 tons of aircraft moving into stride like a racehorse out of the gate. Tony held it earthbound till the runway mid-point. Then he let T-for-Tommy carry us into the night.

Within minutes Gee-set trouble was apparent. Instead of three position line signals, I was getting one. I flipped the set off, let it cool a few moments and booted it up again. There was still just one gremlin pointing the way. I ran through the trouble check-list, step by step, without getting an answer.

Not to worry, I had given Tony the heading for our North Sea crossing. The first leg took us over the Humber snout 20 minutes flying time from take-off. Jack Ogden, map-reading up front, gave me the opportunity to concentrate on the radar box. He would soon see if we were on track.

'Grimsby and the Humber mouth just to starboard,' he duly announced. By then I had prowled the floor beneath my nav table, up the flight deck beneath Tony's feet and beyond, checking for a pinched cable or loose connection. The lines were intact but the Gee-set still blinked with one eye instead of three.

'No Gee,' I told Tony.

'Do we need it?'

'Not really. Jack has a pair of eyes upfront we've never had before and Butcher Harris has the moonlight turned-up full. Worst comes to worst I'll have to start navigating again.'

'So we go without Gee?'

'Can't think why not,' I said. Tony polled the others. They agreed.

Ten minutes later we had a second chance to abort. At 10,000 feet we switched onto oxygen and routinely checked our masks. Walker's wasn't working. Tony sent Thurlow back to look at it.

'The valve seems to be periodically sticking. I think I've cleared it,' the engineer reported.

'You going to be okay?' Tony asked.

'Yeah, why not,' Walker replied. 'Thurlow's left me a portable tank if mine packs up.'

'So it's go for Cologne,' Tony confirmed. We were in full agreement.

At 02:03 hrs, Ogden looked down through three miles of moonlight silvering scattered cloud. He was making his first operational landfall and trying to be businesslike about it. But the confirmation of navigational theory is always a surprise. 'The Hook of Holland is dead beneath us,' he announced. It was as if he had just discovered sex.

We were within half a dozen miles of our assigned path and two minutes ahead of our ETA. I recalculated wind-speed and direction and gave Tony a small adjustment in course and airspeed. Taking our exact place in the queue was vital. The 'bomber-stream' concept was based on putting all aircraft on the same track so that, closely bunched together, we would over-whelm German defences.

RAF boffins had determined that within each night-fighter patrol 'box' a German radar controller could direct no more than six enemy 'plane interceptions each hour. There were only so many Luftwaffe night-fighters available. Once our path was determined, they had to be brought into it. Then each of them had to be vectored onto a single bomber.

A year before Bomber Command had despatched a hundred aircraft along various routes to an assigned target over a four-hour period. In the spring more than 200 aircraft had been targetted to bomb Lübeck within two hours. Now a thousand aircraft were crossing the Netherlands in a narrow path, scheduled to move through each successive fighter box and across the target at the rate of 11 planes per minute.

From Bomber Command bases in Yorkshire and the Midlands, from advanced flying stations and operational training units in the south of England and from a half dozen coastal command bases, we had been mar-shalled to sweep in across Schouwn, Overflakkee and Putten polders; over the ancient towns of Breda, Tilburg and Eindhoven. Midway across the 140-mile stretch, we would look down on the Wilhemina Canal aglow in moonlight and know we were on track.

Roermond was the last and critical turning point. From there the final leg ran 42 miles south-east to Cologne. On a bend of the Maas River, it was readily identifiable this moon-bright night. We were among 11 aircraft scheduled to be on that target at 02:40. That meant crossing the Maas at 02:27.

Two minutes ahead of that I left my nav table and climbed to the flight deck to stand beside Tony for a better view.

Except for the bomb run I had never before left my table while over enemy territory. In a Whitley I sat behind the pilots with good visibility; there was no need to move around. You could see nothing from the navi-gator's station in a Halifax. Ogden had been doing fine at map-reading but Roermond was a critical tracking point and I was going to double-check it.

In truth, I had to feel involved. The Gee set had packed up on this epic test operation, Ogden's map-reading had reduced my navigation to a few twists of the dials on a course-setting calculator. And for the first time I would have no role to play on the actual bomb-run.

Now I shared the panoramic view with Tony. The muted hum in our head-sets was isolating and the moon-washed heights seemed to detach us from the world below. We were moving across a moon-blue canopy that dropped to darkness on all horizons. Except to the south-east. If you looked intently in that direction there was a suggestion of the colour of fire.

THIS IS IT!

Half a dozen miles ahead and three miles below, the Maas River was silvery in the moonlight.

To starboard at our altitude, perhaps three or four miles away, a Whitley and a Wimpey were headed home. They were about half a mile apart, almost in line-astern formation. 'Geezus, I sure would hate to be in a twin-engined kite on a night like this,' I told Tony.

'Well they're going to be home before we are,' he said.

That was our last conversation. The intercom hum was swallowed by a vacuum, ripped by the bark of aerial cannon, shattered by disintegrating noises. A fiery curtain cut through the fuselage floor somewhere back of the bulkhead, unfurled into incandescence and swept forwards. Orange and yellow, leaden and vaporous, I watched the aerial cannon-fire pass down the Halifax centre-line.

For perhaps five seconds balls of fire danced around us. I watched them pass between Tony's body and mine; saw them pouring through the navigation table and stool that I had so recently vacated. Then there was silence and the stench of cordite. Still the four Hercules engines droned on and the aircraft ploughed steadily forwards.

'Christ that was close!' I exclaimed soundlessly. Whatever the damage, it had not shaken Tony's hold on the aircraft. There he sat, our cherub-faced skipper, implacably in control.

Then he took his right hand from the wheel. He thrust his arm forwards and formed his fingers into a fist. He inverted the fist, thumb downwards. And he levered it from the shoulder in a straight-arm movement that could not be misconstrued. Three times he repeated the signal, levering his arm like a railway semaphore. It was a classic gesture in his inimitable style. 'This is it,' he was telling us.

I could still see no actual flames and there was nothing in the elfin face to suggest fear or finality. But the gesture was indisputable. The escape hatch was under my nav table and the drill was that I was the first to go.

'Bale out!' Thurlow bellowed the message to Stacey back of the bulkhead door. I carried it down to Ogden in the nose. In retrospect we would conclude that English in the mid-upper turret and Walker in the rear one were beyond hearing. The enemy cannon-fire had been deadly centred.

With the reflex action born of 300 nights of rehearsal I knocked the chart table back on its hinges and thrust two forefingers into the big red detonator buttons to trigger the Gee-set and chart container's destruction. Then I reached for the escape-hatch release ring, twisted it and felt it resist.

Ogden reached from behind me and turned the hatch handle – correctly – the other way. Together we pulled the hatch clear. Then he grabbed my parachute from its stowage and thrust it at me. If he saw me on the tenuous edge of panic he ignored it. I didn't realize that he had been nearly blinded by the curtain of fire that took us down, nor that four tons of incendiaries were burning upwards from the bomb bay into the fuselage.

I clipped on my chute and looked back up the short stair to Tony and Thurlow beside him. Thurlow was supporting his left arm with a cannon-shell through it. Tony glared at me impatiently. Then both returned their sights to what they could see of the 'plane. Fire was reflected in their eyes. Still the Halifax seemed under control.

'It would be a helluva thing to bale out while the others got home,' I told myself.

Tony dismissed that notion with a final glance. 'There are seven guys to get out, you know, and you're the first,' his eyes instructed me.

Ogden and Stacey were waiting for me now. Thurlow had his own parachute in place and was holding Tony's. I gestured a sort of salute, clutched the parachute ring in one hand, the oxygen bayonet and communication-cord socket in the other, thrust my legs into the hatchway and slipped into the night.

I don't recall counting to 10, nor pulling the release ring, nor being snapped from free fall. What I remember first is strangling in mid-air. I had forgotten to remove my helmet. Oxygen tubing ran up one set of shroud lines, the intercom cord up others. My head and throat were caught between the converging lines. Frantically I thrust my thumbs inside the tubing and communication cord to wedge them clear of my chin. Welts creased both my cheeks for days after to remind me of my stupidity.

Then I heard the roar of an aircraft. It began in some unfocused corner of the vast and silent sky. And it built pitch, volume and intensity with the awesome force of a galaxy exploding. Whether it was the twin engines of a Messerschmitt fighter tracking its Halifax prey or the four Hercules of our own aircraft screaming earthwards I would never know. But it was detonated out of crystalline air to envelop my conciousness with a single reality. The aircraft engines spun sharp-bladed propellers that would mince me into oblivion.

I could sense the crushing edge of the sonic blast tearing the sky apart to wipe me out. It was then that the atheist's grandson prayed. The awesome roar became a great black shadow – the beat of a thousand valkyrie's wings. It advanced, enveloped and released me. It passed in the night and I was left to hang limp as a half-drowned puppy. My eyes followed the shroud lines, saw the canopy filled to its fluted edge. Then I looked earthwards. The moonlight faded on all horizons but to the south-east the night was broken.

A fiery column arose from Cologne. The column appeared several miles square at its base and it rose perhaps 20,000 feet into the sky. It was a pyre of smoke and burning debris, flak bursts and bomb bursts, fiery bits lifted on hot updrafts, structures afire, flaming gas from broken mains and fuel tanks exploding as the night wore on.

From my omniscient perch I could sense the crackle of flaming timber, the crashing of masonry, the ominous roar of gale-force winds feeding the base of a fire-storm. I could imagine the greasy char, oozing from bunkers that had become crematoria, starting to run in the city's gutters.

Hanging from parachute straps, I watched Cologne burning 60 miles away. The fiery pylon rose on the horizon of blacked-out Europe. Dependent on your viewpoint it was at once a torch of hope – the promise of liberation for enslaved millions – or a preface to Armageddon.

Turning in the wind I scanned the sky for my crew-mates. But there was only empty space and silence rolling back to engulf me.

11

An de Werdt

BUDEL, 1 June 1942

There are three stages to the hawk's demise; the instant when an arrow breaks its wing, those long moments as it flutters earthwards and that interminable time as it scrabbles for an earthy place to hide.

My transition from predator to prey was quick and merciless. For five seconds cannon-fire tore 'plane and crew apart. Then for a dozen minutes I had dropped through the silent sky feeling detached and omniscient as the gods. Now the earth reclaimed me, clutched my feet and held me vulnerable.

Where I had anonymously waged war from the black heights in the company of thousands, now I stood alone, conspicuous, disarmed and earthbound. I had seen no sign of life as I neared the ground but I had no illusion about dropping undetected into war's cockpit. Golfers beat the bushes tirelessly for lost balls. I was sure the Luftwaffe was no less determined to validate its shots.

I was in a clearing of thick grass flanked by a forest of ash and elm. In full leaf, the trees offered cover just a minute's desperate dash away. But first my parachute had to be retrieved. There it lay, 17-feet shroud-line distance away from me, reflecting moonlight from 500 square feet of canopy. Gathering it up was like smothering a searchlight.

Convinced that the Wehrmacht was scouring the area, I could imagine marksmen sighting down their rifles at me; almost hear the jackboots plodding woodland paths in my direction. About 25 feet into the trees I dumped the parachute in a hollow of ground and moved deeper into the woods. There, lying full-length in a dank gulley, I waited to be skewered with a bayonet. When, after five or six minutes nothing happened, the absurdity of my position brought me to my feet again.

Anticipating that one in seven downed airmen would survive, the Air Force had given us an escape kit and cursory advice on how to evade capture. As instructed, I buried my parachute, harness and helmet a few inches deep in the forest floor. Along with them I got rid of three shillings, a six-pence and a London Underground transfer. 'Don't help the enemy outfit his spies for Britain,' we had been told.

The same British intelligence officer had explained the escape kit contents. The size of a cigarette package it contained a good map of Western Europe imprinted on a silk handkerchief, a little compass disguised as a collar-button and the equivalent of about $200 in Belgium, Dutch, French and German money. There were three or four malted-milk candies to sustain energy and tablets to purify ditch-water for drinking. Finally there was a three-inch-long hacksaw blade.

The candy and ditch-water pills were to help keep us off the beaten track for a day or two. The money might buy passage for those with the language skills to travel overtly. The hacksaw blade seemed certain to get a downed airman shot as a saboteur.

In accordance with international convention we were instructed to retain our two identification discs. One was made to sustain high-temperature fire and explosion while the other, we were assured, could remain immersed in the drink for weeks and not go soggy. I could feel my tags – and Joan's St Christopher medal – hanging securely from my neck.

I pushed the Air Force chronometer up my wrist to hide it under my sleeve; I had no intention of abandoning it. A time-piece seemed more essential than ever. Moreover, it gave me navigator status and I suspected I might need all the stature I could muster if I was caught. As an afterthought I kept the key to my room in the Mess. It was an old-fashioned key with 'RAF' embedded in its clover-leaf top. With that to identify me should occasion arise, I stripped the brevet, rank badges and Canada flashes from my battledress jacket and buried them as well. There was not much I could do to disguise my brown felt flying boots except cover them with my battledress trousers and rub dirt on the zippers.

These preparations had taken less than an hour but already I was anxious to be moving under the cloak of night. The chances of evading capture seemed slim enough but the odds would be insurmountable should I be spotted in broad daylight near where we had been shot down. I was as ready as I would ever be to hit the road, or at least a cross-country trail. But in what direction?

My last image when we were attacked was of the Maas River shining in moonlight 10 to 15 miles ahead . We had been on a leg from Rotterdam to Roermond that would take us south of the Luftwaffe base at Eindhoven. In the minute or two between the attack and my bale-out, the Halifax had continued towards the Maas River. From my escape-kit map I guessed I had come down somewhere within drifting distance of a place called Weert, 15 miles south-east of Eindhoven.

Weert, at least, was as good a starting point as any and I dotted it with a pencil point. Had I recalled all of our evader briefing I would not have put any mark on the map by which an enemy interrogator might retrace my steps. It was one of the few slips I made yet it could have had fatal consequences. In fact, we had been over Maarheeze, six miles closer to Eindhoven, when a Luftwaffe fighter set us afire. Another Halifax had been shot down at Weert 20 minutes earlier.

I was virtually certain that I had not drifted east of the Maas into Germany but I had no way of knowing whether I had dropped into Belgium or the Netherlands which meet just half a dozen miles south of Weert. Would I encounter border guards if I stumbled across the boundary line between the two Lowlands countries? With daylight I began to pick up bits of printed material – bread wrappers and hand-bills. They all seemed to be in the same language, which did not seem to be German. I had yet to learn that on both sides of the Belgian-Dutch border the people spoke the same Flemish tongue.

My ultimate destination had to be the Channel coast a hundred miles to the west. Hopefully, long before that, I would meet up with Belgian or Dutch underground workers who could put me in touch with one of the escape chains we were told existed in Occupied Europe.

For the moment I was prepared to head due west, hoping to keep clear of Eindhoven with its war industry and major Luftwaffe base. At the same time I didn't want to blunder into guards on the Belgian-Dutch border. For the first hour or so I kept to the woods wherever possible, otherwise tramping across fields and polders. But progress was slow. When I came to a roadway heading west I took it.

Encountering no one in these early morning hours, I strode on with increasing confidence. About an hour before dawn I was suddenly aware of a horse and cart approaching from behind me. I dove into long grass beside the road trusting I had not been seen. The driver was alone and appeared to be dozing with the reins slack in his hand. Perhaps he was following safe practice in the occupied countries – not seeing what was not one's business.

With daylight I began to encounter people walking or riding horse-drawn vehicles. They seemed to be rather well-dressed for farm-work. Almost as if they were all going to church, I thought. They were, of course. This last day of May was a Sunday.

Studiously showing disinterest in my identity they would mutter a passing greeting. 'Hal,' I would reply trying to adapt 'Hello,' 'Hail' and 'How-are-you' into a universally indistiguishable obeisance.

About 9:30 it began to rain. The water poured down relentlessly for the next two hours. My battledress was sodden; my skin clammy. Twice I stepped from the roadway to empty the water from my flying boots. Now shelter was an immediate need. Walking further in this sort of weather was not only irrational but looked it. On the road in this downpour I would only invite suspicion.

I was among some 240 aircrew shot down the previous night. The odds were that about 35 of us had baled out safely. Most were quickly rounded up but a few of us had so far evaded capture. Perhaps a half dozen RAF airmen wandered among the half billion people of Occupied Europe that Sunday morning. It was a solitary experience.

Luck would largely determine if, and for how long, we stayed out of German hands. In Holland, in particular, there were a few brave and resourceful patriots dedicated to sheltering Allied airmen and getting them back to Britain to fight again. These people were organized into chains that passed the evaders from one clandestine cell to the next.

Linking up with them, however, was a matter of chance. Unless an alert escape-group participant spotted an aircrew member descending by parachute – and got to the airman well ahead of the Germans – there was little likelihood he could be safely spirited away.

There was another, even more remote, possibility. We might seek out someone prepared to aid us. Asking that help, however, was a tricky business. If we blundered onto a German sympathizer's doorstep we faced capture. If someone took us in they accepted an ungodly risk. Found with a downed airman in their home a Dutch, Belgian, French or Scandinavian family invariably faced a firing squad.

To reduce the chances of bringing death to their doorsteps we had been briefed on where to seek help in Occupied territory. Priests, nuns and Protestant clergy would provide shelter and put Allied airmen in touch with underground agents if they could do so safely. But they would certainly not risk detection if we put them in a position to be exposed. Doctors, teachers and other professionals were frequently members of the Underground or the escape chains. While they were on the look-out for evading Allied airmen, it was unlikely we would spot them.

We were forewarned not to contact burgomeisters or other civic officials; the Germans would not have left them in authority unless they were sympathetic to the Nazi cause. Local police might want to help us but they were closely watched.

'If you do seek assistance use common sense,' a British intelligence officer had lectured us. 'Pick a smaller home rather than a big one, in the country rather than the city. But don't head for some isolated property that is apt to be a German command post. And when you knock on a door be prepared to have it slammed in your face. Under the best of conditions it takes a very brave person to shelter an evading airman. They know what will happen to them – and every member of their family – if you are found on their premises.'

It was about 11:30. Rain had driven me off the road into the shelter of trees. Still I kept moving. Pushing through brush and high grass I was suddenly waist-deep in a small stream. Sloshing up its bank I was again on a roadside. There, weighted by soaking clothes, desperate solitude and a brooding grey sky, I dropped to my knees and peered through the driving rain.

I was on the edge of a sandy, secondary road; not much more than a tree-lined lane connecting half a dozen small farms that made up the hamlet of Budelerberg, 12 miles south-east of Eindhoven. The smallholders' homes were long, low, brick structures designed centuries earlier to house families alongside their animals. A structural wall separated the household from the stables while they shared a common roof that rose sharply over part of its length to form a hay-loft.

A nexus of family farms had evolved from peasant holdings in centuries past. Now they were harnessed to the wartime economy imposed on Occupied Europe. In this third year of war these smallholder families still managed to hold back enough of their own produce to sustain a rudimentary diet. But they were feeding the Third Reich's population much better than their own and the disparity would get worse month by month.

Under the uneasy eyes of occupying forces in this Brabant district – a bread-basket of Europe since the 12th century – women and children did the farm work while fathers and grown sons manned the Philips electronics plant at Eindhoven or worked at the Luftwaffe base on the edge of the city. Whether in the factories or farmlands on which Germany was so dependent, the Dutch were under *Sicherheitspolizei* vigilance. From the English Channel to the Volga, the Nazi security service prowled corridors and backroads in search of spies and saboteurs, uncowed patriots and partisans.

I knew nothing, of course, about the *Sicherheitspolizei* nor its web of Gestapo and Kripo agents watchful as spiders in every dark corner of Europe that spring. Nor could I anticipate that their commander Reinhardt Heydrich would lie dying of assassins' bullets in Prague that week-end. The manhunt for Heydrich's killers had the entire Continent on edge. It was not a good week to visit Europe but I had been in no position to postpone my flight.

I was aware that families who sheltered Allied airmen risked death. It gave me pause but did not deter me. Armed forces and civilians, all of us marched to the drums of war that season.

The house to my left and a quarter mile ahead seemed a little more remote from the others. I approached cautiously, paused just long enough to shake off rain like a drenched dog and put my knuckles to the door. A golden-haired girl of about eight answered, captured the rain-soaked stranger with saucer-wide eyes and stared silently.

'Father, mother?' I asked.

She disappeared without closing the door. Then she was back with her mother. An de Werdt, 36-year-old wife, mother and Dutch farm-woman, eyed me with instant recognition. Mid-way through the second war of her lifetime she was about to become an active participant.

'Soldat!' she said. It was a statement of recognition not an enquiry.

'Yes. Well, airman anyway,' I agreed thrusting my RAF mess-room key at her. It confirmed what she already knew.

Half a century later I am again embraced from the fathomless depths of this woman's eyes as if it were yesterday. I can still see An de Werdt's instant realization that she was being summoned from passive civilian life to combatant action. Nothing had ever conditioned her for such a role. No kin or acquaintance had ever spoken of the Underground, of active resistance, of sheltering a downed flyer.

Fate had not forewarned her but a Dutchwoman's sense of duty shaped her instant response when I brought the smell of death to her threshold. She was at once aware and undeterred. With the slightest inclination of her head, An de Werdt stepped aside and ushered me in.

There would be a moment during Gestapo interrogation atop Amsterdam Police Building a week later when my mind's eye fixed on the de Werdt family as they had surrounded me in their summer kitchen. Instantly I suppressed the scene and the characters; buried them so deep in subconsciousness I had great difficulty in reviving them a generation later.

An de Werdt, Martha the eldest of her three daughters, her 13-year-old son Jan and her 10-year-old nephew Harry van Seggelen were there when I arrived. Her husband Joseph was working a Sunday shift at the Philips works, so she sent for her brother-in-law to try and break the language barrier.

'I had been to church with my cousin and afterwards returned to his mother's house, to my aunt An,' Harry van Seggelen would recall 30 years later. 'It was about 11:30 when someone knocked at the door of the summer kitchen. Martha opened the door and called her mother. My aunt gestured for him to come in and he identified himself by showing a key on which there were the letters "RAF".

'My aunt sent for her brother-in-law since she could not understand the man. When he came in the airman seemed scared he had been betrayed but this, of course, was not the case. While he was eating in the summer kitchen my cousin and I were ordered to stay on the look-out and to warn if anyone was approaching.

'I can still recall my aunt asking him for a souvenir and his answer was something like "Puff! Puff!" as if he wanted to explain that everything was lost in the aircraft. Finally he handed her a tiny compass the size of a Dutch silver dime.'

Van Seggelen's account brought back my own memory of the desperate attempt I made to dissuade the de Werdts from keeping anything that would mark an airman's passage through their home.

'Burn, bury, destroy every shred of my clothing,' I kept telling her with frantic gestures.

Implacably, she had replaced my battledress and underclothes with her husband's and brother-in-law's clothing, painstakingly sewing each item of my escape kit into the seams. The compass, worn as a collar-button, was additional to the one in the escape kit. How could I refuse this sole request?

The foreign money – and the damn hacksaw blade – were sewn into the seams of the heavy tweed jacket, a dark red shirt of rayon material and the sweat-band of good, dark-grey trousers. Long white two-piece underwear, that reminded me of pyjamas, completed the clothing. Then as an after-thought her husband had given me his only neck-tie. Brightly striped in red, green and yellow, it seemed to glow conspicuously in the night. Ruefully I buried it early in my flight.

In one of the first letters An de Werdt wrote, when Royal Dutch Air Force Colonel Arie deJong reunited us a generation later, she said: 'I still remember you standing before the mirror with my husband's cap on your head and trying it over and over again and you kept saying "Yes, yes"'.

They had provided the ubiquitous peaked cap worn by Dutch males in this farm country and I had carefully stuffed the handkerchief-map into the peak of it. Her brother-in-law's boots fitted surprisingly well at the outset. We could not anticipate that my feet would swell in subsequent days till I thought they would burst the footwear.

A few words of French augmented my English. However, they spoke only the Dutch-accented Flemish of Brabant province. For hours we gestured at each other, repeating words in our own tongue and matching them with the familiar objects around us. We consulted the map and they located me between Weert and Maarheeze. Again and again they tried to explain that a Belgium canal system running through Antwerp to the Channel passed seven or eight miles south of Budel.

Thirty years later, An de Werdt's granddaughter translated in faultless English how I had misunderstood her grandmother's instructions. 'They kept telling you to go south to the canal about two hours walk and to ask a Belgian barge captain to take you west with him!'

That day, half a lifetime later with the de Werdt family, *Eindhoven Dagblad* editor Ruud Groen and my wife Lynne in tow, An had walked me to the roadway that would have taken me to the canal. Jabbing with her forefinger she again pointed the way.

'It was so close, so easy and you were so dense,' her granddaughter translated finding the kindest word to describe my stupidity.

116

Joseph der Werdt had returned from Eindhoven at suppertime to find the drapes suspiciously drawn and his family harbouring a British airman. 'My uncle was much more afraid of getting in trouble with the enemy than my aunt,' van Seggelen recalls. 'So you had to be hidden upstairs in the hay loft. But my aunt also had fears that I, being not yet 10 years old, would talk about the event.

'She took me aside and said: "Harry, if you ever talk about what you have seen they will kill me, your uncle, the whole family and you, too. But if you never talk about it, I promise that when the war is over you will get a real silver guilder." '

When it was dark they brought me down from the hay loft, thrust two thick cheese sandwiches into the pocket of the tweed jacket and escorted me out of the gate. Then they pointed me towards the canal and wished me godspeed.

When the war was over An de Werdt gave her nephew his first silver guilder. She unearthed my flying-boots from their hiding place beneath the barn floor and sold them to a man who worked with her husband at the Philips plant. The little compass was deposited on the mantel of their fireplace. It was there when Lynne and I visited a generation later.

'Did she burn my battledress jacket and pants?' I asked her granddaughter. An de Werdt sensed my question. A broad smile creased her strong face.

'No she did not,' her granddaughter translated. 'She says you should know that is not the way we do things in the Netherlands. She cut your uniform apart and dyed the material a different shade of blue. Then she made a coat for her eldest daughter. My aunt must have been the only girl in Nazi-occupied Holland who wore an RAF airman's battledress to school for three years.'

Mothers in Allied lands showed their courage and morale in many ways those war years. 'The news is good these days and you are all doing good work,' my mother wrote her only child the last day of May 1942. 'But it is also a bit terrifying to us here when we know that each time there are naturally a few losses. We keep our fingers crossed and are as hopeful as we can be.'

She apparently left the letter half-finished while she prepared supper. Then she had continued: 'Just heard on the radio of the mass raid of 1,000 'planes over Cologne last night with a loss of 44 'planes which, of course, is a small amount considering all that went out but nevertheless there are many sons in each. But so it goes and we hope and pray that if you were among them you are back safe and well, darling.'

12

Flight of A Grounded Airman

WEERT to MIDDLEBEERS, 1–3 June 1942

A witness at the Nuremberg trials described an SS death squad's 'special action' in the wake of the German Army's advance across Poland in mid-war.

A soldier sat on the edge of a clay pit, a cigarette dangling from his lips and a machine-gun cradled almost casually between his arm and his lap. Naked families descended steps that they, themselves, had dug on the opposite side of the pit. They came forward holding hands, stepping down into the cauldron of blood and shattered corpses; near-dead voices keening the hum of hell.

And the soldier would swing his gun in an arc of about 100 degrees, keeping the barrel dipped a little below the pit edge to terminate another 40 or 50 lives in a dozen seconds.

This, said the witness, went on and on. The soldier sat stolidly smoking between bursts of annihilation as new ranks of naked victims formed up, walking hand-in-hand to oblivion through an endless morning.

I do not believe that I could have been conditioned to kill like that. Nor could I have aimed the steel bumper of a Gestapo squad's Mercedes staff car at the legs of elderly yellow-starred Jews fleeing for their lives across an Amsterdam street in morning sunshine. I was in that Mercedes, my hands palming its low roof at a Gestapo officer's Luger-in-the-neck insistence.

Just nights earlier I had purposefully flicked the six fusing switches on the bomb-aimer's panel to arm four tons of high explosives. With complete concentration I had checked and rechecked the bomb-sight settings. Then I had searched the pathway of flares, dummy fires, fiery debris and pyrotechnics that were miniaturized three miles below to fit the finger-width of my bomb-sight aiming wires.

Slowly I call off directions to Tony at the controls. 'Right about 10 degrees . . . easy . . . easy. No! a bit too much. Left-left, hold it. Hold it now. Steady . . . steady . . .' The release toggle is cradled in the palm of my right hand. Four ounces of thumb-pressure rains death on human heads below.

I on the Perspex floor of the bomb-aimer's turret, the soldier on the lip of the clay pit, we dealt death on command. But I was isolated by my preoccupation with bomb-sight settings, by the cloak of night and by that long parabolic arc of the bomb's trajectory. The German soldier swinging his machine-gun in a lazy arc, sighted just below the faces that stared back at him.

We were agents of very different regimes. The comparative immorality of our roles is a matter that I have not personally resolved. A reporter by trade, I can only tell it as it was.

The one instance which still surprises me was my ability to lie in the teeth of the *Sicherheitspolizei* following my capture; to mislead them as a mother hawk ground-hops, playing the broken-wing trick to distract the hunter from her nestlings. Through a long June afternoon of 1942, high in Amsterdam police headquarters, I lied desperately to shield the de Werdt family who had sheltered me.

A few nights earlier they had cautiously opened their front gate, peered into the dark road and pointed my way south. Within an hour's walking – as I understood them – I would reach the canal that wound west to the Meuse River system through Belgium. They were sure a Belgian barge captain would whisk me safely to a Channel port.

But by midnight I had reached neither the canal nor a major waterway. Either I had blundered off course or misunderstood their gestured instructions. Scanning the escape-kit map I decided to sharply alter direction and make Tilburg, about 30 miles to the northwest, my next destination. It was on a relatively straight-line route to the Channel coast that would keep me from blundering over the Dutch-Belgian border.

My altered route took me cross-country across polders and wet fields. Then I was on a footpath that passed through alternate stretches of forest and clearings. Moonlight played on the trees and bushes giving them life that danced in my imagination. In a clearing a hundred yards ahead the bared branches of a tree seemed to point skywards like the barrels of a Bofors anti-aircraft gun. As I advanced the illusion sharpened in focus. Then, at the base of the gun-like image, there was movement more human than tree-like.

Not 50 feet away I was stopped in my tracks by reality. It *was* an anti-aircraft battery and it was manned by at least two square-helmeted soldiers. For an eternity of several seconds I stood frozen just within the shadow of the trees.

Then I backed off, literally trying to fit my shoes into the foot-steps I had taken. The crunch of every twig underfoot, the brushing of leaves across my shoulders, seemed to shatter the night's stillness. Once I tripped on a tree-root, fell heavily backwards against a tree and was certain the anti-aircraft crew must know someone had blundered into their domain. But there was no pursuit. I must have back-tracked nearly half a mile in the woods before I had the courage to head on a westerly route again.

I was on a tree-lined roadway. The trees seemed reminiscent of some country lane I had walked back in Canada. Then the picture they conjured came into focus. It was 'An Avenue of Trees' by the 17th century Dutch painter Meindert Hobbema. Every Ontario school-child of the 1920s studied that painting in art class. Now it was as if I had been whisked back into a page of my third-grade school-book.

An hour later I was on a main road; it seemed the only road that ran parallel to the Dutch-Belgian border. It was after 3am when I detected low on the skyline and some miles ahead what appeared to be the vague trace of a red inverted-V sign. As I walked on, it slowly sharpened in shape and deepened in colour. Another hour's walking repeated the image as if there were two red inverted Vs at right-angles to each other. They stood out in dreaded clarity. These were the red-neon obstruction lights that defined Eindhoven airfield control tower.

As I continued, irrevocably committed to the highway along Eindhoven airport's boundary, Luftwaffe aircraft returning from a raid on Britain moved into the circuit, signalled for landing permission and were, in turn, given the green-light to proceed. It was an uncanny replay of the landing procedure that we, ourselves, had performed so often in the early morning hours after an operation. Now I was on the other side of the looking-glass.

Plodding on, not daring to pause by the roadside, I watched enemy bombers coming in to land. In minutes the Luftwaffe crews would be describing the weather over Britain, the searchlights and defences over southern England's targets. Reporting how *their* bombs had fallen. Then they would be heading for breakfast and a dry, warm bed. I shrugged off the early morning damp and pushed thoughts of food or sleep from my mind. At this moment I was as far from home as I would ever be.

I could picture the reception an unkempt German flyer dressed in civilian clothes would get if he was nabbed in the early morning hours alongside Leeming's boundary fence. Now just getting safely past Eindhoven airport, which seemed to stretch for miles alongside me, was going to take forever. When I finally did pass it, Eindhoven industrial area began to take shape. With the first streaks of dawn, but well before curfew ended, I was the only person tramping the factory-lined streets.

Starting into another block of silent plants and warehouses, I spotted a uniformed policeman coming from a factory entrance at the bottom of the street. He seemed to give me no more than a passing glance as he approached. But I was clearly the only pedestrian abroad during curfew hours. We were both on the same side of the street and as the distance between us shortened I crossed diagonally to the other side.

With all the purposeful stance I could muster, I bee-lined for a factory entrance as if I had been sent on an errand to it. The policeman continued up the other side of the street while I hovered for perhaps 20 seconds in the shadow of an entranceway. Then I continued, resisting an ungodly urge to look over my shoulder at the Dutch constable. Perhaps he was suppressing an equal urge to turn and follow my footsteps. What I didn't realize, of course, was that in this third year of war no Dutch policeman was going to pursue a potential saboteur.

By 7:30 I was well into the countryside past Eindhoven. I had been walking almost continuously for nine hours and the shoes, which had seemed to fit comfortably the previous night, were gripping my instep and toes like a pipefitter's vice. I had to find someplace to lie down and remove those shoes if only for an hour or so. My limping gait caught the attention of two farm youths in a nearby field and they headed towards me. My instinct was to run but it was as if I was being nailed still by my feet.

'Need rest – lie down – sleep,' I told them gesturing a head-side pillow with palms of my hands pressed prayer-like beside my ear.

'Yah,' they understood yet, clearly, they were not in a position to offer accommodation. Perhaps fellow workers deeper in the field could help. What followed was a series of inquiries shouted across perhaps an acre of Dutch farmland as one farm-hand queried the next. Certain their shouts would summon German captors and virtually pinned by pain to the spot I tried to quiet them.

Finally, one of them pointed to a barn about a quarter mile away. I staggered a few steps towards it. Then they were virtually dragging me along. It was about 1pm when I awoke. I was again in a loft, almost covered in straw. My shoes had been removed and it was minutes before I could locate them in the hay beneath me. Getting them back on over swollen feet was sheer agony but had to be done.

Laced into the shoes, my feet seemed anaesthetized as I climbed down the loft ladder and headed for the road. The agony quickly returned. It was as if I was being crucified, feet-first, with every step that I took.

Fifteen minutes on the road – it seemed as many hours – brought me into the village of Winterle not more than a half dozen miles west of Eindhoven. A few homes, a couple of shops and a cafe stretched along two blocks of the main road.

Which of them might offer help? I was almost directly opposite the cafe when I noticed it. Its windows were shuttered and the entrance door closed. Beneath one window a bicycle had been left leaning against the wall. That bike became the sole focus of my attention.

Mindful of cowboys jumping to their saddles in hundreds of Western movies, I took a hop, step and spurt across the road. The roar of Saturday matinee kids cheering Tom Mix' heroic leap to action rang in my ears as I mounted the bicycle seat. No longer mindful of my tortured feet, I was peddling furiously out of sight when I heard the hubbub behind me.

'Stop, thief!' has much the same intonation in any language. I recognized the Dutch version as I peddled away.

Once again, as on my arrival by parachute two nights earlier, I headed for a patch of woodland. My lungs seemed about to burst and my feet were again aflame when I sighted a well-wooded stretch to the right of the road. Dragging the bike deep into the woods I laid it behind a large tree trunk and piled leaves over the handlebars to cover their reflective shine. Then, once more, I lay on the forest floor hoping not to be skewered by captors.

It was about 10 minutes before two Dutch policemen, riding tandem on a motorbike, went by scanning each side of the road for a bicycle thief. Half an hour later one of them came back on the motorcycle, returning to Winterle empty-handed.

'I better wait till dark,' I decided. 'At least for another couple of hours.' In fact, I remained hidden for about 90 minutes in all; long enough to remove the carrier-basket and the bicycle-lamp from the handlebars in an effort to disguise the bike; enough time for my feet to stop their painful pulsating.

But it was not long enough to escape three years internment as a POW. I was back on the road astride the stripped two-wheeler for no more than five minutes when the second policeman returned from nowhere riding another bike. 'Halt,' he commanded. I waved and peddled on attempting to ignore him.

'Halt,' he repeated, turning to come abreast of me. Then he was waving the ceremonial sword that the German occupying forces allowed the Dutch constabulary to wear in lieu of real weapons.

Where was I going? he wanted to know. Tilberg, I told him.

Where was I coming from? Tilberg, I answered again hoping my response fitted his question.

Did I have identification papers? he demanded. In Tilberg, I assured him.

'Look! Do you speak English?' I asked as he approached to collar me.

'Yes,' he said in surprise.

'Look, I'm a British airman. Shot down two nights ago.'

'So! There were several brought down Sunday night.'

'And if you let me go now I'll get back to fly again and drop more bombs on the Germans.'

'That's true,' he agreed after some consideration. 'But the stolen bicycle. I was sent to find it and the man who stole it.'

'Well, here's the bike so you won't return empty-handed.'

'Yes. I must let you go. My name is John Schikopf and I live at Middlebeers. After the war you write me?'

Yes, I assured John Schikopf, I would. The sound of gravel crunching beneath bicycle tyres fades in memory as I remember him riding off wheeling the stolen bike beside him. The same gravel-crunching sound grows loud again a few minutes further down my mind.

Why did I not hide out in the woods again? Why would I continue down a roadway in broad daylight within a mile or two of where I had stolen a bicycle in wartime? Perhaps painful feet addle the head. Perhaps I expected John Schikopf to summon some miraculous help from the Dutch resistance movement. When he returned not 10 minutes later, however, there were no more questions to be considered.

'Quislings, German sympathizers who live in Winterle, saw you on the road. I have the bike but if I don't bring you in I'll be shot for certain.'

I was in no position to argue. Pain surged through my feet. I was dog-tired and utterly confounded. I remounted the stolen bike and rode on beside him to Middlebeers. We said little but I kept thinking it was all part of a ruse to outwit the Germans. Any minute the Resistance would whisk me to safety.

It didn't happen, of course. Schikopf had given me a chance to escape and I had muffed it. Now I was headed for captivity. I was delivered to the burgomeister at Middlebeers town hall, an overweight man in his forties. His self-satisfied smile spoke assurance that his authority would last forever.

'Do you speak English,' I asked.

'Certainly.'

'Then understand that I am a British airman shot down two nights ago.'

'Ah, yes.'

'So what do you plan to do with me?'

'I have no choice but to hand you to the Luftwaffe at Eindhoven.'

'No choice?'

'No, we are not free to handle such affairs.'

'But what the police went after was a bicycle thief and you have him. Why not simply throw me in jail for stealing a bicycle,' I argued.

'Impossible,' said the burgomeister putting authority and sweet reason in his smug smile. But he allowed Constable Schikopf to take me to his nearby home to await the Luftwaffe. Enroute I dashed between out-buildings and raced on torturous feet to a cross-road, Schikopf in pursuit. I dived into a ditch in a frantic effort to escape but it was futile.

The policeman and the bicycle thief shared embarassment as I climbed ignominiously out of the ditch and accompanied him back to his house. Perhaps we both recognized my futile dash for what it was – a stylized gesture of reluctant surrender.

Schikopf and his bride had moved into their bungalow following their marriage just a couple of months earlier. Now they invited me to wash and shave away two days beard and to join them for supper as we waited the Luftwaffe's arrival. Their dining room overlooked a small terrace through French doors and the lawn was soon covered with more than a hundred townspeople.

Villagers swarmed across the lawn and into the dining room. 'English flyer! Englander!' they cried, reaching to shake my hand and clap my back. 'When comes the invasion?' 'When comes liberation?' they asked.

A fortnight earlier Nazi forces had penetrated east through Crimea to take 100,000 prisoners. That week they had broken the British Libyan front. And my presence was evidence enough that the Third Reich controlled all Western Europe. What could I tell them?

A Luftwaffe major arrived in a staff car and the crowd of villagers on the Schikopf lawn reluctantly parted to let him through. He strode into the dining room to take me in custody. I stood and we walked through the French doors wordlessly.

As we stepped into their midst, the hundred townsfolk shouted almost in unison. 'When comes the invasion?' 'When are the Englanders coming?' they wanted to know.

I raised my right hand forming two fingers into a Churchillian V-sign. A hundred villagers returned the victory salute. The Luftwaffe major scowled and grabbed my left arm possessively.

'When comes the invasion?' they kept roaring.

'Soon. The invasion will come soon,' I told them, our hands all bobbing V-sign defiance at the Luftwaffe major.

'Soon you will be liberated,' I insisted, choking on the futility of my response that desperate spring.

I was initially interrogated at Eindhoven airport by the Luftwaffe major who had brought me from Middlebeers. He was misleadingly relaxed. I gave him my name, rank and number, as the Geneva Convention demanded and I confirmed that we had been shot down two nights before.

Where? I professed not to know. Fighter or flak? I thought it was one of his fighters, I said. Was I the pilot? No, but I declined to explain my place in the crew. What of the other crew members? I could honestly say I had no idea what had happened to them.

The Dutch farmer's peaked cap lay on a corner of the major's desk where I had placed it on our arrival in his office. When I remembered that the silk map was folded carefully into its peak I involuntarily reached to recover the cap.

It was the sort of reaction trained interrogators immediately pursued. The major snatched back the cap and felt carefully through the lining.

When there was nothing there to explain my concern he examined the cap more closely under his desk-lamp. It took only a couple of minutes to find where I had slit an opening into the peak; for him to fish out the map and to examine it beneath the desk-light.

Almost immediately he found the one pencil-mark I had made to pin-point Weert. In minutes he had 'phoned to tap German air defence records of that sector over the past few nights. Now he was telling me, 'So you did come down from the thousand bomber raid on Cologne. And your crew were Sgt. Anthony Moore, Sgt. Harold Stacey, Sgt. Frank Walker, Sgt. Donald Thurlow, Sgt. Jack Ogden and Sgt. Marshal English.'

The names dropped lifeless on the worn rug of the Luftwaffe office. Nights earlier these had been my brothers in that black womb heavy with bombs. Now they were only names. Who lived? No answers to that were sought nor given. Only one's name, rank and service number were communicable. I was volunteering nothing else.

The interview terminated within minutes after that. The major was aware that RAF aircrews were as committed as their Luftwaffe counterparts to resist interrogation beyond identifying themselves. And Hermann Goering had unquestionably imbued the Luftwaffe with the notion that his aircrew and RAF airmen were all players in the same league. Like medieval gladiators, we were expected to kill each other but within the bounds of good sport.

In the washroom a Luftwaffe fighter-pilot loaned me his comb. 'Thank you,' I said. 'Thanks a million. That's what you say, isn't it,' he responded with a wide smile.

I spent the night in a small cell. It was similar to the holding cells in court buildings that I was familiar with as a police reporter. It was not uncomfortable and I had been provided with coffee and cigarettes before I was locked up. As I stretched out on the thin paliasse covering the cot I let my body sag in fatigue. There was a terrible sense of finality to my incarceration. It was matched, however, by a sudden awareness that I had survived my air-war career.

In four nights ending 4 June, Bomber Command sent 2,368 aircraft to Cologne, Essen and Bremen. Ninety-seven of them, containing some 600 aircrew, were shot down on those four raids. That meant about 85 of us probably survived and perhaps a dozen evaded capture. So some 70 or more aircrew that week joined the ranks of RAF POWs who would number more than 10,000 by war's end. By the following week there were about 40 or 50 of us in the cells of a big military prison in Amsterdam awaiting despatch to POW camps in Germany.

The cells were narrow and barred by heavy wooden doors. The doors had massive hasp-and-lock assemblies identical to those commonly found

125

on the doors of cold-storage plants. The door-closing mechanism must have weighed 15 pounds, yet it was supported by two quarter-inch-diameter bolts which went through the door panel. The bolts were secured by large hexagonal nuts. Those on the inside of my cell door were relatively loose. With nothing more instructive to do I readily removed these lugs and hid them in the straw paliasse. Then, lying on my back on the cell floor, I put the soles of my shoes against the bolts and thrust the whole mechanism into the corridor.

The door-closing assembly fell to the stone floor outside my cell with a resounding crash that seemed to echo through the prison corridors. Resuming a prone position on the cot I waited my captors' response. It was not long unfolding. A guard opened the inspection-hole flap, confirmed that I was still there and screamed Teutonic oaths. I feigned sleep and he turned up his lung-power.

I asked, *sotto voce*, what the problem was and was told graphically by two sturdy guards. Standing each side of the opened cell door, they gesticulated at the peep-hole and the lock-assembly bolt holes.

'Nonsense,' I said. 'I couldn't very well escape through those holes. Could I?'

The block captain arrived next, decided he was not going to be aggravated by a British swine *luftgangster* and left it to the two guards to again secure me.

They postponed their retaliation until I needed their escort to the toilet. Then they let me wait. Watching through the peep-hole in the cell door as bladder pressure built anguish on my face they ignored me. Just short of the bursting point they bowed me out the cell door and simultaneously kicked me. Their boots hit the cheeks of my ass in unison and with a force that propelled me several feet down the corridor.

The escapade had broken the week's monotony but it had an unanticipated result. It brought me again to the attention of senior Luftwaffe officers. One of them apparently wondered why I alone among the shot-down aircrew was in civilian clothes. It was a question to be discussed with the *Sicherheitspolizei*.

13

A Long Day in Amsterdam

AMSTERDAM, 9 June 1942

The *Sicherheitspolizei* insisted they were Field Security Police, not Gestapo. The Luftwaffe had had second-thoughts about my identity and the polizei had reacted in their own unsubtle way. I was aroused about 6:30am by four very large men in leather jackets and riding boots, their wide-brimmed hats framing duelling-scarred faces. One, with the malevolent sneer of a pre-war Hollywood film heavy, held a cocked Luger in my face while his companions searched me.

The Luftwaffe had done little more than turn out my pockets the previous week. A map hidden in my cap had not surprised the major because RAF aircrew had been carrying escape kits for some time. But as the Gestapo ripped maps and money from the cuffs and seams of my civilian clothes it confirmed their suspicions.

They had come to investigate a suspected enemy agent. Now French francs, Dutch guilders, German marks fluttered to the cell floor as they tore at my clothing. It is fifty years since it happened but I can still hear the pinging sound as a three-and-a-half-inch hacksaw blade bounced on the cell floor.

'Saboteur!' one them exclaimed.

It was then that the plug-ugly heavyweight pressed the Luger muzzle into the nape of my neck and they marched me out. There was a brief stop in the corridor while one of them signed a Luftwaffe document. I did not need to read German to know that he was signing a receipt for one prisoner who was not necessarily to be returned.

Ushered into the back seat of their staff car between a pair of them and watching the other two take their places in front, I had more than a sense of *deja-vu*. I had, in fact, had a preview of this experience. Half a dozen years earlier I had been 'taken for a ride' by a four-man squad of United Automobile Workers during a sitdown strike at the Chrysler plant in Detroit. It was a foretaste of my ride with these four Gestapo-men six years later – with notable differences. I was sympathetic to the UAW cause at the time. They had not thrust a Luger in my neck and the Flying Squad did not attempt to mow down citizens in the street with the front-bumper of their car.

In a 40-minute passage through Amsterdam's streets this mid-war morning, such distinctions etched to the depths of my consciousness the contrasts possible in the practice of humanity. I was again reborn; dumped from my disciplined Allied serviceman's cocoon into the streets of a European city where Nazi gangsters chased human prey with fast cars.

Six weeks earlier – a month before he was, himself, gunned down – Reinhardt Heidrich had decreed that Western European Jews identify themselves with yellow Stars of David worn prominently on their lapels. My escort still found this amusing. Twice enroute across Amsterdam from the military prison the driver violently swerved the Mercedes staff car to aim its heavy front bumper at the legs of elderly yellow-starred Jews.

The targetted couples ran for their lives across broad streets to the shelter of building entrances. Twice the staff car mounted the curb to pursue them, its two right tyres screaming mechanical invective. Were the screams directed at the doctrine-mad Gestapo driver or at his hapless quarry? In a lifetime of 40 minutes I had been borne from the ordered field of RAF-Luftwaffe battle into the racist gutter of the Nazi gangster world.

Then we were at a six-storey building and mounting a wide staircase with large urns of flowers on each landing. The Luger was still in my neck and my mind raced a logical pathway. Funereal flowers . . . funeral parlour . . . morgue. These efficient Teutonic bastards, I reasoned, had brought me to the most convenient spot to shoot me.

But first I was to be questioned. Mid-room in a large office on the top floor, I was seated in a straight-back chair. Two of my captors were joined by a middle-aged, avuncular man. Minutes of ominous silence followed until a secretary arrived with a shoe-box-size carton.

'Sandwiches, lunch,' I thought. But the carton held handcuffs, leg-irons and a length of chain. The chain joined the handcuffs behind me swooping between my thighs to the leg-irons. Since the human body is symmetrical the chain nudged my rectum when I was seated.

Back on the squadron an intelligence officer had once lectured us on how to cope with enemy interrogation. 'Stay cool. Keep your dignity. Stare out a window with indifference,' he had told us. Atop Amsterdam police building this day I wondered if that wingless sonofabitch had ever sat with a chain up his ass.

Then for half an hour a Gestapo interrogator screamed at me in German. His simian chest would swell as he sucked life from the room. His lungs refilled, he would expel Nazi anger in Wagnerian thunderclaps. 'Sie sind ein saboteur!' he roared. 'Ein saboteur fir Churchill. Englischer hund!'

Each accusation was a crescendo leap enroute to a death sentence. Fear flooded my defenses, ebbing towards panic. Fear flowed into desperation and swept back with a wave of matching anger. Shaking the chain on its short leeway – at risk to my genitals – I stood roaring for an intepreter.

Ultimately they produced one. He had been a New York street-car conductor for 20 years before the Hitler regime called him back to the fatherland and his English was still pure Bronx. It was unnerving to hear my Canuck speech falling on German ears in Bronx-accented words in an Amsterdam police building this wartime day.

'Tell them I am an RAF airman shot down on His Majesty's Service. I am to be treated as a prisoner-of-war,' I demanded. Did the words sound as pompous and futile in translation? I wondered.

'You are in civilian clothes. You are to be shot as a spy,' I was told.

'I'm an airman.'

'Prove it.'

'My dog-tags prove my name, rank and number.'

'Churchill gives such dog-tags to all of his saboteurs.'

So we circled each other through a long hour of impasse. The avuncular man broke the deadlock. 'Tell us the names of your crew,' he said.

The Luftwaffe major had identified my crew when a mark on my map put our demise in the vicinity of Weert. With regard for King's Rules and Regulations I had declined to confirm them. Now I must weigh an infraction of service rules against the prospect of death. Or was this all an elaborate ruse to pry information out of me? 'Tell me my crew-mates names and I'll tell you if they're right,' I quibbled.

Perhaps the absurdity of this word-game amused them. But they did contact the Luftwaffe at Eindhoven by phone. Again the names were dropped one by one on the charged air.

'Sgt. Anthony Moore,
   'Sgt. Harold Stacey,
      'Sgt. Frank Walker,
         'Sgt. Jack Ogden,
            'Sgt. Marshal English,
               'Sgt. Donald Thurlow.'

This time I acknowledged them. There was a further call across Amsterdam for confirmation. But the second call prompted more questioning. 'What position were you in the crew?' I was asked.

'I was the navigator,' I admitted.

Now a third 'phone call was made. I had no idea of its import. My identity, however, was still conspicuously in doubt. For nearly 20 minutes we sat in utter silence. Then their 'phone rang and my aircrew status was apparently confirmed. Now the handcuffs were removed, the leg-irons unfastened. Coffee was ordered. Polish cigarettes in ersatz American-packaging were passed around.

A week later at Dulag Luft – the first step to POW internment in Luftwaffe custody – I was reunited with Don Thurlow, our flight engineer. He filled in the 20-minutes in which my fate had hung suspended. 'When they first came to my cell and asked me if I knew you, I denied it. We're not supposed to tell them anything except our own identity, are we?'

'That's true.'

'So when they came back a second time you really had me in a quandry.'

'And vice-versa,' I agreed.

'They said the Field Security Police were holding a guy in civilian clothes who claimed he was Warrant Officer Silver and the navigator in our crew. Now they said if I still denied knowing you they were going to shoot this guy. I still wasn't sure if this was a trick to get information. But if they weren't kidding you needed confirmation so I gave it.'

'Damn decent, Don' I told him.

Thurlow had confirmed my identity and the Luftwaffe had never really doubted it. If the Luftwaffe wanted me back in their custody that was okay with the *Sichereitspolizei*. But for the moment these guardians of Nazi-held European security were faced by an airman who had plucked civilian disguise out of nowhere within a day or two of being shot down. On a note of chilling cordiality – one respectable enemy to another – the interrogation resumed. Where had I obtained my civilian clothes, they wanted to know.

That was the moment when terror struck, when I could see the de Werdt family stripped naked for Gestapo annihilation. Fear of their discovery enveloped me with such dread that June afternoon I unreeled truth and fiction from parallel spools in my mind's eye. It was as if the real and the cover story were being projected from tandem projectors on a split screen of memory and imagination.

Weert and Winterle – as the Luftwaffe had already established – were the start and finishing points. The reality and the evasion had to cover the 20 miles between them. That was not much distance to be explained by two days travel even in ill-fitting farmer's boots across rain-sodden polders.

But if the real film leaked from my mind it would detour just three miles from a straight line through Winterle and Weert. It would cross a creek near Buderlerberg village to a collection of farmhouses. Gestapo thugs following that route would have no trouble locating the farmhouse at 10 Berg.

For a frightening instant I again saw An de Werdt stolidly sewing my escape kit into the seams of her brother-in-law's Sunday pants, into her husband's maroon shirt. In that instant I rewound the film and shut down that projector. It was 40 years before I replayed it.

'So tell us what happened when you were first shot down?' the Bronx interpreter demanded. From Weert I had slogged northwest, I told them. *Not west towards Budelerberg*. Why? Because I wanted to get away from the

130

three-country boundary; to put as much distance as possible between myself and the German frontier. *Logical!*

'And the clothes. Did you buy them?'

I had stolen them, of course, I said. *Careful! Complete wardrobes don't hang on Dutch clotheslines these days. You don't find shoes to fit on every doorstep!* Then like a marathon swimmer adjusting for the long haul I paced my response. I had hidden, watchful, for much of Sunday morning, casing a group of houses where a road crossed a canal.

'The people went to church, I guess that's where they went. I got the peaked cap and underwear from the first house. The second place had nothing. *Keep it plausible.* I got the trousers and jacket at two other houses . . .'

But the shoes. *Explain how you got the bloody shoes!* I had spotted them on a doorstep towards suppertime. They were caked in mud like someone had left them to clean later. *Logical.* It was risky creeping up on them but my flying boots had blistered my feet beyond endurance. The shoes proved tight but I had no choice.

The middle-aged Gestapo-man who might have been anyone's kindly uncle nodded understandingly from time to time. It was as if he, himself, spent Sundays swiping clothes from Dutch farm-houses. He saved his final question until my route and clothing caper had been established beyond recall.

'And did you steal a needle and thread as well?' he asked beningnly.

Fear again swelled to anger. Rage filled my head. These goons had ripped off collars, cuffs, sweat-bands from my Dutch clothing. 'If your men had been less anxious to tear my clothes apart they could have got those things the way I put them in,' I roared.

'And how was that?' I had slit seams and poked them in with the hacksaw blade, I explained.

The avuncular one smiled benevolently. Whether he was marking my deception with professional respect or growing disinterest I shall never know. Perhaps fact and fiction had become indistinguishable in the Thousand-Year Reich.

It must have been apparent that an organized Resistance movement would not have despatched me to steal a bicycle from a village cafe-front at high noon. But the notion that An de Werdt, a domesticated, apolitical Christian woman would put herself and her family at mortal risk because her sense of morality allowed no other course – that would not have occurred to them.

Perhaps there were more important things for this branch of the *Sicherheitspolizei* to do on this wartime day; more Jews to chase down with their Mercedes on Amsterdam streets, more civilian hostages to be taken in. In late afternoon they returned me to the Luftwaffe prison.

But first – like bureaucrats the world around – they covered their backs with paper. 'So now you must sign a confession,' the Deutch uncle told me.

'Sign what!'

'You must retell what you have explained and a stenographer will copy it all down and type it out. Then you must sign it for our records.'

So they took me back over my story, my route, my theft expedition. There was a large wall-map of the Lowlands and I was allowed to consult it to clarify where I had been. I would suck in a place name and regurgitate it a few minutes later. But it had not been easy to pick places at random that were remote from Budelerberg and still feasibly within range. Half a century later I remember a place called Rosevalde because it reminded me of U.S. President Roosevelt. But I was afraid it was too far off my escape route – real or imagined – to be credible.

Earlier, as a suspected Churchill saboteur I was to be thoroughly inter-rogated then shot. But it was all to be done within the formal niceties of their anti-espionage craft. As a downed airman stupid enough to don civil-ian clothes I was out of their league, a mere nuisance who had distracted their attention for much of the day.

Now while we waited for the stenographer's transcript that I would sign, real American cigarettes – not the bogus Polish ones – were passed round. Lemon pop was poured. Now the ex-Bronx tram conductor had someone to talk at in English.

'England is kaput,' he told me, spinning a world globe. 'Look what Rommel is doing in the desert. Russia is kaput. Look where our panzers are in Crimea. And where is America?'

The global picture he painted that June week of 1942 was certainly dis-heartening but I was not going to give comfort to this smug Gestapo bastard. 'I'm really not in a position to answer,' I said. 'Perhaps after the war we can argue the toss.'

Soon after I was returned to my military prison cell, a guard opened the inspection flap and asked 'Essen?'

'Nein,' I said, I hadn't eaten.

When another hour went by without food, I complained. The cell-block officer was summoned. 'When you were returned by the polizei my man asked if you wanted to eat and you told him no. Now you must wait for breakfast,' he said.

It had been that kind of day you could live without – 14 hours of mis-understanding.

14

The Two Reds

LUFT III, 1942

'For you, the war is over!'

Every kriegy was greeted with that line by his German captors. He might hear it as he touched enemy ground, from the polizei who clapped him in custody or from the first Luftwaffe officer to interrogate him.

It was invariably well pronounced and sincerely said. At once, it announced captivity, the end of personal hostilities and grudging congratulations. Implicit was the envious observation: 'You came close to being a dead pigeon but it's the caged birds who'll survive.'

The logic of that was irresistible. In 10 months I had survived members of two crews, four aircraft and probably 300 squadron-mates. Life was immeasurably safer on the ground and I was not apt to fly again this war. In due course I would participate in escape endeavours, moved by boredom and half-convinced of their futility. But I was not dragged behind barbed-wire kicking and screaming that June week of 1942. I walked through the compound gate of Luft III curious as any 25-year-old attending his first high-school reunion.

Others were not so docile. The arrival of the two Reds – Gordon and Noble – each in his own fashion, was legendary. James Reid (Red) Gordon was the third of W. Earl Gordon's four sons to join the Air Force. 'W.E.', as he was known in the quiet reaches of Islington, was a civilizing force in that Metro Toronto suburb pre-war. He had founded the Knights of the Round Table to smooth the behavioural edges of boys such as his sons without dampening their spirit. W.E.'s knights combined Rotarian manners with Boy Scout zeal. Remarkably they harmonized wind, piss and lung-power, directing their primal instincts into acceptable channels.

Young Reid was as flamboyant as his red hair; endowed with enough energy and good-fellowship to lead sing-songs, impromptu football scrums and organized sociability for six decades. When the twin-engined Wellington he was piloting across Libya was shot down, Red Gordon hit the deck running, so to speak. Six weeks later he jumped from a train window as it pulled out of Marburg near the Yugoslavian-Austrian border. 'The train hadn't picked up speed and they soon had me back on board. It was no big deal,' he said.

A month later, he and fellow-kriegy Ed Mullins jumped from another train window. The train was moving at about 20 miles per hour and Mullins hit a tree. 'That slowed our travels and we were caught five days later,' he explained. Christmas Eve 1941 Red Gordon and John Snowdon cut their way through the wire at Stalag VIII-B, Lamsdorf. They were half frozen before they hopped a train heading north through the Polish winter. Two days later railway police pulled them from an open coal car. They were too stiff to move.

Reid learned from experience; he made his fourth escape in summer. He and an English POW walked out of Luft VI at Heydekrug wearing French berets and carrying a ladder. The overt simplicity of that effort got them clear of the camp. It was the river, bordering Luft VI like a moat, that was their undoing. To swim across it they removed their clothes. On the other side they sprinted for freedom. They were running fast and naked when they encountered a German school-girls' picnic.

'The girls raised an alarm, the goons unleashed the guard dogs and we began to run even faster,' Reid remembered. 'It was late summer but with those dogs on my heels I felt like little Eva going across the ice from slavery.'

Reid Gordon's ability to wrap a smile around adversity, his whiskey baritone voice cracking in song, the endless jokes, banter and after-dinner wit, played a big role in keeping his fellow kriegies free of barbed-wire depression. Post-war Reid took Positive Thinking on a revival tour. He hit the service club dinner circuit with an indefatigable mix of Norman Vincent Peale and Dale Carnegie. He probably did better with it than they did.

In September 1980 Red Gordon lost his left lung to cancer. The whiskey-baritone was muted but the smile encircling his round Scot face was undiminished. Now he was obliged to garner strength in the voice box over several minutes before telling a joke. Four years later he lost his voice completely. But the spirit never dimmed.

A few minutes after 10am Friday 15 November 1985 Reid pursed his lips for a good-bye kiss from his wife Betty. It was a day past their 40th wedding anniversary. The life-long, all-encompassing smile for humanity creased his face a last time. That done, Reid relaxed into final sleep.

Carmen Douglas (Red) Noble preferred to be called Joe and he generally got his way. He grew up in the relatively harmonious environment of a Southwestern Ontario town where boys fought for periodic exercise rather than on principle. But Joe had a red-head's temper which he kept stoked on the off chance he would find a target worth roasting. Air warfare fully engaged his energies till he was shot down in the summer of 1942. For the next three years our German captors drew his fire.

Early in his first tour as a 40 Squadron navigator/bomb-aimer, Joe was in a Wellington that ran out of gas returning from an operation and crash-landed near their base. Joe pulled the pilot from the wreckage before it took flame. The remainder of his first 30 ops were relatively uneventful. But of his subsequent stint instructing new aircrew at an Operational Training Unit, he would say, 'it was like watching paint dry from a dangerous observation point.'

As Shag Reese, the Welshman who teamed with Joe in latter-day escapades, recalled: 'Teaching was not his bag and Joe possessed the persuasive powers to get out of it. Soon he was back in action on 214 Squadron Stirlings. He was on his 57th operation enroute to Osnabrück when an Me-110 attacked. After three encounters both the Stirling and the Me-110 were in flames and falling out of control. Two crew-mates were dead and three had baled out. Joe and the captain were about to jump, themselves, when the aircraft exploded. Joe found himself in mid-air, then on the ground with burned face, hands and minor injuries.'

Joined by his front-gunner, Joe used his escape-kit map to guide them 70 miles to the Dutch border in six nights walking. By then Joe's right hand was infected and in considerable pain. But like so many others they failed to contact help. 'They pressed on until they were stopped by two Dutch policemen whose limited English nullified Joe Noble's persuasive powers,' as Shag put it.

'When the police indicated they would have to turn them over to German authorities, Bailey the gunner bolted from one policeman's grasp while Joe immobilised the other with a blow that did further damage to his swollen right hand. Astride the policeman's bike and riding virtually one-handed, Red sped towards the Belgian border. He got across the first bridge under the noses of border guards. Four police captured him at the second bridge.'

Joe Noble was hospitalized for a month before joining us in Luft III's North Compound. It was enough time to restoke his fires. His next bid for freedom was a leap from a hut roof to a cart-load of fir branches. Guards saw him jump and quickly removed him. His third try was in a garbage can but the refuse shovelled onto him contained hot cinders. He was not burned but near suffocation when they carted him off to the camp cooler. His fourth escape attempt was in a party of 24 kriegies marched out the camp gate by fellow POWs disguised as guards, marshalling their delousing party with wooden rifles. Red was enroute to Danzig by train in the role of a Norwegian worker when a routine check unmasked him.

Joe Noble shared his final bid for freedom from Luft III with Shag Reese. They were scheduled to be the 78th and 79th kriegies out of the Great Escape tunnel when the man ahead of them was nabbed at gun-point.

As Russian armies swept close to liberating us in mid-January 1945 we were evacuated from Luft III and marched through Silesia for a week before our captors loaded us into cattle-cars for a camp near Hamburg. On the third night of our march through sub-zero weather, a number of us found shelter in a hay-filled barn loft. Shag Reese and I can still hear Red Noble's voice cutting the frigid air.

'No smoking,' he roared. 'If I catch one sod smoking I'll stick a pitchfork in him.'

In the spring when we were again evacuated just ahead of advancing Allied forces, RCAF Group Captain Larry Wray was the Senior British Officer among several thousand of us. Our German captors still carried the guns but Larry Wray assumed virtual authority in the last hectic weeks of the war in Europe. To help him exercise that authority he made Red Noble his right-hand man. The soft-spoken group captain had found the most trenchant voice to relay his commands.

Both Larry Wray and Joe Noble remained in the RCAF post-war. Joe was a Wing Commander in charge of the RCAF base at Rockcliffe when he took retirement. He was still in his fifties; age had not mellowed him and he suffered fools intolerantly. For a time he was city manager of Oshawa, Ontario. Experience left him unequipped to cope with his elected employers, however. For a while he was personnel director of Toronto's public health department. But civic workers don't readily adapt to armed-forces style chain-of-command communication.

Joe Noble died in 1989 in Collingwood where he and wife Betty had retired. Their two daughters and four grandchildren remember his soft voice at bedtime, his firm hand taking them in tow. They never heard him as we had on dark nights in mid-war, bellowing like Thor to bring the heavens down on the cursed Hun.

There were ultimately 10,500 Allied Air Force POWs at Stalag Luft III and the satellite camp Belaria just down the road. In 1941 Russian POWs – worked at gun-point and near starvation – hacked a 13-acre clearing from Silesian pine forests at Sagan, a rail point near the Oder River midway between Berlin and Breslau. Within this acreage stripped to its sandy base, four separate compounds were defined by 20-foot-high guard towers, searchlights and 10-foot twin fences which sandwiched rolled concertina wire between them and were topped by barbed wire. A low wooden guard-rail ran 30 feet inside each fence line marking a *verboten* area. Within this 'death strip', the sandy soil was kept well raked to display any errant footprint. But it was unlikely any POW would have escaped the guards' vigilance long enough to leave a footmark.

Our guards were mostly middle-aged and some were World War I veterans. Suprisingly few of them seemed to resent us as *Luftgangsters* who had threatened the lives of their women and children. We were simply enemy forces to be kept securely behind barbed-wire. Since guarding us in the remote barrens of Silesia was preferable to facing the Russian armies to the east, the *postens* who manned the Sagan gun-towers and plodded the perimeter between them remained ever vigilant. We were impressed with the need to neither surprise nor provoke them.

Oversleeping one morning, I awoke to find my room-mates already well on their way to the twice-daily roll-call parade. Throwing on pants, shirt and shoes I leapt through a hut window in a bee-line rush for the parade site.

'*Verboten,*' a gun-tower guard screamed.

Since the voice was coming from above and behind me, I assumed it was aimed in my direction. But some 1,500 fellow kriegies were now forming up and I had no wish to delay proceedings. I was running fast to join them when the guard called '*Halten-zee.*' Again I ignored him.

'*Halten-zee,*' he told me now. '*Icht gib schiessen.*'

I don't believe I had ever heard those German words before but their meaning was instantly evident. The guard's voice vibrated with a life-and-death tone yet it was resolute. Either I stopped in my tracks or I was going to be a dead kriegy. The heads of 1,500 POWs turning to see my response left no doubt that I was the object of the guard's command.

Stopping was an involuntary response, virtually a reflex action. It was followed by a great wave of embarassment. I was conditioned by movies and the popular press to put my hands up at gun-point. I had done so without a qualm at the first thrust of the Amsterdam SS-man's Luger in my neck. But now under the eyes of 1,500 fellow kriegies, a hands-up posture seemed much too servile a gesture. And I had only been commanded to halt.

Looking back up the tower-guard's angle of sight, I saw a German serviceman more frightened than I. Now we, two, shared the audience attention. Standing in my tracks I had forestalled the guard's need to shoot me. But I had not met the customary stance of surrender. In the endless seconds that followed I offered a compromise gesture. My hands came up from my sides to my hips. So I stood, arms akimbo when the lager-officer Hauptmann Pieber strode forward to take me in charge.

Initially, the Luftwaffe tended to send all airmen kriegies to Luft III. NCO aircrew occupied one compound and officers another. By mid-1943, however, Allied aircrew losses were evident in the growing numbers at the Sagan camp. The NCOs, myself among them, were shipped up the Baltic coast to Luft VI at Heydekrug near the Latvian-Lithuanian border. Four months later a dozen of us, who had advanced from NCO to Warrant Officer rank during our service, were moved back to Luft III. Our captors had found the crown-marked rank of the king's warrant holders as confounding as we did but nobody argued.

Enroute by train from the NCO to officers' camp in the company of four guards, we stopped for more than an hour in a busy Polish rail station. While the guards were distracted a pair of us peeled back the blackout curtains to study the station platform. Slowly a strange group came into view. There were about 30 elderly men and women – the yellow, felt Star of David on their right sleeves identifying them as Jews – flanked by six or eight helmeted German railway police. They were followed by four more Jewish men carrying what appeared to be all of the party's luggage in a single blanket. They were in the care of two more helmeted police.

This singular party of guarded oldsters with their collective luggage in a single blanket was hard to assimilate. Were they homeless refugees being taken to shelter or some undesireables being removed from the Reich's busy rail lines? The answer was not readily available. Only at war's end when we read the accounts of how six million, Jews, Slavic people, gypsies and other enemies of the German Reich had been rounded up for slaughter in the Polish death camps did we realize what we had witnessed. We had seen 0.0005% – five/ one thousandths of one per cent of those six million – being marched to oblivion in the dead of night.

Some months later my status as a commissioned officer – recommended by my squadron commander three days before I was shot down – was conveyed to the Germans. Hauptmann Pieber called me out during morning roll-call to impart the news.

'Herr Silver,' he announced as the ranks of fellow kriegies strained to hear him, 'Through the good offices of the Swiss government, the Protecting Power, and the the International Red Cross, I am instructed by the OKW German High Command to advise you that you were commissioned a pilot officer by His Majesty the King and that you have advanced to flying officer rank. Congratulations, Herr Silver.'

So it was that one of Hermann Goering's racially-élite officers congratulated a Canadian fly-boy – with the pseudo-WASP name of Silver – because I had been commissioned by the King of England to blow holes in the Third Reich.

Had my maternal great-great-grandparents not had the wit to flee Paris and Strasbourg for the American states early in the 19th century and my paternal grand-dad to whisk his family from Fiddler-on-the-Roof country to the Ottawa Valley a dozen years after Confederation, Goering's Nazi pals would have undoubtedly melted me and my latter-day kin down to soap like that party we passed in the night at a Polish rail station in mid-war. When I got to thinking about that I developed a life-long nervous twitch.

The German High Command considered that all aircrew, regardless of rank, warranted special attention to keep us within barbed-wire boundaries. Consequently, Air Force NCO prisoners were not recruited for working parties as Army NCOs frequently were. Regardless of rank Air Force POWs were closely watched for the duration. There was virtually no difference in living conditions between the NCO and Officer compounds in the camps where the Luftwaffe held us.

Unlike the class-stratified RAF and the US Army Air Force, where officer and 'enlisted men' had little contact except on operations, Canadian aircrew were a single breed. On both RAF and RCAF squadrons, Canadian NCO and officer aircrew ate and slept in separate messes but socialized – as we worked – together. A dozen years after the war our ex-Air Force POWs could not remember where we had first met each other – in the offlager or NCO compound. Nor had it ever mattered.

Sociologists might ponder the fact that Supreme Court Judge Ed Houston, a veteran of the Canadian criminal court system, the Hon. Eric Winkler who served as Diefenbaker's Whip in the Commons before joining Premier Bill Davis' cabinet in Ontario as House Leader, Percy (Pinky) Gaum, the gutsy health and welfare minister in George Smith's Nova Scotian government of the late 1960s, and Roger Rousseau, the veteran Canadian diplomat and ambassador to half a dozen countries before Trudeau co-opted him to rescue the 1976 Olympic Games from organizational disaster, were all shot down into kriegydom as NCOs.

What all Air Force kriegies shared was exclusivity – we were the 15 per cent of aircrew who survived – and the restless energy of healthy youth honed to fighting fitness who had been zapped in mid-flight. For two, three or four years we jogged the circuit, booted balls, skated the surface of the fire reservoir and feverishly dug tunnels. We studied and planned post-war careers; read books and wrote them; learned to play civilized games and unsociable musical instruments; argued politics and philosophy. What we didn't do until the Normandy invasion was count time. I don't recall seeing a calendar at Luft III until after 6 June 1944.

We were a singular society – all-male and all equal. Food was always in just short enough supply to replace sex as the dominant preoccupation. For most of our incarceration at Luft III we received the 10-pound weekly Red Cross food parcels with remarkable regularity. The Germans provided fibre-thick bread, potatoes, swedes, cabbage, token bits of unidentified animal flesh, meatless sausage, honey distilled from coal tar and a herbal tea that appeared to have snails and straw in it. We filled up on the German rations and watery soup, generally before bedtime; relied on the Red Cross fare to keep us healthy and used the herbal tea for shaving water.

From experience we can say that food does substitute for sex in the minds of a womanless society – but to a limited extent. There came a time when every red-blooded one of us dreamt of home and saw Canadian womanhood rather than a pound of butter beside the bed.

Since we had all arrived in virtually the same dicey, derring-do way, we made a lousy audience for shot-down stories. I recall the arrival of an Australian fighter-pilot in our room in the summer of 1944. He had, himself, shot down more than a dozen Huns; was well decorated and had been much publicized.

Most new arrivals had a need to ventilate and wind-down. So we would politely feign interest for the first night or two. This beribboned ace was still at it into the second week. By then the other seven of us were taking to our bunks, turning our faces to the wall and sustaining silence when he continued to regale us. For our mutual sanity it was agreed that he would be better living with other newcomers still at an impressionable stage in their lives.

Kriegy life meant sharing minimal living space under maximum stress conditions. Day and night, in fair season and foul, we were thrust together in such close proximity that every skin blemish was counted. Tolerance and an enhanced sense of equality were essential to survival. A sense of humour helped.

We were not all born equal, of course. Becoming aware of that was the first essential. The second was adjusting our inequalities in plus and minus increments. Those with a bit more going for them, as a matter of personal endowment, soon shared their confidence and living skills. The less endowed were quick learners. Thus we tended to avoid first-person pronouns and to share the common wisdom. Once we had seen each other naked to the soul we could no longer cloak our human vulnerability.

'When your room-mates have seen you bare-assed down to your last hairy wart you don't try and slip on a persona with your shirt and pants,' as one ex-kriegy explained. 'We were immunized to bull-shit in our first week in the bag.'

15

Don and Wally

NORTH CAMP, LUFT III, 1943–44

We were all survivors, of course. But some must have felt God's restraining hand on their parachute harness as they neared earth.

Jimmy Abbott was a 21-year-old from Owen Sound flying a Spitfire IX at 26,000 feet over Holland one summer day of 1943. His RAF squadron's job was to 'delouse' a flight of Flying Fortresses as they returned from a German target; that is, to pick the Luftwaffe fighters off the American bombers' tails.

As Jimmy went after two Me-109s, a third enemy plane – the invariable Hun-in-the-sun – raked him with cannon fire. Black smoke and hot oil from shattered piping filled the cockpit. The Spitfire shuddered, its engine sputtered and coughed towards extinction.

Jimmy's reaction was to kick the aircraft into a spin, letting it tumble more than 20,000 feet earthwards. When he tried to pull it out the engine was dead. With reflex response he unclipped his Sutton harness, shrugged off his shoulder straps, jettisoned the hatch cover above his head and flipped the Spitfire on its back to throw himself out.

But he didn't make it. He hit something and lost consciousness. 'Next thing I remember,' he told us as we pounded the circuit at Luft III, 'was the aircraft right side up again and my parachute straps hooked around the radio mast behind the cockpit. I was hanging along the right side of the fuselage. My chute was open – but not open . It was just a thin string of silk trailing under the tail wheel. I tried to lift the chute but couldn't. Then I tried to pry myself up and got my toes so they were touching the tail-plane. Then I tried straddling the fuselage but the slipstream pushed me off again.'

'The aircraft was at sort of an approach angle and the ground was looming up. God must have had full control,' he explained. 'I saw the horizon disappear under the wing, a bunch of trees, a house. This is the big moment, I thought. Dying doesn't seem so bad.'

He awoke in a hospital bed with bits of cannon shell in his leg and shoulder. Eye-witnesses told him they had seen his Spitfire plough into the ground and explode in flame. Still tied to its side by his harness, Jimmy Abbott was cut free by a fearless rescuer. He and his German captors came to the reluctant conclusion that as as he slid back along the side of the

141

Spitfire he had counterbalanced the diving aircraft – weighing its tail down until it crash-landed from almost level flight.

It was a very iffy explanation but none of his fellow printers at the Owen Sound *Sun-Times* post-war ever came up with a better one. Nor could they guess what happened one Christmas Eve a dozen years later when Jimmy's car skidded on an icy stretch of road and killed him.

Don Morrison was posted to Canadian fighter squadron 401 in November 1941, the week of his 20th birthday. When he was shot down a *second* time, exactly a year later, he had destroyed seven Luftwaffe fighter 'planes and was credited with 'probably' knocking off another six. The first time Don baled out was into the Channel during the Canadian Army raid on Dieppe. Plucked from his dinghy by an air-sea rescue launch he helped to fish other survivors from the drink. The second time he was shot down he left a shattered leg in his burning Spitfire.

A log entry 10 days after joining 401 Squadron notes that 'F/Lt Jeep Neal and self jumped some Me-109s. Lots of fun. 3 probables and one damaged.' Morrison shared one of the probables with his flight commander. Four days later he was credited with one and 'probably' two Focke-Wolfe 190. Two weeks after that he shot down a Me-109F and damaged another.

He remembers the February day the German pocket battleships *Scharnhorst* and *Gneisneau* escaped from the Channel under a low blanket of cloud. 'We spotted a battle convoy as we broke cloud. We couldn't miss it. We were flying between two battleships. 'Don't you think we're getting a little close,' I suggested to Jeep Neal.'

'Don't worry, they're ours,' the C/O assured.

'But they weren't ours,' Morrison recalls. 'The fireworks those two German battleships displayed were the most impressive I've ever seen.' Later that day he shared destruction of a Me-109F with another 401 pilot. A few days later he was credited with yet another FW-109 probable.

In May Don was flying yellow four position – the tail-end Charlie of a four-plane formation. 'I was the last man out over the French coast when a Me-109F dived out of the sun at us. There was a loud explosion on my tail and the Spitfire was thrown into a sudden, violent climb. I saw the 109 break and dive and I rolled over to follow him. As soon as I built up speed my aircraft nosed up again very violently and I realized that my tail plane had been damaged by a cannon shell. It was forcing the aircraft upwards where I didn't want to go. There were a lot more Me-109s up there so I kept rolling and diving. By the time I had the whole sky to myself I looked for some of the air-sea rescue boats we had spotted on the way out.' But they had disappeared.

Squadron records relate that Morrison nursed the Spitfire 20 miles back to Shoreham on the Channel coast. 'I decided on a wheels-up landing because I had to push the control column forward with my feet to get the nose down,' he vividly remembers. 'We landed with little extra damage except a broken propeller but I wondered how Jeep Neal would feel about it. It was his new aircraft that I was flying.'

In June he shared another FW-190 destroyed with a squadron mate; was awarded the DFM – 'quite a surprise' – and he was commissioned. The following month he led 401 Yellow Section on sweeps that shot up aircraft and trains in occupied France. One August day he passed out for several minutes at 22,000 feet when his oxygen line blocked. Battered against the aircraft interior as it fell out of control, he regained consciousness to find himself dangerously close to ground.

Ten days after that he shot down a drifting barrage balloon over Dover in the morning. That afternoon while escorting USAAF Flying Fortresses on their first raid of the war, his flight encountered 'lots of FW-190s' off the French coast. 'It was a terrific scrap. I got off two squirts but there was no time to see results,' his log entry noted. The flight claimed one aircraft destroyed and four 'probables.' Of his three flight members one was killed, another was missing, a third wounded.

Two days later he was in the thick of the air battle over Dieppe as Canadians soldiers fought an impossible assignment on the beach. Morrison was about to get his fifth confirmed kill and wreck his own aircraft in the process. 'As I closed to about 25 yards, I opened up with a two-second burst of cannon fire. As both the enemy aircraft and I went into thin cloud he exploded. Suddenly my windshield and hood were covered with oil and there was the clatter of debris striking my aircraft. I imagine it punctured my radiators. The engine started to cough and the aircraft shuddered violently.'

Don looked across the Channel towards their base at Lympne in Kent and realized he would never make it. 'We had heard that ditching the aircraft in the sea was rarely successful. Paddy Finucane had been killed just a couple of months earlier when he tried. So I decided to bale out. I pulled up but the engine cut completely and I only managed to reach about 2000 feet. I took off my helmet, undid my safety straps and tried twice to jettison the escape hood. I trimmed the aircraft fully nose down and kicked the stick forward expecting to be shot out like a watermelon seed. Unfortunately, my parachute pack caught on the hatch hood and suddenly I was hanging out of the cockpit from my hips, looking down over the Spitfire nose at the Channel which was coming towards me very quickly.'

'A really big kick popped me out. My forehead clipped the radio mast and I rolled over backwards as I pulled the ripcord. The chute opened just before my feet hit the water. As I came to the surface I released the parachute, inflated the dinghy and climbed in.' Two squadron mates circling to mark his position remember him waving that he was okay. A third 401 pilot alerted the air-sea rescue service.

Morrison was picked up by rescue boat HSL-177, 17 miles off Dieppe. It was just after 11am. He was given dry clothes and treated for a cut over one eye. 'They wanted me to stay in a sick-bay bunk but there was just too much going on. I watched the action from the bridge,' he says.

In a post-war article he described the fighting between German bombers and the naval convoy returning from Dieppe and how the crews of the air-sea rescue launches, including HSL 177, plucked survivors from the sea. 'Fuel and ammunition were exploding around them and the men were screaming with pain. They all seemed to be badly wounded and several of us dived overboard to help lift them up the boarding nets. We picked up 14 survivors,' he reported.

The official account is that 'A few minutes after being picked up in the Channel, Morrison plunged overboard and rescued a man from certain death by drowning. During the remainder of the day he manned a machine gun on the rescue launch.'

The Spitfire that replaced the one lost at Dieppe was Don Morrison's eighth. He named it for his fiancee, *Jean VIII*. Two months later it was succeeded by *Jean IX*. In the interim he had destroyed another FW-190 and been credited with the probable destruction of three other enemy fighters. One encounter in late August was memorable. 'Escorted 12 Fortresses to France. Squadron engaged by 50-plus (enemy planes). Terrific scrap. Four probables and two damaged,' he told his log book. One of the probables went to Morrison's credit.

On the morning of 8 November 1942, a dozen Squadron 401 pilots were briefed to provide cover for 36 Flying Fortresses making an attack on the locomotive works at Lille. Morrison led the four-plane Yellow Section that escorted the bombers. Whether his oxygen supply failed or the shock of near fatal injuries wiped the slate of his memory clean, he only knows what others witnessed.

As the squadron intelligence record described events, 'F/L Morrison reported that he saw two FW-190s behind and below the bombers and led his section to attack.' Morrison and his wingman, P/O Doug Manley became separated from the other pair. A few moments later 'Yellow-4 saw one FW-190 going down in flames which he thinks was shot down by Morrison and Manley.

'Yellow-3 and 4 then saw six aircraft 2,000 feet above them and they began to climb when the six aircraft dove past in front of them. They were identified as two FW-190s chased by two Spitfires, who were in turn chased by two more FW-190s. The fifth aircraft, a FW-190, was seen to fire on one of the Spitfires which began a spiral dive and descended in smoke. The other Spitfire was not seen again. Ten of our aircraft landed safely at Kenley at 1300 hours but Yellow-1 and 2, F/L Morrison and P/O Manley are missing.' In fact, Manley was killed as he tried to crash-land his aircraft. Morrison and Manley were jointly credited with a FW-190 destroyed.

All Don knows is that 'I was shot down between St Omer and Calais, leaving my leg in the plane as I baled out.' Shock mercifully blanked out the details. Baling out and pulling the rip cord was a conditioned reflex.

As he put it in a kriegy postcard from Germany to Jeep Neal: 'Greetings from a jail-bird. I woke up in a Luftwaffe hospital 10 days later and actually wasn't feeling too well. But the German doctors had apparently done a pretty good job of surgery.'

Two French farmers had wrapped the flier with the shattered stump of his left leg in his parachute, used a ladder as a stretcher and taken him across a small stream to German soldiers billeted nearby. They, in turn, had applied a tourniquet, commandeered a truck and rushed him to hospital. 'The first thing I remember when I regained consciousness was a German guard telling me my leg was kaput. I had had enough high school German to realize what he was saying and my reaction was better a leg than my head.

'A couple of days later I awoke again to find a German doctor wielding a pair of giant pliers to amputate the big toe on my right foot. It had been burned beyond repair. They had given me no anaesthesia, not even a painkiller. But by then I seemed to be beyond shock, pain or emotion,' Don recalled.

The first POW he talked with in Luft III was Wally Floody. To prevent the Germans from planting a phoney kriegy among us every new arrival was identified and vouched for by someone who had been with him in training or on a squadron. Nearly three years earlier Don Morrison and Clarke Wallace Chant Floody were among half a dozen young Canadians processed from civilian life into the RCAF at a Toronto recruiting office. Their respective dog-tags were numbered R80521 and R80527.

Morrison, lightly-built and medium height, was just short of his 19th birthday when they were sworn in. 'I didn't drive a car. I was still making drug-store deliveries on my bicycle when I graduated from high school that spring,' he admits. Within a year he had mastered Tiger Moths and Harvard trainers and the early 'Marks' of the still evolving Spitfire. In the next half year he went from sergeant-pilot to beribboned flight-lieutenant commanding one of 401 Squadron's two flights.

Floody, six-feet four-inches before he donned football boots or miner's gear, was a 22-year-old survivor of hard times and six months married on the October 1940 day that he and Morrison were enlisted. In mid-Depression Floody had quit high school a month or two before his final exams to go north to work in Kirkland Lake gold-mines. He was working on an Alberta ranch when war was declared.

The next day Wally and a pal headed back east to enlist. They persuaded a train crew to let them ride in the tender and shovel coal for their passage. 'It was the first time I ever rode in style,' Wally would recall. Between stints as a Kirkland Lake gold-mine worker and an Albertan ranch-hand, he rode box-cars (and the stabilizer rods beneath them) to get a Depression-era view of America. He had ridden the rods to California and Mexico, a year earlier.

'When we were posted to Brandon in October 1940 I had never been west of Windsor, Ontario,' Morrison observes. 'Wally was a well-seasoned traveller. He was inches taller than any of us and he could bellow from a gargantuan chest. In his hurry to get to war he found that shouting in an authoritative manner opened the doors ahead.'

Flooded with aircrew applicants and expanding airfield facilities as fast as men and material could be organized, the British Commonwealth Air Training Plan was still moving into high gear in the fall of 1940. They were certainly not inclined to recruit married men without flying experience but Floody had pitched his voice to be heard while modulating it just below an aggressive tone.

In Brandon, the recruits were shuffled off to do six to eight weeks guard duty pending the opening of new training facilities. All except Floody. 'Wally claimed he had had plenty of military indoctrination in a high-school cadet corps. Uttered loud and clear from six-foot altitude, his claim was accepted. So he skipped toting a rifle around an airfield perimeter in the depths of Western Canadian winter and wound up in pilot training a month or two ahead of the rest of us,' Morrison notes. 'Floody had arrived on 401 Squadron and been shot-down on his first operation more than a month before I got to the station.'

In the two years since they had been sworn in at Toronto, Morrison had become – in the words of 401 Squadron commander Keith Hodson – 'probably the best known of any pilot here and a legend throughout the RCAF overseas. His rise was spectacular but well-deserved.'

Floody had flown quickly into captivity where he would dig his way to fame. In the spring of 1943 when some 1,200 officer POWs were moved into the new North Compound at Luft III, *Big-X* Roger Bushell commissioned Wally Floody to engineer three potential tunnels – *Tom*, *Dick* and *Harry*.

'Because I had worked for a mining company and was a commissioned officer, the RAF types assumed I must have been a mining engineer with lots of experience when I joined up,' Wally explained. 'In fact, I had gone straight from high school to the gold-mines back home where I worked on the surface. I was never underground until we started to dig tunnels in the camp. In any case there was a helluva difference between drilling for gold in Northern Ontario rock and digging through sand in Silesia. But I wanted out of the bag and I wasn't going to argue with anyone about my lack of tunnelling expertise.'

Floody's stature had brought him ready recognition for athletic performance during high school days. He had neither sought nor achieved academic honours. Now half a dozen years since most of us had forgotten the terminology of higher mathematics, Floody was pacing the compound circuit to cast covert glances at trignometric angles; algebraically estimating horizontal distances beyond the barbed-wire on basis of known heights within it.

Size was more a hindrance than help when he squeezed his frame into a Spitfire cockpit. When he began digging tunnels he was a mere 175 pounds. He had lost a fifth of that weight when Wings Day 'grounded' him, so to speak. They had already hauled Wally out of suffocating sand-falls on several occasions when Wings, as the Senior British Officer in North Compound, decided that a live Floody directing tunnelling from the surface was better than an emaciated digger prematurely buried in Sagan sand.

The tunnel-master took it all in stride. 'I got a little too far in advance of the shoring crew and it seemed that a couple of hundred tons of sand dropped on top of me,' he recounted. 'So with much hollering on my part they pulled me back a little greyer, wiser and quite a bit more cautious the next time I went down.'

That was just one occasion. During earlier efforts in East Camp Floody had been trapped under half a ton of sand. Fortunately his face was pressed against the edge of the shaft of any earlier tunnel. Stale air sustained him for the hour it took to dig him out.

The shafts of the three tunnels were almost complete when Floody and two digging mates began excavating the three work-rooms where they would begin the long horizontal stretch for freedom. The crack of a bed-board – one of the quarter-inch-thick boards that shored up the loose sand – signalled a break near the top of the shaft. As sand poured down it twisted the frames that lined the sides of the shaft releasing more and more dirt. Floody's companions climbed clear but he was pinned waist deep in the sand. They were just able to haul him clear before the roof literally fell in.

In June 1943 Wally was hauled back by his ankles when the tunnel roof of *Tom* collapsed. The following day he was buried again but this time a make-shift miner's lamp was tipped over. By the time he was hauled clear, hot fat that fuelled the lamp had blistered his thigh. But *Tom* was 105 feet long at this point and he was soon back lengthening it.

When the Germans discovered *Tom* in the autumn of 1943, Roger Bushell ordered the other two tunnels closed down to reinforce the German security chief's conviction that he had finally frustrated escape efforts in North Camp. In January 1944 Big-X had work resume on *Harry*. Wally was setting the pace for his digging crews by clearing up to 12 feet of sandy soil from the tunnel face each day. Then he was buried again. Once more he was rescued from suffocation.

A few days later a sand-filled metal jug fell from the trap edge and hit his head a glancing blow. A direct hit would have split his skull. It was then that Wings Day grounded him. Ten days before the Great Escape, Floody and two other key players were purged to the Belaria camp. So he was not among the 76 who got out – nor the 50 who were shot when recaptured.

On the spring day of 1944 when German goons swept into North Camp to collar them Floody refused to accept the belated reality that for him, the war was over. When word of the tunnel break reached the Belaria compound half a dozen miles down the road, Wally was overwhelmed by the unprecedented success of the Great Escape that he had engineered and the realization that he was not among the 76 who had got clear of Luft III. When he learned that three had got back to Britain while 50 of the 73 others had been shot on Hitler's orders, he experienced the survivor-guilt reaction common to Air Force kriegies – 'Why wasn't I shot, too?'

'Was the effort really worth it?' he would be asked again and again in the post-war years.

'People who asked that were thinking in terms of getting just three of our guys back. If that had been the purpose I don't think I would have been interested in tunnelling,' he would tell them. 'We knew we were never going to get a lot of kriegies back to fight again. Our purpose, as Bushell constantly reminded us, was to continually harass our captors and tie down as many of them as possible. When news of the Luft III tunnel broke, every German in uniform was called back from leave. It was the first time this had happened since the war began. Every train in the country was stopped and searched. Every 15 minutes German radio announced that *terrorfliegers*, as they called us, were running loose in the Third Reich.

'More than 60,000 Luftwaffe, Army, Gestapo and SS men were assigned to recapture the RAF escapees from Luft III. The slowdown we caused to the German economy by that one tunnel break was equivalent to dropping a couple of divisions of paratroopers in Occupied Europe. It was enough to panic Hitler into demanding the wholesale slaughter of the recaptured prisoners.'

Don Morrison was among a small group of amputees and severely-wounded POWs repatriated in the fall of 1943. He was home for Christmas and a month later he married his high-school sweetheart, Jean. He spent the last year and a half of the war as a RCAF recruiter and morale builder; one of the select few articulate heroes whom the government would turn loose to crank up war-weary Canadian society.

By war's end Morrison had taken his 'tin leg' in stride, neither admitting nor accommodating a handicap. As a young father, he bounced his son and daughter on his 'good' knee, discarding the other leg at the pool-side to join them in swimming. When family income allowed, Don resumed week-end flying. Nearly half a century since he left one leg in a burning Spitfire his other one still holds a steady foot on the rudder bar.

For nearly 15 years Air Canada's chief trouble-shooter and problem-solver at Toronto International Airport was a moon-faced guy with a disarming smile, no-flap manner, corny jokes and a sailor's gait. Don Morrison still leans into his stride, feeling his way with the four-toed foot that Luftwaffe physicians salvaged from awesome burns. He is a great believer in utilizing available resources for maximum effort.

In recent years he has headed the loose-knit ex-Air Force POW Association in Canada, helped to keep the Fighter Pilots' Association alive and served on the National Council of Veteran Associations. The Council named Morrison the first recipient of their service award in 1987. It recognized the lead role he had played in persuading former Veterans Affairs Minister George Hees to make Canadian veteran benefits the best in the world.

For Wally Floody the last year of World War II was anti-climatic. It took him those dozen months to wind-down. Then he was ready to celebrate survival. For the next 45 years he never let any of us within the kriegy community forget that we had survived long odds; that among wartime fly-boys we were the one-in-seven who came home. 'Every day of living has been a bonus,' Wally would remind us. And to assure our continued celebration of survival he organized the Air Force kriegies' organization.

Pressed to describe his wartime tunnelling expertise, he called it 'creative engineering – you pick the most adaptive people, dig in the most suitable site and learn from experience. Like realtors and restaurant proprietors we learned that location was everything.' Post-war his sense of location and timing fell short of infallible. For three post-war years he tried manufacturing power lawn-mowers in Britain where a mass market of grassed front and back-yards failed to materialize.

Back home in Canada he and radio announcer Herb May operated a two-plane air service out of Toronto Island Airport, flying as far afield as northern Ontario to stunt fly and tote cameras as Rochelle Hudson and Jack Larue starred in *Bush Pilot*. The stars flickered fitfully in that picture and Floody and May went on to other things. A decade later Wally was recruited by Hollywood producer John Sturgis to provide technical advice on filming Paul Brickhill's story of *The Great Escape*.

The picture was filmed in and around Munich. For about a month in the summer of 1962 Wally worked on location to assure the film's authenticity. He was persuasive because, except for the finale, the picture was impeccably accurate. Brickhill would later lament that 'Back in Sydney (Australia) I watched Steve McQueen riding into the sunset on his bloody motorbike and I went out and got sloshed.' But Floody pragmatically accepts that cowboy bike ride into the sunset. 'Steve McQueen made the picture commercial. That scene helped make money for Paul.'

Back in Toronto Wally involved scores of ex-POWs in the premiere hoopla that launched the movie. Box office receipts from the first night's performance went to the ex-Air Force POW Association who put it to philanthropic use. This was the start of a group which within a few post-war years became a tight-knit community of about a thousand Canadian families. For a generation periodic reunions in Canada and Britain were planned in Floody's Bay Street offices or frequently as he hosted the boys to a round at Merry Mary's bar in the Royal York Hotel.

Keeping the ex-flyboy POWs and their kin together became much more than a pastime for Wally and Betty Floody. For two years their house was home to George Harsh in his wheel-chair. The erudite American who looked like Dean Acheson emerging from Roosevelt's cabinet and had headed the security force for *The Great Escape* shot but failed to kill himself one Christmas Eve. George never walked again but was taken everywhere by the Floodys. In other years Wings Day was a frequent visitor flying in unannounced from Britain to make the Floody home the base of his North American adventures.

In the 1980s Floody and Morrison cut a wide arc visiting incapacitated and bed-ridden kriegies, assuring that all who were ambulatory attended the ex-POW reunions; that all ex-flyboys and their kin were getting by.

By the summer of 1989 nearly a half-century's survival celebration had etched deep into Wally Floody's liver. The indefatigable champion of Canadian fly-boys was grounded in an invalid chair. For the last few weeks Don Morrison arranged for a half dozen of us to lunch each Friday with Wally in his Toronto apartment.

The conversation thinned. Not that we had run out of words but they were no longer necessary among us. For a lifetime Wally had practised good fellowship. As he slipped away he expected us to carry it on.

16

Bader, Bushell & Wings

LUFT III, NORTH CAMP, 1942–44

Douglas Bader, the most illustrious kriegie of us all, despised every moment of his three years and nine months in the bag. It was the only time in his life when his will was thwarted, his movements curbed. He resisted every restriction, every hour of his captivity. When we were liberated he flushed the POW experience irrevocably from his mind. It was something so anomalous to his self-determination he could never admit it had happened.

A privileged Brit, Douglas Robert Steuart Bader was readily accepted by the RAF for pilot training at Cranwell in 1928. Thus he joined the young airborne knights whom Britain, France and Germany were preparing for tournament. He soloed before his 19th birthday and celebrated his 21st at 23 Squadron, Kenley where he was picked by C-Flight commander Harry Day for the RAF's famed aerobatic team.

Wing Commander Day, Flying Officers Bader and Geoffrey Stephenson made up the aerobatic team that starred at Hendon Air Show in 1931. All three flew into captivity a dozen years later. Wings Day honed the team's performance to execute five synchronised aerobatic routines with near perfection. Anything less would have sent them hurtling into fatal collision.

Aerobatics were prohibited below 2,000 feet but Bader was inclined to do slow rolls at 50 feet. The trick was to keep the Bulldog engine purring as you rolled the plane over. When another pilot tried stunting at low altitude and wrote himself off, Wings Day told Bader and the others: 'Fighting area regulations say that you must not aerobat below 2,000 feet. Well, you know my views about some regulations. They're written for the obedience of fools and the guidance of wise men. Now if you're going to aerobat below 2,000 feet, first of all – don't. If you decide to ignore my advice don't do it where any senior officers can see you and remember three things. First, make up your mind exactly what you're going to do, then get properly settled down and then get your speed right so you don't spin off or lose height. The only thing you have to worry about then is if your engine stops. If it stops – you're dead. But if you're going to start worrying about that then stop flying anyway.'

The advice seemed a bit ambiguous. But in November when Bader was spotted doing low-level aerobatics and 'beating-up' the airfield, Wings hauled him in and warned him to stop showing off. Paul Brickhill – who first met both Bader and Wings Day at Luft III – made a canny assessment in *Reach for the Sky*. 'Day wondered whether perhaps he should have slapped Bader down harder. He was getting into a dangerous phase of over-confidence which comes to many pilots after a year or two. With his Hendon success on top of a volatile nature he was too outspoken. Day recognised it more as coltish, super-vitality and that under it lay sensitivity. Perhaps he could be slapped down too much. You could not force him; he would only become stubborn.'

Two weeks after Day's admonition, in mid-December 1931, Bader and two other pilots flew to visit RAF colleagues at another field. As they prepared to return to Kenley someone suggested that Bader 'perform' on take-off. When he declined, someone else claimed he was 'windy.' Tight-lipped and flushed with anger, he stalked towards his 'plane.

They watched as the Bulldog swept just over the boundary fence, rocking a little in low thermal currents, the engine screaming at full output. The nose lifted slightly then the 'plane began rolling to starboard. As he had done countless times before he had the stick well over and the top rudder applied to hold the nose up as she came round. Then the stick went forward to keep the aircraft up. Now he was throttling back to keep the engine from flooding as she rolled upside down.

Despite the oft-practised manoeuvre, Bader sensed that the Bulldog was dropping. He was desperately bringing her round when the port wing-tip brushed the grass. There was a spurt of flying turf, the propeller and cowling shattered, the engine tore loose and the aircraft seemed to cartwheel and crumple behind it.

At Royal Berkshire Hospital in Reading they amputated Bader's right leg just above his smashed knee. A couple of days later he lost his gangrenous left leg six inches below the knee. Subsequent surgery trimmed an inch or two more from the stumps.

Douglas Bader had brought an exceptional physique and an uncanny will into the Royal Air Force. On the RAF boxing team he won 19 of 20 fights by knockouts; he was a star at rugger and relaxed at cricket. On the playing field or in the air he applied an incredible mix of energy, concentration and self-confidence. He expected to win. It never occurred to him that he could be defeated by man or circumstance. His wilfullness approached megalomania. Within weeks of losing both legs he was learning to use artificial ones – not just for walking but testing them on the brake and clutch pedals of his MG coupe.

Even his well-placed connections and egocentric drive could not keep him in the peacetime RAF, however. By summer he was out of the service on full pension. His adjustment to a civilian desk job with an oil company must have been difficult. But by then he was married to Thelma Edwards who became the lifetime arbiter of what he was to conquer or endure.

In the spring of 1939 when Hitler began his march on Armageddon at the Czechoslovakian border, Bader began to press his Old Boy connections to get back in the air. 'I am afraid that during peace-time it is not possible for me to permit you to enter a flying class of the reserve,' Air Marshal Sir Charles Portal replied. 'But you can rest assured that if war came we would almost certainly be only too glad of your service in a flying capacity after a short time if the doctors agreed.'

As war clouds thickened Bader banged harder on the RAF door. In October he was summoned by his old Cranwell commandant, Air Vice-Marshal Halahan who welcomed him back for ground duties. 'It's only a flying job I want, sir. I'm not interested in anything else,' Bader insisted.

Wordlessly Halahan sent him for a medical examination with a confidential note to the examiner. 'I have known this officer since he was a cadet at Cranwell. He's the type we want. If he is fit, apart from his legs, I suggest you give him A.1.B category and leave it to Central Flying School to assess his flying capabilities.'

At the end of November – eight years since he lost his legs – Bader soloed again. By January he had advanced to flying Hurricanes. A month later he was practising formation flying in 19 Squadron Spitfires. A fortnight after that he was posted as flight-lieutenant and flight commander to 222 Squadron. In that capacity he helped provide air cover for the Dunkirk evacuation. In mid-June acting Squadron Leader Bader was named commanding officer of the all-Canadian 242 Squadron.

The Canadians had chalked up their share of Luftwaffe kills but were badly demoralized by inadequate leadership prior to Bader's arrival. He seemed hardly the Brit to win colonial goodwill but the Canadian pilots and their stiff-necked commander quickly developed a rapport based on mutual respect for each other's flying skills. 'He left no one unmoved; they either half-worshipped or they detested him,' Brickhill said.

Within a month of his arrival Bader had, himself, shot down a Dornier. By the end of September the war's only double-amputee flyer had 11 destroyed enemy aircraft confirmed. Early in 1941 Bader persuaded his Fighter Command bosses to let him merge several squadrons' aircraft into co-ordinated sweeps across the Channel. So he became Fighter Command's first wing leader.

As a Wing Commander operating from 616 Squadron at Tangmere, he led 100 Spitfires escorting Blenheim bombers in a 'Circus' sweep of the Cherbourg peninsula. On 2 July he shot down another Me-109. It was his twelfth confirmed kill and it won him a bar to his DSO.

Five weeks later it was an Me-109 that cut Bader's Spitfire in two just south of Le Touquet. One leg had been trapped as the Spitfire was smashed. Bader hastily unlaced it to bale out. The artificial limb was recovered and returned to him in hospital at St Omer. Bader soon put it back in service. Three nights after his capture he slid down knotted bedsheets for 40 feet from his hospital room. Escorted by a friendly Frenchman, he walked 40 minutes on his bunged-up legs to a hiding place in a barn. Bayonet-probing soldiers winkled him out of the straw the following morning.

Bader was sent to Offlag VIB at Warburg and for the next year and a half he led fellow POWs in a concerted programme of 'goon-baiting.' At a decided disadvantage himself, as far as escape was concerned, he never abandoned hope he could somehow get away. Meanwhile, he directed his restless energy at keeping the Germans on edge. Brickhill has described how 'Bader goaded his captors into drawing their pistols and then disarmed them by pricking their ire with maddening charm and last-minute surrender.'

In the spring of 1942, the Offlag VIB kriegies were moved from Warburg to Sagan where they took over one of the six huts forming the nucleus of Luft III's first officer compound. The Great Escape was still two years ahead but Bader's old flight-commander and aerobatics leader Wings Day had a highly organized programme underway. It had two objectives – to feed intelligence information back to Britain through the coded letters of nearly one hundred kriegies and to stage escape attempts that would tie down the maximum Luftwaffe manpower in guarding us.

Day's program was based on the integrated efforts of a highly disciplined kriegy population who never made waves without reason. Bader's egocentric goon-baiting kept our captors edgy, vigilant and reactive to no purpose. At the same time he was convinced he could still walk to freedom if he once got clear of the camp. The Luft III escape committee quickly vetoed Bader's one-man escape schemes and Wings Day confirmed their decisions.

Now in the summer of 1942 the legless air ace who had helped to fulfil Britain's war-weary need for heroic figures in Battle of Britain days was misplaced in the ranks of his fellow officers at Sagan. Squadron Leader Roger Bushell, the Big-X director of escape operations, Wally Floody responsible for driving three tunnels under the Germans' noses and George Harsh, charged with keeping the tunnelling secure from discovery, were unimpressed with Bader's prima-donna theatrics. They were appalled by the reaction it provoked in our captors.

Staff Sergeant Herman Glemnitz, in charge of the blue-overalled guards constantly ferreting beneath the huts, poking in refuse piles and stalking clues to escape plans, was half-convinced that escape was impossible from the new compounds at Luft III. From the outset Roger Bushell sought to reinforce Glemnitz's confidence; to keep him relaxed. Now Bader's wilful goon-baiting was provoking an angry response. Incensed, the ferrets were more determined than ever to uproot kriegy escape plans.

As Senior British Officer, Wing Commander Day had assessed the kriegy potential during their first year at Dulag Luft. When the Luftwaffe began to concentrate Air Force prisoners at Luft III, he realized the opportunity to direct our energies into a meaningful assault on the German war effort. As Sydney Smith put it in *Wings Day*, 'He felt the time had come to change into higher gear; to interpret the motives for escape, intelligence and security organization in terms of war effort rather than as a fairly safe game with the International Red Cross as referee. Just because they had brushed with death and fallen into enemy hands, prisoners-of-war should not be thought of as semi-neutrals.'

Wings, himself, had engineered short-lived escapes in company with one or two other kriegies. While they relieved frustration and gave a brief view of the German wartime scene, he realized these singular efforts were inconsequential. Now, he told new kriegies coming into the camp: 'A mass escape – more than five men at a time as far as the Germans are concerned – mobilizes thousands of police, troops and civilian volunteers. Escape activities pin down a maximum number of guards who might otherwise be at the front and a number of officers and NCOs who could certainly serve Hitler more profitably if they were free to do so. Escape alarms create panic and despondency among the civil population.'

When Roger Bushell and Wally Floody cited the impact of Bader's goon-baiting on the security essential to mass-escape tunnelling, Wings Day readily agreed. He had admired the legless flyer's wilful efforts but there was no way to accommodate them at Luft III. Within a matter of months the Germans, themselves, decided that Bader should be moved to hospitalized quarters in the vast VIIIB camp for Army POWs at Lamsdorf. It was a decision in which Wings Day and the German commandant concurred.

Bader reacted badly. He threatened to throw himself into the water-filled, fire-fighting reservoir and let the Germans try to fish him out. The Senior British Officer at this point was Group Captain Massey, a middle-aged Canadian who had been shot down midway through his second war. 'There's one thing we might consider,' he told Bader now. 'It only needs a spark to start an incident and someone may be shot.' Bader finally went quietly and Luft III officer POWs returned to their collective and disciplined efforts.

'Wings', as he would always be known to fellow kriegies, was the last of the Edwardians. Edward VII had set the style for that restless breed of Englishman who went out in the mid-day sun to show the flag at the

155

corners of the world. Wings Day's grandfather formed an army for the White Rajah of Sarawak. Wing's father was the Rajah's top man in that kingdom of the China Seas. Wings was born there two years before the century ended.

Melville, as his mother called him, came out of Borneo into an English public school speaking fluent Malaysian but clueless on a cricket pitch. Not too ruggedly structured, he still managed to become a top school cricketer and was headed for the rugby team when a classmate accidentally discharged a blank cartridge wad into his back during cadet manoeuvres. This was indicative. The man we knew in the bag was never a bystander; if a shot was fired Wings was not inclined to step aside.

He was 18 and still growing when he joined the HMS *Britannia* as a Royal Marines second lieutenant. They called him the 'boy sprout' and he had bloomed seven inches taller by the time *Britannia* was torpedoed off Gibraltar. The growing boy rescued two marines from the blazing lower decks to win the Albert Medal.

For half a dozen post-war years Marine Lieutenant Day escorted Royalty to India, the Prince of Wales to Belgium. There was a touch of action at Smyrna where he helped evacuate Greeks from Turkish massacre and at Memel where the British fleet settled the Lithuanians down at League of Nations request. Wings was 26 when he became airborne with the Fleet Air Arm; 29 when he headed the RAF aerobatic team at Hendon Air Show. In those same three years, romanticist Flight Lieutenant Day enjoyed the first two of his marriages and fathered the first of his two daughters.

Those were the days when Britain, France and Germany stretched their fledgling wings in Schneider Cup races, in aerobatic display at international air shows and in growing flying-club memberships. Flight Lieutenant Day was the bird to set the pace. There was the memorable fly-past watched by the Royal Family in which he led the aerobatic team *under* London Bridge. The Queen reputedly was not amused.

Forty-five years later Group Captain Day, OBE revisited Buckingham Palace to trade in his Albert Medal for the updated George Cross. Slightly scarred from a car prang two days earlier, he arrived impeccable and undaunted. This time he was gentler on royal sensibilities. When the Queen showed concern for his bandaged forehead, Wings reassured her, 'It is nothing, madam, but evidence of my haste to get here.'

Squadron Leader Day was officer commanding an advanced training squadron of Furies, Harts and Ansons in 1939. At 41 years of age he was destined for a staff job with Bomber Command when War Orders were issued. He was otherwise inclined and persuasive. Two months before war's outbreak Wing Commander Day took over a strategic reconnaissance squadron of Blenheims. The war was five weeks old when he led them on their first operation over France. Three Me-109 pilots claimed a share in shooting him down. Had they known the ground war he would wage in five years and seven months as a kriegy, they would not have boasted about bagging him.

His first escape from Dulag Luft was short-lived but instructive. At Barth he organized escape operations, instituting 'ghosting' to keep roll-calls untallied and the 'duty pilot' stooge routine that beset the besetters. More than a hundred tunnels riddled Barth before he was moved to Sagan where the first Luft III compounds were opened in April 1942. Within weeks Wings tried walking through the compound gates in German NCO guise but was recognized. In the punishment cell he and another prisoner cut through the iron bars. That got them purged to the satellite camp at Schubin.

At Luft III Wings left a firmly established X-organization in Roger Bushell's hands. Big-X was a prominent British barrister in his early thirties when he went to war with the RAF in 1939. He was shot down early in the game and within weeks had repolished his French and German language skills to wartime intelligence demands. A skiing accident years earlier had given his right eye a sinister cast. Roger learned to offset it with a studied smile. He could charm his German captors. Unlike Bader, he did so consistently. Big-X possessed a profound hate for Nazi Germany which he sustained at fever pitch behind a benign mask.

He was a polished actor, beaming affably at our Luftwaffe captors. Only if you caught the glint of his ski-scarred eye might you wonder if he was ever angered. In fact, his hatred of the Third Reich burned white hot. In the summer of 1942 Bushell was ushered into Luft III offlager wearing a civilian suit which his captors had incredibly let him keep. Six months earlier while being moved from Barth to another camp he had sawed through the floor of a cattle truck.

In their half year's freedom he and a Czech kriegy had travelled far afield. They were caught in Prague in a round-up that followed the shooting of Gauleiter Reinhardt Heydrich. The Nazi preoccupation with finding Heydrich's assassins may have spared the two escaped POWs. When Bushell name-dropped associates of Goering he had encountered on Swiss skiing jaunts pre-war, his captors returned him to Luftwaffe custody. He was not the sort of chap I would have wanted wandering around my country in wartime if he was not on our side.

In March 1943 Wings Day was the last of 33 kriegies through a 150-foot tunnel from the toilets at Schubin. He had walked two days through Poland when he was pitchforked to wakefulness in a barn loft. That escape got the Nazi police chief at Posen shot; the camp commandant and his security officer were suspended. 4,000 German troops were diverted to search duties for a week. Wings had at last tasted blood.

Purged back to Sagan – to the newly occupied North Compound – Wings found that Roger Bushell had not been idle. *Tom, Dick* and *Harry* tunnels were well underway. Under Wings and Bushell's combined direction *Harry* was completed in March 1944. It funnelled 76 kriegies for 348 feet from hut 104 under the camp prison building and a roadway to the edge of a woods. This was The Great Escape.

Wings and his travelling companion, Polish Air Force fighter pilot Peter Tobolski made it through Berlin to a French workers' barracks on the Baltic coast within sight of Swedish-bound ships where they were caught. Purple-faced with rage and clutching Wing's Hungarian identity card, a German police colonel advanced screaming invective. By this time Wings had polished a disarming tactic in the face of choleric captors. His six-foot-two frame stiffened to Royal Marine parade-ground stance. 'Stop shouting. I am an officer and a colonel,' he roared back in German. 'I have served my king for five and twenty years. Politeness please or you, too, can be damned.' Realizing long after that he had translated 'king' as 'kaiser,' Wings rationalized. He told me: 'The King and the Kaiser were cousins, you know.'

Tobolski was one of the 50 Luft III officers shot in the wake of the Great Escape. Wings was sent to Sachsenhausen Concentration Camp – 'a place from which there is no escape,' SS Police General Arthur Nebe assured him. Within days of Wings arrival, he together with erstwhile Luft III krie-gies Major Dodge, Sydney Dowse and Jimmy James were tunnelling through sandy soil beneath their barracks. Four months along on their 115-foot tunnel they were joined by Commando Lieut-Colonel Jack Churchill. Wings was crippled with a swollen knee but the others tunnelled on – about two feet a day, 7 days a week.

Late in September Wings persuaded an SS doctor to drain the water from his bulbous knee. Two nights later they escaped. A day and a half after that he and Dowse were routed from a half-bombed Berlin cellar. Returned to Sachsenhausen, Wings, Dodge, Dowse and James were put in the Death Block where Police General Nebe was now also imprisoned. Implicated in the July plot against Hitler, Nebe was hung on piano wire.

As the mass bombing raids on Berlin heralded the Allied advances, Sachsenhausen was evacuated. Now Himmler was collecting VIP prisoners as potential hostages and the RAF foursome were among those moved to Flossenberg. There other Hitler-plot conspirators, Admiral Canaris, Hans Oster and Pastor Bonhoffer were strung on piano wire. Less prominent prisoners were shot.

As massed formations of Flying Fortresses and artillery fire marked the inexorable Allied advance, Wings stalled another evacuation. But on 15 April they were moved again. They spent two nights at Dachau then another night's travel through blazing countryside brought them to the Reichenau camp. Here Himmler was collecting the ultimate hostage party. One segment of it included the RAF foursome, Peter Churchill, Polish and Danish resistance leaders and two Italian partisans. After 10 days the party was moved out in five buses and an army truck. Now it embraced 136 VIPs from 22 countries including Dr Hjalmar Schacht, Pastor Niemoller and Molotov's son Vassili. A 30-man SS detachment conducted the convoy. Another 20-man SS liquidation squad rode shotgun with a case of grenades to augment their *schmeissers*.

They went south through the Brenner Pass, stopping indecisively at Niederorf in the Alpine foothills. Here a 14th German Army unit disarmed the SS while partisan groups created chaos. Wings got word to a U.S. Army unit who liberated them.

There were about 400 of us, a third of the North Compound population, who worked on the tunnelling projects that led to the Great Escape. I was neither skilled nor inclined towards digging though I did go underground to man the air-pump on a subsequent tunnel built from the theatre. Like scores of others during the 13 months that *Harry* was being dug I was a 'stooge'; that is, part of the countless apparently idle bystanders watching the goons assigned to watch us.

The main gate from the German *vorlager* into our compound was dead centre in the north-side fence. The *Harry* tunnel began from hut 104, about 90 feet south of the gate. The end room here accommodated two officers and its window afforded a good view of the *vorlager* gate. To maintain this view during the night-time hours before curfew, kriegy craftsmen had carefully positioned a knot-hole in the blackout shutter. Alternating every few minutes with a fellow stooge before my eyes lost focus, I manned this knot-hole vantage point in twice-weekly shifts. Our job was to identify immediately and announce the entry of any German. One of us would instantly alert our stooge boss, a mild-mannered New Zealander who invariably was playing bridge just two rooms away. It was his responsibility to alarm George Harsh's camp-wide security system.

To prevent any light from the room leaking from our blackout-shutter spy-hole, we were supplied with a square of black cloth fastened on one side to a large knitting hoop. The hoop was constantly pressed over the knot-hole while the viewer was cloaked in the black cloth that issued from it. It occurred to me one night after several months stooging that my war effort at this point verged on the absurd. His Majesty's Service was paying me a flight-lieutenant's wage – plus flying pay every day spent in Germany – to play twice-weekly cloak and dagger without the weapon.

Big-X took a much more serious view of the job. Midway through my shift one night I saw two of our captors coming into the camp. My shift partner immediately went to alert our New Zealander boss. He was in the toilet at the time and there was a five or six-minute delay in sending out word to shut down escape operations. Fortunately, the lapse in issuing a warning did not endanger the system. But it might have, said Bushell. The minutes'-long gap in security epitomized the carelessness that caused losses in wartime. We were at war and he was determined to exemplify the lack of vigilance.

I was one of seven or eight kriegies at the inquiry that Bushell conducted. I was simply asked to relate what I had seen and done. So was my shift-partner. The New Zealander admitted his absence from his post to relieve himself and agreed it was 'careless.' He was a quiet, conscientious officer who might well have gone through life without critical experience. But on this mid-war day in the depths of a German POW camp he drew Bushell's wrath.

It was as if he had lanced a tumour long festering in Big-X's depths. For nearly three years Roger Bushell had banked his fiery hate of his Nazi captors behind a studied mask of good-fellowship. Now, within the secure bounds of a kriegy room he unleashed his fury.

'You had a responsibility and you aborted it. You endangered months of work by hundreds of your fellow officers,' Big-X screamed. 'Men have been shot in wartime for less negligence. You should be now.'

His verbal assault on the New Zealander lasted no more than 10 or 12 minutes but those of us who witnessed it can hear the anger still venting. Half a century since, I still see the young officer bleeding from a thousand verbal cuts. Bushell was relentless. As the Great Escape drew closer to reality he was determined that everyone of us must understand the price of its security.

The quiet young New Zealander paid that price that afternoon. In a dozen minutes we watched Roger Bushell studiously drive him – literally – insane. Our shift boss was among a half dozen Luft III POWs repatriated later that season. A medical examining party on behalf of the neutral Protecting Power had declared them suffering from 'barbed-wire psychosis.'

Wartime zeal unleashed awesome emotions in uncompromising men. At war's end Douglas Bader quickly put his kriegy years behind him. But not before he tried to redress his Luft III experience. His brief stay in North Compound was the only occasion when Air Force colleagues had not concurred with his aims. Roger Bushell was dead – one of the 50 despatched with an SS shot to the back of the head. And Harry Day had been elevated beyond reproach to Group Captain, GC, DSO, OBE. That left Wally

Floody as the escape-team member to be blamed for opposing the legless hero's goon-baiting. But Floody had gained status among Canadian authorities. The RCAF were disinclined to consider Bader's claim that tunnel-maker Floody had been insubordinate.

Bader rejoined the Shell Oil organization post-war in a public relations capacity. It was a job that let him continue to fly. More pertinent, it gave him the time, resources and freedom to play an even more important role in peacetime. The legless fighter ace epitomized what a double amputee could accomplish by sheer will. For the next four decades he used his fame and energy to become *the* role model for British amputees. Thousands of these men and women walked through fulfilling lives on artificial legs because he had personally encouraged them.

A dozen years post-war the Shell company sent their legless ambassador on a goodwill mission to Canada and the States. I did public relations work for Shell Canada at the time and I was assigned to accompany Bader during a whirlwind one-day Toronto visit. I hired a limousine and picked him up before 8am to speed through a hard day's agenda. Bader made two hospital visits to hearten legless war veterans and civilian amputees trying to get on with their lives. He cordially worked through half a dozen media interviews I had arranged. About 5pm as we sped back to his hotel, I sought to make polite conversation.

'I remember the day in North Compound at Luft III that you threatened to jump in the fire pool,' I said without preamble.

'Really,' he replied. 'And what's the next stop on today's agenda.'

I was in London in the summer of 1968 when ex-kriegy Sydney Smith's book *Wings Day* was published. The publishers held a reception at the RAF Club for British booksellers. Wings invited me to attend. The booksellers were fascinated by his two-war's career and the famed flyers with whom he had interacted. 'You were Douglas Bader's flight commander when he lost his legs. Would you tell us about that?' one of them asked.

'Well, if the silly bugger had done what he was told he would still have them,' Wings replied.

A 'planeload of Canadian Air Force kriegies were in Britain on one of our perennial jaunts in the summer of 1982. That same week-end Second World War airmen held a tribute dinner for our wartime Bomber Command chief Arthur Harris on his 90th birthday. Douglas Bader toasted service colleagues at that London dinner then died on his way home. There was irony in that since Bader's death gave him a presence among visiting ex-POWs that he had studiously avoided while he lived. The ultimate individualist, a leader not a team-mate, Bader found our compound camaraderie as intolerable as his confinement in 13 acres.

Like Bader, the head of the Canadian Air Force kriegies Don Morrison was in a public relations job and continued to fly post-war. But Morrison walked shoulder to shoulder with the human race, disarming the disaffected with sheer good humour.

'What makes you and Bader so different,' I once asked.

'Well I shot down fewer aircraft and I only lost one leg,' Don told me.

17

The March

SILESIA, January 1945

Time throbbed a beat louder that last week of 1944. Time was the living world beyond barbed-wire and for years it had been beyond our hearing, beyond hope. Then in June Allied armies landed on Normandy beaches and we hung up calendars again.

A month later the Russians took Minsk, entered the Baltic states, cleared the enemy from the Pripet Marshes and menaced Nazis armies in East Prussia just 350 miles to the east of us. 'The enemy is at the gates of the Reich,' cried German broadcasters. Not quite! It was autumn before East Prussia was invaded. By then the U.S. First Army was battering the Siegfried Line, British and Greek troops had recovered Athens and the Allied winter offensive was about to begin on the Western front.

As we counted time again those last six months of 1944 we kept advancing a lamp-blacked pyjama cord on a big 'Ops Room' map at Luft III. Inch by inch the marker was moved out of the Normandy beachhead and into Brittany; up towards the Seine, east to Paris and up from Marseille. Paris, Brussels and Lyons were behind the pyjama cord by Labour Day.

The frustrating thing was that we could only move the pyjama-cord marker in line with official Wermacht communiques aired on camp loudspeakers twice a day. And Goebbel's ministry was double-talking. *The enemy was stopped in the depths of our lines . . . our troops advanced (back) to prepared positions . . . the traitorous Romanians . . . Yugoslavian treachery.*

For the actual situation we had to wait on the once daily BBC newscast. This was received on our clandestine radio set and delivered to each barrack block by Con Norton. Every afternoon block security would post stooges and we would crowd into the washroom. Norton would stride in, his South African voice tamed by years of British broadcasting, to read the BBC news to us. When not in use the radio receiver, built from bits and pieces pilfered and bribed from our captors, was hidden in a toilet water tank. How ironic that the 'pukka gen', as old RAF types called reliable information, came out of the toilet more or less.

That last week of 1944 Patton's army and Allied air forces were beating back the last German offensive in the Belgian Bulge and Churchill was settling the Greek civil war. The Russians, however, were still stalled some 300 miles to the north and south and east of us. Where we sat at Luft III – midway between Berlin and Breslau, 35 miles west of the Oder River – it was the Soviet Army's push that would really count.

East Prussia was a long way off and for weeks our pyjama-cord marker had hung stationary on the eastern side of the map. The endless horizon of reforested pine trees beyond the goon towers never changed but you could feel the Baltic winds coming closer. It was going to be a long, cold winter. We were neither prescient nor optimistic, yet as time throbbed louder that last week of the year we imagined we could hear the rumble of Soviet tanks on frozen ground.

Half a century later that Christmas Eve of 1944 remains atop my mind. The brew bubbled through Brownie's still making the valves hiss in the slide-trombone cooling coil. Four of us were solemnly pounding prune pits with wooden mallets to get at the almond-like kernels. Someone was grinding Red Cross parcel biscuits into flour. He was obviously a new POW. The old hands soaked biscuits and German bread alike into a glutinous, rib-sticking glop.

Now all those lush prunes that Brownie hadn't opted for the brew, all that Klim milk powder hoarded to make a lathered topping for Christmas puddings, all that egg powder for Christmas morning breakfast was to be consumed. Despite half-parcel issues that winter and stuff being stashed away 'just in case', we had quite a bash. Maybe we were feeding our bellies to keep anxiety out. That last Christmas in Germany we ate like there was no tomorrow.

While Brownie's still was bubbling, the Red Army was surrounding Budapest and General Patton was writing the scenario for George C. Scott's starring role at Bastogne. While we cracked prune pits Ruhr industry was grinding to a halt under our erstwhile colleagues' bombardment. And somewhere out there on the other side of Poland some 300 Russian divisions sat stolidly keeping their powder dry.

If things were not all that Christmassy at Luft III they were less so elsewhere. At Hitler's headquarters, General Heinz Guderian was begging reserves from Belgium for the Eastern front. Hitler told him no and Guderian told his diary: 'I was rebuffed and spent a grim and tragic Christmas Eve in those most unchristian surroundings.'

At Auschwitz, 200 miles down the Oder River from Sagan, Rudolf Hoess had shut down the gas chambers, not because it was Christmas Eve but because the crematoria were falling behind with disposal. And Hoess was busy packing.

At Luft III the rumours began to sharpen that holiday week. The snow-filled air seemed to anticipate the clank of Red Army tank treads, the squeak of frozen boots and trundling gun-carriers. The silently falling snow carried a foretaste of the sweep they would make across 150 miles of flat-lands between the Vistula and the Oder.

The Klim Club plan to stash Red Cross food into *George*, a fourth tunnel in North Compound, was part of exigency planning should the SS try to liquidate us if the Russians got too close. The tunnel – which started from under the seventh seat east in the third row of the camp theatre – now reached beyond the wire. It had been completed in those months after they sent the 50 escapees' ashes back in tin urns and told us that 'attempting escape is no longer considered a game.' Some of us figured that if it was no longer a game then it was seriously worth doing. I worked underground, manning a row-boat style, kit-bag pump during *George's* construction.

With Wings Day purged to Sachsenhausen and 55-year-old Group Captain Massey with his bad leg repatriated, the Senior British Officer in North Compound was RCAF Group Captain Larry Wray. Years earlier he had flown Canadian map-makers on the first aerial surveys of the Northwest Territories. Now he organized us into kriegy commando groups as a precaution should things get ugly.

'No flap,' he said. 'But be sure you have clean socks and a good pair of boots. Get some exercise every day. We may soon be walking.'

For Group Captain D.E.L. Wilson, responsible for the 10,500 British kriegies in the Sagan-Belaria complex, and for Larry Wray and the other four compound SBOs, that last week of 1944 was the most harrowing of their careers. SS-chief Heinrich Himmler was already making the first moves towards consolidating his hostage potential – the tens of thousands of Allied POWs and hundreds of VIPs from the captive nations. There was good reason to believe that he would not leave us to Soviet liberation.

On the other hand there was no certainty that the Soviet armies would sweep across the Oder in our direction in the foreseeable future. Nor could our senior officers expect that our liberation and safe passage back home would have much priority in the last and most critical months of World War II.

Soviet authorities had never recognized the Geneva Convention concept of prisoners-of-war for either their own or enemy captives. With up to 20 million dead and every live Soviet citizen fighting for their own freedom, the welfare of British kriegies and 4,000 Americans at Luft III was of small concern to the advancing Russian generals. The ultimate question was whether our German captors would – and could – evacuate us from the jaws of a Soviet advance. Reluctantly we were being conditioned for a winter march.

Now the experts on toting and haulage, on survivor gear and high-energy rations, came out of the woodwork. Our barrack rooms buzzed that last night of 1944 with heated debate on how to sling a haversack fore or aft, whether small packsacks high on the shoulders were preferable to big ones slung down the back; whether a D-bar from an American Red Cross parcel packed more energy when mixed with oatmeal than sprinkled with English Bemax. Almost everyone had an opinion – except the Polish airmen among us. They just kept fanning their tea-makers with little windmills. Let the Brits get all packed up, the Poles were used to travelling light this war.

A day or two before Christmas the temperature dropped to within a few degrees of zero and remained there. Now the dry snow steeped the camp and barren Silesian countryside to oneness. It blanked out the barbed-wire coils between the electrified double fence and it capped the guard towers, even the searchlights. The camp and countryside had a greeting-card look. So we skated on the two frozen fire ponds and paced the compound to toughen our feet.

Memory dims the first few days of 1945. Except for General Patton's success at Bastogne there was an ominous lull. It was like the barometer dropping before a cyclone. We filled the vacuum with rumours and conjecture. Would Uncle Joe's troops sweep this way? *They say they've got these big tommy-gun-toting Ruskie dames on their gun-carriers.* Would the Jerrys evacuate us in time? *The commandant has told Berlin he's got to have 400 trucks by tonight.* Would Himmler's goons be waiting as we went out the gate? *Those same bastards that sent 50 recaptured escapees back to us in tin urns.*

Then on 12 January Uncle Joe launched his last great battles. We can still hear Con Norton relaying the CBC reports that followed. Crowding the washroom between the sinks and urinals a hundred or more of us had to nudge each other in the ribs to keep from roaring hallelujahs. Norton's best BBC voice propelled the words like bullets. 'Konev's Army has broken out of its Vistula bridgehead south of Warsaw . . . it is heading for Silesia . . . *coming our way.* Zhukov's Army is crossing the Vistula heading for Berlin . . . and beyond Zhukov, more Red Armies are driving for the Gulf of Danzig' – *across that bloody corridor that was the Fuhrer's last demand at Munich five years before.*

Now the pyjama cord on the Ops Room map lagged so far behind reality we just waited for Norton to give his washroom newscast each day. By the time Warsaw and Cracow fell to the Russians on 17 January most kriegies had done their packing. So had Rudolf Hoess down the road at Auschwitz. In the six weeks since he had shut down the gas chambers, Hoess' *sonderkommandos* had packed 99,922 children's garments and underclothes, 192,652 women's wear articles and 222,269 men's clothing items for shipment back to Germany.

19 January, the Russians take Lodz – halfway to the Oder River. 22 January they are within 10 miles of the Oder, less than 50 from Luft III.

The Ops Room map is useless now. Goebles' guys are still trying to adjust the German focus to their side of the Vistula.

25 January, a month since Brownie's still bubbled its last brew, Russian armies are around Poznan and Breslau. The Russkies astride Poznan are heading for Berlin but those at Breslau are coming our way. Rumour, wishful thought and heroic speculation churn in super-heated air. *It's too late for the goons to get us out. Wow! Home by Easter via Leningrad . . .*

Nope, we're marching at six o'clock, the Oberst just told the Groupie . . .

Change of plans, chaps. We're staying till morning.

For nearly a month the sleighs had been taking shape, fashioned from bed-boards and wall strapping. Packsacks to hold up to 40 pounds of food and clothing had been filled and refilled. As each rumour wafted our way the travel gear was emptied and reassembled.

27 January, the camp commandant says he has been told by the German High Command in Berlin that Luft III is not to be evacuated. But Group Captain Wilson has learned that German personnel have already been issued with two days' emergency rations. That accelerates our own preparations and the rumours proliferate. *We're marching at noon . . . at 3pm . . . .*

Nope, the Reds have cut the road south of here . . .

No, duff gen that. We're leaving at 9 tonight.

In fact, it was an hour into Sunday morning, 28 January, when 1,938 of us began leaving the North Compound. We went through the lager gate, up to the warehouse where guys were heaving out Red Cross parcels – two to a man. So we had to reorganize all those packsacks slung fore and aft, repack the sleighs and maybe heave away the last of the inedible, unwearable momentos.

I'm a curious clod, always have been, so I made some notes that night and on the march. For the record, we went down the road towards Spremburg wearing or carrying an average 1.1 pair of trousers, 2.5 sweaters, 1.5 pairs of boots, 1 extra pair of heavy socks, 2 suits of underwear, 2 towels, 1 jacket, 1 scarf, 1 great-coat, 1.5 pairs of gloves, 2 shirts, 1 belt or braces, 1 hat or balaclava, 2.2 blankets, 3 Red Cross parcels – or their equivalent with at least one intact, 1 pound of chocolate, 1 pound of miscellaneous food and 900 cigarettes.

Group Captain Wilson chronicled our march from Sagan. The Americans quit their compounds in the two hours before midnight. We began to evacuate North Compound at 1am. Central and East Compound kriegies were on the road by 7 in the morning. The camp at Belaria was not evacuated until the following day.

'The compounds were left in a state of chaos,' Wilson duly reported. 'Prisoners' belongings worth an estimated £250,000 were abandoned.' He might have mentioned the manuscript for my one and only work of fiction, an 80,000-word book recounting allegedly humorous Air Force anecdotes. Even before Christmas when we knew that the Russians were poised for their last great drive to the west I had mentally weighed each item to be carried if we marched. I figured my manuscript scrawled in notebooks was expendable.

A lot worse dribble survived to gain bookstand and library-shelf space post-war. But fiction was not my forte and the humour was somewhat juvenile. On a mental scale I balanced the manuscript against another pound of concentrated food or two more pairs of heavy socks. When we marched I left the manuscript notebooks on my shelf in hut 119, North Compound. I understand that a great tank battle was fought on the site of Luft III a week or two after we vacated it. I would like to think that my manuscript pages gave a bit of traction to Russian tank treads.

There was just one snag to my decision. My manuscript was half of a joint enterprise. I had persuaded Bob Buckham to do a score of illustrations for the book. He had put a lot of talented hours into creating cartoons that were truly funny but they were geared to my text and quite meaningless without it. Bob was not going to be pleased when he learned that I had abandoned their usefulness. At 6 feet 4 inches, he was a head taller than I and better built. You could tell by his purposeful stride that he was a dedicated guy. He had put a lot of effort into those illustrations done on large sheets of art paper.

The last of North Compound kriegies cleared the camp at 3:15am. Sunday morning 28 January. Four out of five hauling their gear individually or collectively on sleighs, the rest of us pack-sacking it, we headed into light wind-blown snow. I remember the cold and sleeplessness, the sting of ice-laden wind and the endless pain of toes in slush-filled boots.

But I still recall with equal clarity the great sweep of space embracing us beyond the gates as we marched away from Luft III. After 30 months within a dozen acres we were suddenly loosed on the open road. The horizon was murky but at least we were moving towards it again.

We were not deluded; the guards still carried guns and we would not have ventured off the roadway into oblivion. We were being marched into war's long night yet it was a new darkness that enwrapped us. What we were experiencing was not liberty nor even a pseudo-freedom. But the beat of time throbbed louder in our ears. Somewhere out there in the blackness ahead lay the pages of war's last chapter. You could hear them unfolding in the dark distance.

Nine hours after leaving the camp we reached Freiwaldan 17 miles south-east of Sagan. 'We were told we would be billeted here for the night,' Group Capt. Wilson duly noted. 'But little attempt had been made to find accommodation and the two halls allotted were totally inadequate. After waiting an hour exhausted and half frozen, prisoners began making their own arrangements for billeting with civilians willing to take them in. Luftwaffe Major Rostek promised to do all he could but an objection from either civilian or military authorities led to the Germans' decision that the march be resumed.'

'We reached Leippa, four miles further on, about 5pm.' Wilson would recall. 'Eventually about 700 were crowded into one barn while the rest waited. It was another four hours before more barns were found. During the wait several POWs collapsed. They were found in the ditch by a search party organized by the prisoners themselves. 60 officers had to spend the night in straw in the lee of a farmyard wall. Many of them suffered frostbite and vomiting. The column had been on the move for over 16 hours without organized meals.

'Darkness fell shortly after our arrival and the night was one of the coldest of the year. Clothes and boots of prisoners waiting in the snow and slush were ice-covered. It was almost impossible to obtain water and almost impossible to prepare even cold food in the darkness with numb hands. An issue of a third of a loaf of bread per man was attempted but few obtained it in the darkness. It was so cramped many were forced to urinate where they lay. For some people this night was the severest experience on the march,' said Wilson.

My own recollection was helping to pass fellow POWs up a chain of hands into the black depths of a hay loft. It seemed to take hours and there was not a single body space left. Charlie McCloskey and I moved to the shelter of a nearby stable and crawled into the first stall. Its bovine occupant was not inclined to share her space but we shouldered ourselves sleeping room.

As I stretched out on a thin coating of cow-pissed straw the cold concrete floor embraced me. My body began to shake spasmodically and my teeth chattered as they had the night we had crashed on Great Knoutberry Hill nearly four years earlier. This time I inserted a glove, myself, to keep the tooth enamel from breaking. The glove was soggy with stable dirt. I could still taste the acidic waste when I woke.

The march resumed at 8am Monday. We reached Priebus before noon and paused for lunch – the food we carried moistened by a little water from the townsfolk. At about 6pm we arrived at the Polish town of Moskau, 40 miles south-west of Sagan. Billets were provided in various structures; 600 of us luxuriated in the warmth of a glass factory. Glass-making operations were suspended for the 48 hours we occupied the place but the kilns remained at high heat. The kiln doors were made of some silicate compound that withstood the extreme glass-making temperature but was vulnerable to water.

'Keep anything wet away from those doors. The slightest moisture will explode them,' the French slave-workers warned us. Within an hour of our arrival every kiln door was flanked by tin mugs for tea-making. On the edge of survival we were not readily intimidated.

The kilns cast a defiant glow. Almost everywhere else in Occupied Europe the air-war – combined with manpower, material and fuel shortages – was banking the industrial furnaces. 'The war is lost,' Albert Speer wrote Hitler that last day of January.

'Do you think the English are enthusiastic about all the Russian developments?' the Fuhrer asked Goering that night. 'If this goes on we will get a telegram from the English in a few days,' Goering assured him.

But Roosevelt, Churchill and Stalin were enroute to Yalta. They had no word for Nazi Germany except unconditional surrender.

When we resumed the march 57 North Camp POWs remained for treatment by the French medical officer who exhausted a large part of his supplies for our kriegies' benefit. About 550 Americans left our North Compound group to join fellow USAAF kriegies in another column of the miles-long trek. They were replaced by a like number of East Camp NCOs. Several of these were reunited with officer crew-mates from our compound.

When we left Moskau 90 per cent of our stuff was sleigh-borne. But the blizzard had let up and it began to thaw. At first the sled runners just hit the odd bare spot dragging on the tow rope. Then there would be long scraping sounds accompanied by rude words. By this time the cool types had acquired wheels. There were dozens of small wagons, baby carriages and assorted vehicles when we began the next stage of the march.

Bob Buckham was among the group who had been billeted in the stables of the Castle von Arnim at Moskau. When we marched again I knew I would have to confront him. The traffic-tracked clay road had thawed to a sticky consistency which slowed our pace. When I sighted his 6-feet 4-inch figure ahead, however, it was striding earnestly with league-long steps. Sure enough, he was carrying his outsized artwork rolled into a long-tube slung across his back.

I had to half trot to catch up to him. The physical effort dissipated my anxiety while accelerating fate. In a moment he would know that tube of drawings across his back was worthless. I could visualize his big right hand which so skilfully wielded a brush or sketching pencil closing into a great fist. I could anticipate the taste of Silesian clay on my teeth as I hit ground.

'Bob, how goes it?' I queried catching my breath but not his stride.

'Okay,' he responded with every evidence that things were not. The 'trots' had denatured his usual geniality. The usually happy-eyed Bob Buckham looked downright mean.

'Bob, I've gotta tell you the truth,' I blurted out. 'I left the damn book manuscript behind. I took extra socks instead.'

He never broke stride, never even turned to eye me. 'What the hell do you think I did with those illustrations. All I'm carrying are a few sketches of kriegy life that I just couldn't leave. Screw your book.'

An hour before midnight Wednesday 31 January, we were marched out of Moskau destined for the railhead at Spremburg 16 miles to the east. We made it in two stages over the next 30 hours which Group Captain Wilson duly described.

'The effects of the previous marching – more than one POW had frost-bite too severe to wear boots and finished the march in stocking feet – the darkness, the hilly country and the Germans' failure to exercise normal march discipline, made this the most difficult stage of the journey. The guards soon abandoned any serious attempt to patrol and straggled or marched with the prisoners. The prisoners marched in companies. There was little conversation. Above the sound of muffled footsteps only the grating of sleighs in slush could be heard.'

At Spremberg we were given an hour's respite at the 8th Panzer Division's depot. Soup and hot water were supplied then we were marched to the rail station a mile away. Here we entrained for Milag-Marlag Nord Camp near Bremen on the other side of Germany. Our transport was the ubiquitous 40-men and 8-horse box-cars of two world wars but now they were being filled to absolute human capacity. For the two-day trip across war-torn Germany there was not quite room for us to lie down. We slept crouched in sitting position or wedged immovable between others.

The cattle-car doors remained closed except for two watering stops in the first 36 hours. The second of these was in a great railway switch-yard on Hannover outskirts. Here hundreds of nearby householders worked tire-lessly to provide the train occupants with water. Adults and children hauled kettles and cans and tubs of water to the cattle-car travellers – we kriegies, German wounded from the Eastern Front and civilian refugees fleeing the Russian Army's advance. To the German populace that last winter of war, misery was indistinguishable among friend and foe.

Our train arrived at Darmstadt about 5pm Sunday and we marched the mile and a half to Marlag Nord Camp. The last of our column pulled up at the camp gates about 7pm. And there we waited for six and a half hours, blasted by Baltic winds in near zero weather while the guards searched, counted and recounted us.

As Group Capt. Wilson would report: 'It was raining and the prisoners were standing in mud tracks covered with pools of water. Apart from exhaustion, many were suffering from frost-bite, dysentery and vomiting. Several collapsed and were taken to hospital. For the majority this wait, after eight days movement under the conditions described, proved the breaking point. More than 70 per cent of the POWs suffered gastritis, dysentry, colds, influenza and other illnesses during the following weeks.'

Marlag Nord was a huddle of huts built 20 miles east of Bremen early in the century to detain errant seamen. The cobblestone floors discouraged tunnelling and challenged survival. For much of the 10 weeks we occupied these punitive barracks we slept on palliases atop ice or slush-covered floors. Our captors provided an hour's fuel for the stoves each day which we used in suppertime cooking. Then we would crawl to bed beneath all our belongings.

What we found compensating in the weeks that followed was the fact our captors increasingly shared our misery.

18

Last 100 Days

ON THE ELBE, Spring 1945

The night we arrived at Marlag Nord the last 100 days of the war in Europe had begun and the Churchill, Roosevelt and Stalin were meeting at Yalta. The destruction of Dresden by Allied airmen 10 days later signalled their grim intent.

Ten days after that General Patton's US Third Army entered the German Saar and General Crerar's First Canadian Army invaded the Ruhr. On 7 March General Hodges' US First Army crossed the Rhine into the German heartland. Within another week Allied drives were underway toward Munich, Leipzig and the Hamburg-Lübeck sector that held us. By the month's end British and American armies were sweeping to the south and east of us enroute to Berlin.

In the second week of April – the week Franklin Roosevelt died, the V-2 factory at Nordhausen was overrun, the Russians entered Vienna and the Allies launched their final offensives – we were evacuated once again. This time about 2,000 of us moved off under the effective command of Group Capt. Larry Wray. Allied authorities had advised that POW camp populations were to remain intact until liberated by our own forces. Our Luftwaffe captors were still nominally in charge but their days were conspicuously numbered. So they marched alongside us carrying the added weight of their guns.

Rations had improved at Marlag Nord and we had recovered our stamina with the spring weather. Our step was almost jaunty as we hit the road. Making time was not, however, Wray's intention. 'Not more than three or four miles a day,' he said. The more we dragged our feet the quicker Allied forces would overtake us.

The first to do so were a pair of RAF Tactical Air Force Typhoons that swept down from great height to blast Wermacht tanks, armoured vehicles and anything else that moved on German roadways. They encountered us on the second day of our trek from Marlag Nord.

The scream of their engines was like a high-pitched belch from the bowels of hell. Instinctively I dove to a shallow ditch, my teeth biting earth in a mad attempt to burrow deeper. I could sense the Typhoon shadows, the swish of their rockets and the bark of their cannon fire sweeping across us at great speed. And I realized we offered no identity. To pilots moving at 420 miles per hour, 200 feet above a column of marching men, we were a prime target. As it happened the only vehicle was a horse-drawn wagon carrying a score of our kriegies who were too sick to walk. Eleven of them died in the attack.

That first assault by TAC fighters conditioned our reflexes. We seemed to develop a third ear, an ultra-sensitive human antenna to catch the initial high-pitched wail of a diving aircraft. We would sense it beginning five or six miles up there in a fathomless sky and know we had seconds to track its direction, determine its path, take cover or shrug it off as not our concern.

The second time we underwent a Typhoon attack we were passing a Lunenburger farm. A woman and her young daughter were watching us from the gateway of a stone fence. They were unaware of the Typhoon enunciating the first syllable of its death call. I had sensed it and caught the path of its trajectory before they realized what they were hearing.

'Down, down,' I screamed but the English warning was meaningless. They were frozen in fear. Immovable, they watched me racing in their direction, diving at them like a football tackle. Then all three of us were sprawled behind the stone wall. Cannon-fire splashed its outer side. As I rejoined the column of kriegies a pair of aged elm trees caught my eye. Four or five feet above ground their great trunks had been cut through like lumber milled by Typhoon cannon-fire.

Our encounters in those last weeks were ironical. Most of us had spent years as POWs yet only in these final days of the war did we share the German civilians' experience. Now as we marched through the Lunenburger farm country we began to trade off Red Cross soap, tinned coffee and Spam from our parcels for fresh foods, eggs and dairy products.

Never a linguist, I had acquired no more than 20 words of German. But I was determined to use them in bartering with the farm-folk. A German *hausfrau* was standing at her front gate and I was anxious to trade Red Cross parcel content for fresh eggs. Did she have any? *Haben-zee eyer? Haben-zee eyer?* I asked.

My query threw the good woman into obvious confusion. Her face turned beet-red and she stammered an unintelligible response. Another kriegy, fluent in German, came up behind me. 'What in hell are you trying to do, Silver?' he asked.

'I just want to know if she has eggs to sell.'

'So what are you asking her?'

'*Haben-zee eyer?* Have you got eggs? ' I told him.

'That's the problem. It doesn't quite translate that way,' he explained. 'What you are asking is the state of her ovaries. Has she had a hysterectomy?'

We were one of dozens of POW columns being driven towards the Schleswig-Holstein peninsula, between the Elbe, the North Sea and the Baltic, which the last great battles would by-pass. On 18 April, no more than two or three days ahead of the Allied armies driving east from Friesland, we crossed the Elbe to Hamburg.

As we marched off the ferry onto remnants of Hamburg's cobblestone streets, the awesome impact of the air raids nearly two years earlier was still vividly clear. Back in Britain smashed buildings on both sides of a street had been commonplace and we had seen entire blocks of London crushed in the blitz. Now, however, we trudged through square miles of a city that had been razed in fire-storms and levelled to oblivion.

Here in four summer nights over a 10-day period of 1943 RAF crews dropped 3,000 block-buster bombs, 1,200 land mines, 25,000 high-explosive and 80,000 phosphorus bombs, 3 million incendiaries and 500 drums of liquid phosphorus. The fires merged into raging storms; fiery updrafts created a vast chimney at the city's core. As the central column of burning debris, bomb-bursts and pyrotechnics arose it sucked all oxygen from the skirts of the storm. People suffocated as they ran in the streets, choked on smoke in fleeing cars. They cooked in the air-raid bunkers, their fat collecting in greasy char on cellar floors. At least 60,000 died in a single night and 900,000 were made homeless. Now we walked for hours through levelled rubble where their homes had been.

We were two days getting clear of the Hamburg area. As we tramped the sideroads paralleling the Hamburg-Lübeck *autobahn* it was as if we had been swept offstage to watch the last fortnight of the European war unfold from just beyond the footlights glare. From Cuxhaven to Kiel the German naval guns had been silenced. Throughout this peninsula not a single Luftwaffe airfield was still usable. A half dozen miles from where we camped one late-April day we could see Dorniers, Me-109s and Me-110s apparently taking off and returning to a single landing strip. Soon it was evident they were using the Hamburg-Lübeck *autobahn* – their last runway.

We could trace the battle-lines by the Allied aircraft con trails and the echo of artillery fire just across the Elbe. For the moment Mongtomery's Second Army units were racing past us in a pincer-play with Soviet forces for a final crunch of Wermacht resistance. That done it would take less than an hour's run to free us.

Meanwhile, Larry Wray decided we would watch from our present vantage point. On 27 April, a few miles southwest of Lübeck, he called a halt. Our Luftwaffe captors, as tired as we were, were still nominally in control but only too ready to agree. An SS colonel patrolling the Wehrmacht's flanks, however, insisted we move on. While he screamed death threats Group Capt. Wray dispersed us.

Back at Luft III Wray had created a commando structure in which each room's occupants were a unit reporting to him through block commanders. To the SS colonel we must have appeared as a vague column of shabby-clothed men moving in spurts and starts, scattering for a mile or two each side of the route to trade with German householders. In these last days of the war, he saw us as a dangerous rabble. In fact, we were military-trained personnel still mindful of our status and organized to respond to our commander's word. On Larry Wray's order we melted into the countryside over a space of a dozen square miles.

Waving his cocked Luger, the furious SS colonel threatened to shoot our C/O.

'And if you do who is going to call those men back to order?' Wray countered.

So we were accommodated in the fields of a German industrialist's estate at Trenthorst, 13 miles southwest of Lübeck. It was there that a sergeant of the Cheshire Regiment in his armoured scout car found us just after noon on 2 May 1945. Our Luftwaffe captors had slipped away before daylight.

Mid-day sun reflected from the scout car aerial like a blazing sword blade as it dipped through a ditch and up into our midst. In moments it was lost beneath 2,000 milling men. Only the sun-drenched aerial remained visible. And from its roots in the armoured roof we could hear Brit voices on their radio channel.

'Fox-2 on target, Fox-2 on target,' the sergeant driver buried beneath us was calling.

'How many? What condition?' he was asked.

'Damned if I know. But if there were any more of them I'd be bangers and mashed,' he told his despatcher.

Officers and men of a German Panzer unit had arrived in half a dozen vehicles an hour or two earlier. Wordlessly they surrendered their arms and I liberated one of their cars, a four-door Mercedes that cruised at 145 kilometres per hour on the *autobahn* before its engine burned out for lack of oil.

That didn't happen for two days, however. Meanwhile I was assigned to transport a half dozen just-freed Polish slave-workers along district roads to collect hundreds of weapons that surrendering Wermacht troops had abandoned in culverts and ditches. Within hours the half-starved Poles had liberated a stock of schnapps and were fire-watered to fighting frenzy. They had probably never before handled guns but now their glazed eyes fixed on the biggest and most menacing weapons.

Thus armed they were intent on finding German targets of either sex and of any age. Vainly I tried to dissuade them, citing the international rules of warfare and appealing to their basic humanity. But no one had mentioned the Geneva Convention in their previous five and a half years' experience and their sense of humanity had been eroded in camps and on work-gangs. In any case they were beyond English-language communication.

Fortunately, as the booze took hold their gun-grips weakened and their legs buckled. Wrestling them back into the Mercedes staff-car and returning them to our Trenthorst camp was my one action in World War II that I felt was worthy of a mention in despatches. It might have been in less momentous times.

The Cheshire Regiment scout car was like the foremost pinnacle of a British armada restoring civilized order and culture to Europe. Within hours an army group had set up headquarters within a mile or two of our camping ground. They were an advance element in the occupational forces prepared for an indefinite stay. In their wake came supply depots, transport headquarters and auxiliary services. Among the latter was an ENSA troupe, one of the professional entertainment groups that took music-hall fare to servicemen in the field. Just three nights after our liberation we watched a live ENSA performance in a huge tent strung with theatrical lighting and vibrant with amplified music.

Back at Luft III talented kriegies – including two or three future stars of British stage and screen – had kept us entertained with a varied fare. Now in this tent-theatre we joined the on-stage voices once again in belting out wartime songs. But midway through the evening's performance a basic difference between this ENSA group and our kriegy amateurs became apparent. Suddenly we were aware we were hearing women's voices again, that the high-kicking chorus line was propelled by *real* female legs, that the heroines of the skits were not just hairy-chested guys in drag.

I walked one of the ENSA show-girls back to her billet that night. It was my first live encounter with a female British voice in three years and I found it overwhelming. I had trouble trimming the pitch of my own voice for a girl's ears and my little store of small talk had long since dried up. Here was this magnificent young woman casually making polite banalities and I was sputtering earnest and irrelevant replies.

We had been walking arm-in-arm for several minutes when I became aware that she was holding her right hand in front of her face. A second glance revealed a cigarette between her fingers. Belatedly I realized she was gesturing for a light and I provided it – not with a match but by thrusting the lit end of my own cigarette against hers. It was a habitual response after those prison-camp years in which matches were scarce and cigarettes were lit one from the other. The ENSA girl laughed uproariously. My rehabilitation to the bisexual world had begun.

We waited nearly a week at Trenthorst for RAF Transport to fly us back to Britain. Then I managed to scrounge British Army rail warrants for a dozen of us from Lübeck to Brussels. Our group included George Edwards who remembered the crashes that had punctuated my operational career back on 10 Squadron. 'The Air Force should have made you a ticket agent in the first place,' he told me.

Shortly before midnight on 8 May, the night the war ended in Europe, celebrant Belgian rail-workers had two trains running on the same track in opposite directions. We were on one of them when they crashed just north of Antwerp. Two colleagues – one of them 190 pounds and wearing size 13 army boots – came out of the overhead luggage racks onto me where I lay on the floor between the seats. It was a rude awakening but none of us was seriously hurt.

So we climbed from the overturned rail car and headed for a nearby station structure. Still a bit dazed I opened the door to the brightly-lit interior. At first I could not identify faces in the glaring light but George Edward's voice was unmistakable.

'Geezus Christ, Silver,' he yelled. 'With you on board we should have known it would happen.'

In the early morning hours of 9 May we hitched a ride into Antwerp with an army truck then travelled by inter-urban tram line to Brussels. The war had been over for 36 hours but there was no pause in the celebrations. For blocks in all directions from Brussels main square you could walk on the heads of the people. In late afternoon I made my way to the Atlanta Hotel, an Allied officers' watering spot.

The u-shaped Atlanta bar must have been 40 feet long and the celebrants were stacked three and four deep across every foot of its perimeter. I shouldered into a spot at one end. Air force, army and naval officers of a dozen nations and a hundred different units were there. As my eyes adjusted to the smoke-filled scene I focussed on a familiar face in the murky distance at the opposite end of the bar. The big florid face was borne on the hulking frame of a major in my hometown regiment, the Essex Scottish. It was Doug MacFarlane, editor of the Canadian Army newspaper the *Maple Leaf*.

Four years earlier we had worked in adjacent bureaus of the *Windsor Star*. Doug's exploits – editorial, alcoholic and sexual – were legendary. My own reportorial experiences had tended more towards farce – getting deathly seasick on a storm-tossed rescue mission in Lake Erie, sleeping-in to miss a murder story and getting fired in London, Ontario. But we had been trained on the same team and followed each other's service careers at the outset of war.

Now, down the length of the bar, Doug was shattering ear-drums that had survived years of artillery fire. 'Silver, you cowardly son-of-a-bitch,' he bellowed. 'You've been hiding out the war in a prisoner-of-war camp. Now that it's over you come out to celebrate.'

It occurred to me that while I flew into adversity, MacFarlane had continued to play newspaperman. For the past three years he had contrived to keep his vitally important organs fully flexed while mine atrophied behind barbed-wire. Considerably less endowed than he at the outset it was as if we had raced through the best years of our lives, I moving steadily backwards.

Perhaps Doug appreciated the irony. Certainly he did his best to be hospitable. Soon we were in his jeep headed for the *Maple Leaf* offices across town. Subsequently we would recall that we clutched bottles of brandy in both hands, afraid to place them on the floor for fear they would get broken. We remember, too, that Doug had no driver and we still wonder how his jeep was driven across Brussels on VE+2 Night a half century ago.

I awoke that third morning of peace in Europe on a wicker settee in what served as the *Maple Leaf* newsroom. The wood-weave at the end of the settee scored my head like a crown of thorns. The stacatto fire of typewriter keys hit my skull from ear-hole to ear-hole. Not 10 inches away, war correspondent Ross Munroe was pounding out some deathless despatch. He was typing at the rate of four lines a minute which meant that the typewriter's line-end warning bell rang every 15 seconds. It was as if I was in a church belfry tied to the bell clapper at evensong.

'So you POWs get priority on shipment home and the good jobs will all be taken by the time we active types get back,' Doug ranted. 'Well, don't be smug. I may be out of uniform before you are,' he told me. A fortnight later Major MacFarlane, as *Maple Leaf* editor, tangled with a three-star Canadian general and three weeks after that he was back home in civilian clothes. I was still in uniform and my head was still aching.

At Brussels airport the Dakota transport 'planes were taking off for Britain a dozen times an hour. I signed in with the transport officer and took my place in the queue. In due course I was aboard a 'plane waiting for take-off. Routine as buses departing a terminal the Dakotas nosed onto the tarmac, revved up and hurtled down the runway. As we watched one of them blew a tyre, spun into flame and burned at the end of the field.

Just minutes later our aircraft was revving up for take-off. I tensed myself. In a few seconds we would be racing into the air. We didn't, however. We, too, burst a tyre but it was early in the take-off run and the pilot braked to a safe, if bumpy, stop.

'That was lucky,' a crew member said as we climbed out. 'If that had happened a few seconds later we'd have ground-looped like that other kite.'

'I know,' I said wearily. 'I can't knock luck. But somehow I thought peace-time flying would be different.'

19
Brownie and Harsh

Ex-newspapermen tend to hang together and a lot of people think we should. Newspaperwork was the common background that first brought Kingsley Brown, George Harsh and me together in Luft III North Camp in mid-war. At the time Brownie and George were preoccupied with escape activity and it wasn't till we met again after liberation that we struck up lifetime bonds.

They were among the oldest of the Air Force POWs, both about 35 at war's end; I was seven years younger. Kingsley had had a dozen years newspaper experience in Toronto, in Paris in Hemingway's day and in pre-war Halifax. 'How did you happen to wind up managing editor of the *Halifax Herald*?' I once asked. 'When I got off the boat from France I was broke and the *Herald* was within walking distance of the docks,' he explained.

George Harsh had been introduced to me in the camp as a former columnist for the *Atlanta Journal*. He had written for that paper briefly before coming to Canada to join the RCAF in 1940. But as he tells it in his 1971 autobiography *Lonesome Road*: 'Life started out for me with great expectations. I lost my father when I was twelve and at his death a half-million dollars was put in trust in my name. Then at the age of 17 something went sour within me and I was sentenced to die in the electric chair.

'But there is a saying in this country (U.S.) that 'You can't hang a million dollars' – that there is one law for the rich and another for the poor – and at age 18 my sentence was commuted to life in prison. To be pardoned after 12 years on a Georgia chain-gang and then to find myself six months later a commissioned officer and gentleman in His Majesty's Royal Air Force is at least somewhat ironical.' The irony was that – in my experience – in war or peace, imprisoned or free, drunk or sober, George Harsh epitomized gentility. He was a decent guy.

For half a century Brownie was my friend, mentor and conscience. George was the most fascinating man I ever met. I suppose that the three of us shared an unusual sense of humour and an innate iconoclasm. Yet as a pot-bottom disturber I lacked their enterprise.

Kingsley Brown and George Harsh had already sailed gallantly through the ranks of the Air Force, British nobility and civilian aviation circles leaving them awash and confounded when I joined their drinking session in a Bournemouth hotel room on a June day of 1945.

At this point they were both technically under house arrest, confined to the custody of their fellow officer and kriegy Wally Floody pending possible court-martial. And Wally was somewhere else. 'I was disinclined to play chaperone to two clowns who didn't hold their drink properly,' he said.

The root of the trouble was that a couple of weeks earlier Brownie and George had held their drinks – from one urination to the next – for four days amd four nights. Thoroughly sloshed and still carrying bottles of whiskey in hand, they had arrived at the edge of Poole Harbour at day-break. Half a mile off-shore a British Overseas Airways Sunderland flying boats bobbed at anchor.

Poole Harbour, on Bournemouth's doorstep, was BOAC's global base and the multi-million-dollar flying-boats anchored there included those in trans-Atlantic service. Kingsley had been nearly five years away from his wife Marion and their four adolescent kids. George was not at all certain what America offered on his return but he was anxious to find out. Drink defies circumstance and it simplifies logistics. To the drink-frazzled minds of these two erstwhile fly-boys those great craft just off-shore offered fast passage home.

They found a boy with a boat and for a quid he took them out to one of the Sunderlands. These craft sit two and a half decks above the waterline presenting a formidable profile to those who arrive by row-boat. Neither Brownie nor George was impressed. They bid the boy god-speed, climbed a ladder and disappeared into the giant vessel.

'I hadn't seen an aircraft wireless set for three years but the one in this Sunderland seemed to smile as if it recognized me,' George would recall. 'I managed to turn it on and it lit up with an array of wavelengths. I believe I settled on one for the Chinese Air Force and began to communicate.'

Kingsley had never flown anything bigger than a twin-engined Hampden, a plane perhaps a tenth the size of the four-engined Sunderland. 'But seen through the green glass of a booze bottle everything is relative. I had found the engine switches and much of the instrumentation when they interrupted us,' Brownie told me. 'The interruption was fortunate because while I had released the line that held the craft to the buoy I didn't realize it was anchored by the keel as well. Had I by chance got the Sunderland going I would have ripped its keel out. Ripping the bottom out of one of those flying-boats would have been very expensive.'

BOAC may not have anticipated two drunken fly-boys' intentions but they did maintain their Sunderland fleet under constant vigilance. Four security men were despatched in a fast cutter to remove the intruders. Torn between caution, incredibility and amusement, the BOAC men returned the two apparent Air Force officers to shore.

Recounting their experience that day at Bournemouth, neither Brownie nor George remembered saying a word on the trip ashore nor in their ascent to BOAC's control tower. But they do remember their response to interrogation by bemused BOAC officials.

'It was evident from our uniforms that we were RAF aircrew and that we had not been out of our clothes from some days. And we bore the aura of alcohol,' Kingsley said. 'It was unlikely we could have done much harm before they caught up with us and they were inclined to laugh off the incident.

'George and I were upset, however. Boredom and impatience to be home had spurred our drinking and drink had opened the vista of a home-bound flight. Now were being dismissed like errant school-boys.'

They could not recall who responded first but they said their reaction had been almost spontaneous. 'We broke into German, refused to converse any longer in English and said we should be treated as Luftwaffe prisoners-of-war. We told them we were trying to get back to the fatherland just as British *fliegers* would try to do from Deutchland under similar circumstances,' Brownie explained.

This exchange took place in an office adjacent to the control room. Two or three times the BOAC officials laughingly interrupted the flow of Germanic protest but Brownie and George were now imprisoned in their roles. That stubborn, illogical state in which drink fixes the brain seemed to leave no pathway for retreat. Confounded, their custodians stepped back into the control room to consult their BOAC colleagues. Inevitably, they were obliged to summon British military intelligence.

Years later Brownie could recall subsequent events as if he was replaying a video cassette. 'When our custodians retired to the control room George and I began to explore adjacent offices in the opposite direction. Almost immediately we were in this vast room where two girls in uniform were plotting the position of BOAC's trans-ocean fleet,' he said. 'As each new position was established a flying-boat replica would be moved on a great map by long-handled rake. The map occupied most of the room's floor-space and was surrounded by a low wall.

'We introduced ourselves to the girls, invited them to join us in a drink and secured paper cups from an adjoining washroom before they could find words of refusal. The little wall around the floor-map provided congenial seating and so we were agreeably ensconced when our custodians returned with an MI-5 guy,' Brownie would relate in the same reasonable tone with which he disarmed the sober victims of his outrageous encounters.

The military intelligence officer was disinclined to speak German and quickly terminated the charade. But once called in he could not dismiss the episode as a mere joke by two drink-drenched Canadian airmen. Air Force HQ was advised. Flight Lieutenants Brown and Harsh were charged with conduct unbecoming officers and gentlemen. Pending a hearing before a service tribunal they were remanded to the custody of Wally Floody.

Wally was not the appropriate officer to hold a tight rein. With or without his company, Brownie and George resumed their sociable rounds. It was in a Bournemouth pub a day or two later that Kingsley became involved in a polite but spirited political debate with local residents. It led to another episode.

Pre-war Kingsley Brown had simultaneously been managing editor of a conservative daily newspaper and a card-carrying member of the Communist Party of Canada. Years later he would become executive assistant to Canada's first woman cabinet minister, Ellen Fairclough who was Secretary of State in John Diefenbaker's big-C Conservative government. And years after that he would woo Canada's most affluent citizens in the most politely restrained milieu to raise $15-million for St Francois Xavier University in Nova Scotia. To those of us who accused him of being glib he would insist that he was merely countering our rigidity with a flexible mind.

He was, indeed, a remarkable conversationalist with or without alcoholic stimulus. But booze encouraged his outrageousness. Drink lubricated his political discussion with two men in a Bournemouth bar. It was a spirited exchange though short-lived and Brownie had forgotten the discussion when he got a phone-call at the hotel where we were billeted.

'Are you still inclined to speak on behalf of our man?' the caller wondered.

Brownie was vaguely aware that Britain was in the midst of a national election campaign and that he had been debating politics with campaign workers the previous night. He had not the slightest idea, however, whom the caller represented nor his commitment. Still it did promise new adventure. A week later Flight Lieutenant Kingsley Brown found himself addressing a Bournemouth audience of several thousand people on behalf of Sir Leonard Lyall, the Conservative candidate.

He was sufficiently effective to arouse the opposition Labour Press. 'The hard-pressed Tory party has become so politically impoverished that it is obliged to engage Canadian air force officers in uniform to enlist public support on implicit patriotic grounds,' one newspaper editorial said.

Detained on short leash in Bournemouth pending an Air Force hearing on the BOAC escapade, Brownie spoke on two or three more occasions and was invited to post-meeting receptions where he met Sir Leonard Lyall's aristocratic supporters.

That was how Brownie and George happened to meet two young ladies said to be nieces of the Queen. And they had arranged to take these titled sisters to dinner the evening of that June day we sat drinking in a Bournemouth hotel room.

It was mid-afternoon when our little drink fest was interrupted by a knock on the door. Before we could answer it a hotel chamber-maid used her pass key and, half-entering, asked if she could 'freshen up the room.'

'Of course!' George told her and as she stepped across the room. I caught the look he flashed at Kingsley Brown. This was possibly the most unattractive woman in Bournemouth. She was in her forties, care-worn and haggard, frowzy in her all-purpose dress. All this was digested in George's glance at Brownie. I could anticipate what was going to happen before he said a word.

There was a polite exchange of casual conversation as the woman tidied the bathroom and dusted around us. But I knew instinctively where the talk was headed from the moment George had telegraphed his message to Brownie.

'Would you have a friend?' Kingsley asked her now. His query was pitched midway between polite inquiry and specific question. It was softly put but it leapt the niceties of social preamble. Dinner-time was less than two hours' away and time was of the essence.

The chamber-maid did have a friend who was, in fact, available. That established, Brownie made an urgent phone-call from a corner of the hotel lobby.

I was well out of ear-shot but I could almost lip-read his regrets to the titled lady. He and Flight-Lieutenant Harsh had been grounded by an insensitive Air Force which failed to recognize the inviolability of a dinner engagement. Failed, indeed, to impose the curfew until this impossibly late hour, Flight-Lieutenant Floody had just advised them that they were confined to quarters.

About 10 days after that Brown and Harsh were interviewed by a senior RAF officer. He had just one relevant question for each of them. Did they intend to remain in the Air Force? No, they assured him. 'No,' he agreed. 'I didn't think you would find the peace-time service amenable. We'll try and get you on the next boat.'

They did. A few days later we were bound for Canada on the *Ile de France*. Brownie and I found a sunny spot on an upper deck and reviewed recent happenings. 'If I hadn't witnessed it first-hand I would never have believed it,' I told him now.

'Believed what?'

'That you would – literally – stand-up nieces of the Queen on a dinner date to take out two Bournemouth chamber-maids!'

Brownie gave me one of his solemn looks, an expression that I would come to realize accompanied his profound observations, outrageous statements and subtle jokes alike. 'The titled ladies don't often go short of dinner dates. We spent our hospitality where it would better be appreciated,' he told me.

20

An End-Note

ATOMIC BOMB ROCKS JAPAN, *The Globe and Mail*
ATOM BOMB DEVASTATING – JAP, *Toronto Daily Star*
ATOM MAY END ALL WAR, *The Evening Telegram*

Those headlines announced the dawn of the nuclear era on Tuesday morning, 7 August 1945. I walked into them at a newstand on Toronto's Bay and King Street's corner.

I was on leave and out of uniform but not yet out of the Air Force. After three years in a prisoner-of-war camp I was no prospect for further action. However, until the war with Japan was over that was still a technical possibility.

For all but a score of RAF crews who flew supplies to Brigadier Wingate's forces in Burma in 1943, the war in the Far East was remote. Few Canadian aircrew gave the Japanese much thought as long as the Nazi forces still fought in Europe. After VE-Day the Pacific war filled the news. By then, however, the Americans seemed to have that war under control. We doubted they would need our help. By noon Tuesday, 7 August, we knew we were redundant.

'New Weapon Equals 20,000 Tons of TNT,' said the initial Canadian Press report. That force from a single bomb was equivalent to the combined bomb-loads of 3,000 Lancaster bombers. One news story said Hiroshima sustained seven times as much damage as Halifax had in the 1917 explosion. Another estimated '150,000 Killed by Atom Bomb.'

This single device had killed as many at Hiroshima in a moment as 700 aircraft loads of fire-bombs had burned to death at Hamburg in a night. Yet we had tramped the cobblestones of Hamburg streets to see rehabilitation already underway earlier that spring.

My colleagues and I had taken air warfare a long leap forward from the airborne machine-gun fire of World War I to the radar-guided blockbuster bombs dropped on German cities in the 1940s. In a spring week of 1942 we had mounted thousand-plane raids on Cologne and other Ruhr centres. Yet in the week after that I had been taken by train through the heart of these industrial cities. The rail lines were again intact; factory structures were partially gutted but alive with industry. Dresden sustained five times the Hamburg death toll in a week of Allied bombing. Yet Dresden survived.

Rescue, recovery, rehabilitation occurred at Hiroshima and Nagasaki in the days that followed the A-bomb detonations. In that second week of August 1945, however, there were glimmers of the black truth that falls as invisible rain from the mushroom-shaped cloud. 'Within 500 metres some were protected by buildings and hence not burned,' wrote Dr Michihiko Hachiya who treated Hiroshima survivors within a mile of the bomb-burst epicentre. 'Within two to 15 days many of these developed the so-called radiation sickness and died. Those exposed in the 500 to 1,000-metre zone have shown symptoms similar but the onset of these symptoms was late and insidious. The death rate in this group has been high.'

The significance of the nuclear weapon lay in those 'late and insidious symptoms.' In the fortnight after the A-bomb fell on Hiroshima, a belated hand reached out from the grave of the city to call in 7,000 more corpses. That invisible hand was the residual factor of The Bomb. The full impact of this residual factor is yet to be wholly tested. The atomic bomb was born in the war it ended. The hydrogen bomb, that brings the sun's fury to earth with a thousand-fold the A-bomb's vehemence was born in the Cold War a decade later. No city has yet been surrendered to its testing.

Nearly 40 years ago, however, a 15-megaton H-bomb – 750 times as powerful as the Hiroshima A-bomb – was detonated on a Bikini atoll of the Marshall Islands. The fireball became a 100,000-foot cloud that dispersed down-wind. Then a strange unpredicted thing happened. An hour after the burst, particles began falling 50 miles down the wind's pathway and they continued to fall along an ominous elliptical path. Said the U.S. Atomic Energy Commission in a subsequent report: 'A total area of over 7,000 square miles was contaminated to such an extent survival might have depended upon evacuation or protective measures.'

This was a meticulously controlled test in which all humans had been moved well out of anticipated danger. But the residual hand of the H-bomb had not been anticipated. Within sight of the bomb-burst 23 fishermen aboard the *Lucky Dragon* were dusted by fallout. In three days their exposed skin swelled and reddened. One died; a dozen others were still unable to work a year later.

On Rongelap Atoll – 115 miles from the bomb-burst some 250 Marshall Islanders and U.S. servicemen were also caught by the fallout. It was two days before startled officials evacuated them. About 60 of these people suffered the same symptoms as the Hiroshima survivors who had been within a mile of the A-bomb.

Shelters would have protected the Marshallese from fallout, of course. And in the 1950s as the Cold War hotted up, the Diefenbaker government launched a sky-is-falling campaign to persuade Canadians that they should build basement and backyard air-raid shelters for survival.

These shelters would, indeed, have kept alive anyone not within the target area. We would, of course, have suffered the same 'insidious symptoms' as the Marshallese. Vomit and diarrhoea would have fouled our shelters. In ensuing weeks bowels and bleeding would drain our strength and volition. Two months after the attack we would be primed for pestilence and disease; scratches would continue to fester, wounds still run with pus. Our women would abort at first. Later they would bear misfits and monstrosities with far more than today's three per cent frequency. Then, for every 10-megaton bomb dropped anywhere on earth, 10,000 persons otherwise immune, would contract bone cancer.

The day The Bomb was dropped on Hiroshima, Canada's wartime minister of nearly everything, Clarence Decatur Howe explained this revolutionary new weapon and the Canadian role in its development. A professional engineer given to pragmatic recital of cold facts and hard numbers, Howe said 'The conception of a bomb a million times more effective than the most modern high explosive is staggering. Pound for pound that is the measure of the energy released in an atomic bomb . . . While the first application is for purposes of war, the prospect of applications for peace challenges the imagination. The probability of an enormous new source of power cannot lightly be dismissed. The present situation relating to the use of atomic power is comparable to electrical power when Faraday made his classical discovery of the electro magnet.

'While strictly Canadian effort cannot be compared in either money or personnel with the prodigious effort of the United States, nevertheless Canadian scientists and engineers in co-operation with those from Britain and the U.S. have played a part that guarantees to Canada a front-line position in the further scientific developments that lie ahead,' said Howe.

As he talked, some 350 high-tech personnel were engaged in nuclear development at the National Research Council's hush-hush Montreal Laboratory and two nuclear reactors were under construction at Chalk River in the Ottawa Valley. ZEEP, a prototype nuclear pile, produced enough power to light a 10-Watt electric bulb that fall. NRX, a full-scale research reactor that produced plutonium to fuel nuclear bombs, was operational by the summer of 1947. It was the first full-scale reactor – generating a few megawatts of power – outside the U.S.

C.D. Howe put Canada's Bomb-making role in perspective. We were junior partners alongside the Americans and the Brits but we were part of the nuclear triumvirate nonetheless. As one of the three nations privy to the Bomb's secrets we were now a custodian of the global peace. The Bomb, he said, demanded 'extraordinary security precautions on all phases of the project' and the Bomb-makers would not divulge how it was made 'until international agreement is reached to control this new source of energy.'

The U.S., Britain and Canada, the three initial Bomb-making nations, did establish the United Nations' mechanism – the International Atomic Energy Agency – to control it. But the IAEA was powerless to curb nuclear proliferation during four decades of the Cold War. And Canadian uranium, as well as a nominal amount of plutonium, went into American and British nuclear arsenals.

Canada did opt out of the bomb-making business. From the outset this was the only nation on earth with the knowledge and expertise, the raw material and the high-tech resources, to build The Bomb ourselves and who refused to do so. That gave us a moral status in global councils that Canadians tended to shrug off in recent years.

We tend to hide at the edge of the American umbrella. Yet Canadians were participants in the building of The Bomb. And while our contemporaries were helping to fashion the ultimate weapon in Montreal and Chalk River laboratories we old fly-boys were advancing the means of its delivery abroad.

The last of the gladiators, we had come a long way from our hairy forebears clutching their wooden clubs in tribal protection. We had advanced warfare to genocide and our children stood appalled. Perhaps now that weaponry has evolved to its ultimate potential and tribal fears still fester with primitive hatred, our grand-kids will learn how to quench the fires in mankind's mind.

Index